MINIATURE AUSTRALIAN SHEPHERD

Expert Dog Training

MINIATURE AUSTRALIAN SHEPHERD

Expert Dog Training

Think Like a Dog

Here's Exactly How to Train Your

Miniature Australian Shepherd

PAUL ALLEN PEARCE

ISBN-13: 978-1974542529

What Customers Say About Their Results!

Acknowledgments

For my family and friends that have relentlessly supported my many endeavors.

Preface

From the learning curve of training my first dog and the many that followed, this book contains the methods that have successfully worked for hundreds of thousands of dog owners and trainers including myself.

Table of Contents

Introduction

"We can judge the heart of a man by his treatment of animals." - *Immanuel Kant*

I know that you will find all of the information inside this training guide easy to follow and informative. My hope is that you have yet to purchase your Miniature Australian Shepherd puppy and are buying this guide now to proactively prepare for the introduction of your new furry creatures entrance into your life. Don't worry though, if you already have a grown dog or new puppy at home it is just as effective.

Though this guide approaches training as a serious endeavor, your dog will teach you otherwise. No doubt, the reason that you are bringing a dog into the family is for the enjoyment of their company so while focusing on training always feel free to laugh, smile and enjoy the process.

In an attempt to keep you and the book lighthearted, I have added some humor and fun throughout by infusing my dog's playful spirit. I find dogs entertaining, comforting, and at times my therapist, thank the universe they are such good listeners.

Reading this instructional prior to picking up your puppy will prepare you, benefit your new puppy and help to establish the precise mindset for owning and training a new Miniature Australian Shepherd.

Included inside this books first section is help for new puppy parents that instructs how to prepare the house for the new arrival, socialization, treats, clicker training, and how and when to reward your puppy. Additional information also instructs on avoiding potential negative behavioral issues by doing the right things starting on the first day. Prevention is a savior.

The second section educates dog owners in effective Miniature Australian Shepherd training techniques, understanding and using dog communication, and training handling, housetraining, crate training and teaching the basic commands. Additionally contains a puppy's training milestones and guidance for shaping behaviors and problem solving.

Each command is written out in an easy to follow step-by-step format that uses the highly effective rewards based clicker training. However, if you choose not to use a clicker, you can still follow the instructions and train your puppy by using rewards only.

Section 2 also contains instructions on how to solve jumping, barking, nipping and digging behaviors.

The final section delves into basic care and grooming for Mini Aussies, nutrition and some final thoughts about training.

I'm certain that inside you will find complete and concise proven training support featuring highly useful information culled from years of personal training experience, other professional trainers, various training manuals, research, and years of living with my own canine friends.

Each chapter contained inside this dog training guide compliments the others, shaping your puppy into a well-behaved dog that is welcomed anywhere and a pleasure to be in the company of.

By purchasing this training guide right now, you will be on your way to securing the necessary tools and knowledge to assure your success as a Mini Aussie dog owner and trainer.

I am confident that you will find this guide effective, easy to understand and fun, so move onto chapter one "The First Few Days" and get started preparing for the joy filled journey of dog ownership.

1 The Miniature Australian Shepherd

Mini Aussie, Miniature Australian Shepherd, Mini American

I get excited every time I have a chance to train a Miniature Australian Shepherd because I know it is going to be a fulfilling experience. I really enjoy training this intelligent quick learning breed because they bring such enthusiasm to everything they do. I know you will experience the same.

Charged with liveliness, they are as loyal, endearing a hound as one comes across, and it is always a pleasurable experience to meet their acquaintance. Their innate exuberance to perform is alas every dog owners dream. Feisty, confident and an amicable companion too, what other qualities could a dog family desire from their family herding pet. The only grievous error and owner can make is to ignore or isolate this breed, thus keeping their enormity of fine qualities from blossoming.

For those unfamiliar with the history of the Miniature Australian Shepherd, the common historical account states that the Miniature Australian Shepherd was first developed in California during the mid 1960's from dogs that were smaller than average Australian Shepherds, but similar in all physical and most personality characteristics. The goal was to continue breeding them for their size, intelligence and their dynamic personalities. Smaller statured Australian Shepherds indeed existed prior to the 1960's, which is why they were available to form the Miniature Australian Shepherds that then became Miniature Australian Shepherds. Mini

American Shepherds essentially are Mini Australian Shepherds, but debate can be found in the canine world.

Mini Aussie share most of the same characteristics of personality, coat and eye colors as well as a penchant for herding that their big brother Aussies encompass. In fact, these little dogs are perfect for herding small livestock such as sheep and goats, but if necessary can also handle larger stock.

If that's not your need, just throw them in the vehicle with you and enjoy their company wherever you wander too.

Intelligent and biddable they quickly became favored for both household pets and doubled for those that additionally required their herding proficiencies. They have become quite popular with those that travel with and own horses.

Their size allows them to fit into either urban or rural settings; however, owners must keep them active and exercised. A busy Mini Aussie is a happy Mini Aussie, so try to include them in your daily duties and give them jobs of their own perform, just as wily as full sized Aussies, don't be surprised by their problem solving skills.

Mini Aussies come in a variety of colors such as blue and red merle with or without white or copper trim, black bi or tri that has a solid black body with copper, white or copper and white, red bi or tri with a variance in reds as a base and then copper, white, or both copper and white.

The AKC officially recognized the Miniature Australian Shepherd in 2015 adopting them into the herding category. As of 2017, they are ranked the 36th most popular dog registered with the AKC. The AKC standard states their basic colors as varying.

Mini Aussies are quick learners that are usually easy to train not only basic commands, but also tricks and for sports competitions such as agility, disc dog, herding and Flyball. They are prone to herding and will often attempt to herd small children and other animals so be prepared to do some focused work on acceptable spacing and bumping. They require multiple daily walks or a jog combined with exercises that are more energetic.

Mini Aussies are small sized dogs that are small enough for apartments and able to cope with smaller living quarters, but only if they are sufficiently exercised. They are commonly good with children, other pets, versatile, excellent companions, a bit timid toward strangers but not shy and enthusiastic about their tasks. Additionally, they are devoted and protective of their families and outstanding working dogs that encompass strong guarding instincts with flocks. Their demeanor allows them to adjust to the tasks they are performing by applying the amount of energy and enthusiasm necessary to accomplish the task without losing control.

Due to their natural wariness towards strangers and their exuberance, early and proper socialization is a key component for rearing a healthy minded Mini Australian. Two of my clients Brian and Monica tell the story about their first Mini Australian named Tigre, confirming how too little socialization affected him. Together we were able to turn him into an upstanding canine citizen.

"As busy novice puppy owners we were only able to spend time with Tigre when at home after working, and due to this he was unaware of the many people and places he would later encounter. Unfortunately, this increased his wariness towards strangers and he adopted a heightened sense of territorialism. By the time we realized how severe the problem, he was about eleven months old and it was difficult to have visitors without some disturbance from him.

After some diagnosis help from Paul, we gradually eased him into open-mindedness, but not until many hours were spent introducing him to various types of strangers and worldly situations so that he was capable to meet and greet with a calm happy demeanor, and now we can take him anywhere. Now we understand why early ongoing socialization is a key component to having a healthy dog."

Their grooming needs are minimal. Depending upon what your Mini Aussie has been into, a brushing of their medium length coat once or twice a week and an occasional bath is all that is necessary. If your Miniature Australian Shepherd is in the field a lot then regularly brushing and combing to rid burrs and check for critters will help keep tangles and mats from forming.

Mini Aussies love learning and performing new tricks. If treated well and properly exercised this is a terrific breed to enjoy, and your dog will stay close by in enjoyment of your company.

It isn't hard to understand why they are quickly rising in popularity and enjoying warm welcomes into many Australian homes, but before adding one to your family please know without a doubt that you are able to meet their daily requirements.

Miniature Australian Shepherd Rescue

Miniature Australian Shepherds are often acquired without any clear understanding of what goes into owning one, and these dogs regularly end up in the care of rescue groups, and are badly in need of adoption or fostering. Take the time to understand the breed to ascertain that it is the right fit for your family.

Before adopting a Miniature Australian Shepherd, please be certain that you have the time and means to care for a dog. If you have the facilities and ability, please rescue a dog and enjoy the rewarding experience that it offers both of you.

If you are interested in adopting a Mini Australian, a rescue group is a good place to start. I have listed a few below

http://mascusa.org/breed/rescue.html

http://mascaonline.com/finding-an-aussie/rescue-resources/

Quick Facts

Size – Mini Aussies average 13-18 inches in height and 20-40 pounds classifies them in into the small dog category.

Tail – Mini Aussies have a naturally short or docked tail.

Coat – Medium length double coat that requires brushing a couple of times per week and sheds daily.

Personality – They are loyal, intelligent, protective, versatile for work, adaptable to all living conditions, enjoy close family ties and are commonly easy to train.

Competition – Enjoys competing in agility, herding, Flyball and other competitions.

Herding – Great for herding goats, sheep and even larger stock, many horse people solicit the services of this durable little dog.

Health Concerns – Hip dysplasia, hereditary eye defects such as progressive retinal atrophy, and degenerative myelopathy that is a spinal cord disease.

Exercise needs – Daily rigorous exercise is required encompassing more than one outing per day.

2 The First Few Days

"A dog teaches a boy fidelity, perseverance, and to turn around three times before lying down." - Robert Benchley

Bringing Home the Puppy

The time has come to bring your puppy home. There are a couple of things to keep in mind on this day. First, that you are a stranger. Second, that he or she has probably never been in a car or away from its mom or littermates. As you can imagine this will be a stressful moment for your puppy, so try to make the ride home as free of stress as possible.

Before departing the puppy procurement place, allow your puppy to relieve itself, and during the ride provide a soft comfortable place in a crate or nestled in a humans arms. He may cry or bark during the ride, but that is normal behavior and you must handle it calmly. This will begin to establish that you are there to help. By speaking calmly and evenly, and not speaking harshly, you will show your puppy that you care and are not to be feared.

If possible, bring along the entire family and begin the bonding process during the car ride home. Many times the person that brings the puppy to the home is the person that the puppy will begin forming the tightest bond. Drive straight home so that the pup spends the least amount of time inside the car. Avoid over handling from family members during the ride home; simply allow the pup comfort.

If you have to stop for a pee/poop stop, be sure to carry your puppy to an area unused by other dogs' eliminations and properly clean up afterward. Your puppy is not yet vaccinated and could have worms or parasites in his or her feces and needs to avoid exposure to other dogs' feces that could also contain worms and parasites.

Ride home checklist

- Cleaning supplies, just in case.
- Soft towel or blanket.
- Collar – if you use a collar be sure it is tight. If you can fit one finger between the collar and your puppy's neck then it is correctly tightened. It is good idea to begin the collar adjustment process early as possible.
- Newspapers, paper towels, and plastic bags.
- Smile, good mood, and cheerful tone of voice.
- Crate (optional).
- Pet odor neutralizer (optional).

After your new puppy has performed his first elimination in the predestinated spot in the yard, then bring him inside, unclip the leash and let him do as he pleases and encounter creatures on his own terms.

Never force yourself or other animals on a pup, allow them to find their own comfort level and engage using their own decisions. This is the beginning of the all-important socialization process, i.e. place them in proximity of other creatures and circumstances so they have a chance to engage on their own.

If you have other pets around, you should first consider placing your puppy inside the pre-prepared pen so that there is a barrier between him and others. The first day is filled with acclimation to new surroundings and humans. In addition, you can expect that he will be missing his littermates and mother. Do not over handle your puppy during the first couple of days, allow him time to adjust and engage with others by using his own will.

Beginning with the first day, establish the schedule for feeding, and outdoor relief breaks. Every forty-five minutes to an hour take him to his waste elimination spot and see if he needs to pee or poop, and if after a few minutes he doesn't, then return inside and try again in about 10-15 minutes.

Don't turn elimination outings into play sessions, because you want to train your pup that elimination breaks are only for elimination, this avoids being tricked into going outside for fun time. Of course, you can play a bit or let him smell the yard after he eliminates and you praise him with a "Good boy."

Next, add walks, exercise and training to the schedule, then from this day forward follow that schedule best you can. *Dogs love structure.*

Your new puppy will be missing his littermates and mother, so don't be surprised if you hear some whining and whimpering. Your job is to provide support and comfort but do not over coddle him by running to his side at every little whimper. This separation anxiety will most likely be more prevalent during nighttime so keep your puppy close by where you sleep, either next to your bed or at your opened doorway.

Relentless pining can be a sign of more serious separation anxiety (SA) and should be given quick attention to lessen the symptoms and solve the problem.

Day by day your pup will adjust to the new surroundings and start to understand that he is loved and cared for by his new family and then the separation anxiety will begin to decrease. When a pup understands that all of his needs are taken care of, it will form a human-puppy bond that automatically installs you as the alpha leader and enables him to feel secure and calm.

As you begin teaching your puppy his name, first establish eye contact before saying his name. Remember his name is only to get his attention, not for him to come to you. When issuing commands, say your puppy's name followed by the command, e.g. "Zeke come."

Begin crate training so that he has a safe place to relax and for you to place him when necessary. RULE ONE – your puppy should love his crate so never use it as punishment. If forced to give a time-out, choose a dull place such as a pantry or bathroom. The crate also aids in house-training because dogs are naturally clean and will do everything not to soil their own den/crate.

The first few days you will be busy making regular trips outside for elimination breaks, socializing him to new surroundings, creatures, teaching name recognition, beginning crate training, adoring him and keeping him nearby so that you can avoid indoor accidents of all types. Don't forget to supply ample appropriately sized chew-toys.

First couple of Days and Nights Checklist

- Upon arriving home, take your new pup straight to the predestinated outdoor elimination spot. You will use this spot every time, making it the pups poop/pee palace.

- Clear the indoor area of other pets and place your puppy down to explore. Do not crowd the puppy and if children are present have them provide the puppy plenty of space. Allow him to come to them under his own initiative. Have everyone remain calm and gentle when interacting.

  All puppies act differently. Some take off exploring the house, others just curl up and voyeur the surroundings and might doze off.

  Another *good* option is to place your puppy directly inside his gated area that is already prepared with the proper pee pads, crate with blanket inside, water bottle or small bowl, blanket outside the crate and a couple of chew-toys.

- Keep in mind that if your puppy was flown in or from a shelter that they may have brought stress with them and be extremely tired from the previous day/night. Expect that the following day they will be rested and livelier.

- Separation anxiety is natural and you might hear your puppy whine, squeal, or howl. They might have difficulty sleeping the first few days or weeks. Your puppy has to get used to being away from his sisters, brothers, and mom that used to snuggle together.

- Move slowly when introducing your other pets to your new puppy. The crate, baby gate, or exercise pen puts a barrier between them and allows both to adjust to one another without direct physical contact. I definitely recommend this.

- After about three or four days, take your puppy to the veterinarian for a complete check-up.

- It is very important to show your puppy that they are wanted and cared for. This is of the utmost importance during the first few days.

Elimination Time

- Take him or her out for elimination every half hour. Elimination accidents are common the first couple of days so clean them thoroughly and use pet deodorizers so that there is no trace. Gradually over the coming days and weeks, pups are able to increase the duration between elimination times.

- Always take them to the designated outdoor elimination spot.

- Do not become angry about elimination accidents. If you see your pup going and if possible, pick him up and let him finish outdoors in the spot, and afterward praise him while still outdoors.

- Escort your puppy outside and begin praising when he begins his elimination business, but then let him finish in peace.

- To prevent frequent accidents take notice if you need to shorten the time between elimination trips.
- Track your puppies schedule for eating and elimination, this can help you eradicate accidents and begin housebreaking. Tracking will help you to learn your puppy's patterns.
- After feeding, always take your puppy outdoors.
- Pick up the water bowl around 8pm each night.
- Always praise your puppy when he or she eliminates waste outdoors and not indoors. This will strengthen your bond and begin building trust.
- Before bedtime, always take your puppy out for elimination. A walk assists them in falling asleep.
- Take your puppy out first thing in the morning.
- Allow him to eliminate fully. Most puppies will take several small amounts to finish full elimination.

"Where does my puppy sleep?"

- The first night will most likely be the most difficult for your puppy, but do not isolate because he is vocalizing his loneliness. Try not to keep him far from where you are sleeping. He is alone in a strange place, and you want him to feel comfortable and welcomed. For example, do not put him in the garage, basement or far end of the house away from people.
- Options for not isolating your puppy are a dog bed or blanket on the floor near your bed, or in his crate near your bed or just outside the opened bedroom door. For a variety of reasons, it is advised *not* to have your puppy in your bed.

Even though your puppy is whimpering, do not go to him and pay much attention every time he is vocalizing distress. This can become a negative behavior used by the pup to get you to come to him at every request. A habit you don't want to form.

3 Socializing Your Mini Aussie

"I am in favor of animal rights as well as human rights. That is the way of a whole human being." — Abraham Lincoln

Where, When and Why

Everyone reads or hears socialization mentioned when researching about dogs. What is the reason for socialization? When is the best time to socialize a shiny new puppy? Does it has to do with getting along well with other dogs and people, or is there more to it? Do I let my puppy loose with other puppies, just sit back, and watch? These and many more questions are often asked, so let me provide the answers.

Dog socialization is for your dog to learn and maintain acceptable behaviors in any situation, especially when the dog or puppy does not want to engage. The goal is for your dog to learn how to interact with any normal experience that occurs in life without becoming overly stimulated, fearful, reactive or aggressive. No matter what the circumstance, your dog should be able to go with the flow, keep centered and remain calm. Proper socialization of your puppy is a crucial part of preparation for their entire life and a life-long process.

Exposures to the many things we think are normal are not normal to our little puppies or adult dogs. Mechanical noises, such as lawnmowers, car horns, blenders, coffee machines, dishwashers, stereos, televisions, garbage trucks, and other similar items make noises that dogs have to adjust too.

Beyond mechanical noises are living creatures represented by other household pets, strange dogs, cats and critters in the yard, such as gophers, rabbits, squirrels, and birds. Further, dogs must become accustom to family members, friends, neighbors and of course the dreaded strangers.

All of the things mentioned above and more are new to most six or eight-week-old puppies arriving at your house, so immediately begin the gradual introduction to these items and living creatures.

Continually remain alert to your puppy's reactions and willingness to either dive forward or withdrawal, and never force him or her to interact with things they do not wish to interact. Proceed at their pace by presenting the interaction and then observing their willingness to participate. Observing and learning his body language during this process will help you deeply understand your dog's likes and dislikes from the cues observed from his body language.

When strangers approach your pup do not allow them to automatically reach out and touch, leave a little space and time for your puppy's reaction to be observed, and then you can grant or deny permission based upon you and your puppy's intuition. We all know that many people fail to ask permission before reaching for dogs that are strange to them, so it is your job to instruct strangers in the proper interaction process.

Socialization Summary Goals

1. Learning to remain calm when the world is buzzing around them.

2. Exposure in a safe manner to the environment that will encompass his or her world, including the rules and guidelines that accompany it.

3. Learning to respond to commands when they do not want to, for example, a dog in the midst of a chasing session with a fellow puppy, or while stalking an irresistible squirrel.

Let us begin by looking at how a puppy's social development process is played out from puppy to adulthood.

The first phase of socialization begins as early as 3 weeks and lasts to approximately 12 weeks, during this time puppies discover that they are dogs and begin to play with their littermates. Survival techniques that they will use throughout their lives, such as biting, barking, chasing and fighting begin to be acted out.

Concurrently during this time-period, puppies experience big changes socially and physically. Learning submissive postures and taking corrections from their mother along with interactions with their littermates begin to teach them about hierarchies.

Keeping mother and puppies together for at least 8 weeks tends to increase their ability to get along well with other dogs and learn more about themselves and the consequences of their actions, such as the force of a bite on their brothers and sisters.

Between the ages of 7-12 weeks, a period of rapid learning occurs and they learn what humans are, and whether to accept them as safe. This is a crucial period, and has the *greatest impact* on *all future social behavior*.

This is the time we begin teaching puppies the acceptable rules of conduct. Take note that they have a short attention span and physical limitations. This is the easiest period to get your puppy comfortable with new things, and the chance to thwart negative behavioral issues that can stem from improper or incomplete socialization.

The sad reality is that behavioral problems are the greatest threat to the owner-dog relationship and the number one cause of death to dogs under 3 years of age. It is your responsibility to mentor your dog so a problem does not arise, and that shouldn't be difficult because you adore your pup and enjoy being in his company.

From birth, puppies should be exposed to handling and manipulation of body parts, and exposure to different people, places, situations, and other well-socialized animals. Encourage your puppies exploring, curiosity and investigation of different environments. Games, toys, and a variety of surfaces and structures, such as rock, dirt, tile, concrete, pavement, tunnels and steps are all things to expose your puppy.

This exposure should continue into adulthood and beyond. This aids in keeping your dog sociable instead of shy, and fearlessly capable of confronting different terrains.

It is important for your puppy to be comfortable playing, sleeping, or exploring alone. Schedule alone play with toys and solo naps in their crate or other safe areas that they enjoy. This teaches them to entertain themselves, and not become overly attached or have separation issues from their owners' absence. Getting them comfortable with their crate is also beneficial for travel and to use as their safe area.

Enrolling your puppy in classes before 3 months of age is an outstanding avenue to improving socialization, training and strengthening the bond between you and your puppy. You can begin socialization classes as early as 7-8 weeks. The recommendation is that your puppy has received at least *1* set of vaccines and a de-worming *seven* days prior to starting the first class. At his time, puppies are still not out of harm's way from all diseases, but the risk is relatively low because of primary vaccines, good care and mother's natural milk immunization.

Keep a few things in mind when seeking play dates for help with socializing your puppy. A stellar puppy class will have a safe mature dog for the puppies to learn boundaries and other behaviors. When making play dates, puppies should be matched by personality and play styles.

Games such as retrieve or drop help to curb possessive behaviors as well as to help them learn to give up unsafe or off limits items so that the item can be taken out of harm's way. Another important lesson during play is for puppies to learn to come back to their human while engaged in a play session. *Your dog should be willingly dependent upon you and look to you for guidance.*

Teach mature easily stimulated dogs to relax before they are permitted to socialize with others. If you have an adult dog that enjoys flying solo, do not force him into situations. Teach your dogs and puppies less aroused play and encourage passive play. This includes play that does not encompass dominance, mouthing or biting other puppies.

If you have rough play happening between multiple dogs or puppies then interrupt the rough housing by frequently calling them to you and rewarding their attention, thus turning their attention to you. To dissuade mouthing contact, try to interject toys into the play. As they mature, elevated play can lead to aggression.

Two phases of *fear imprinting* occur in your growing puppy's life. A fear period is a stage during which your puppy may be more apt to perceive certain stimuli as threatening.

During these two periods, any event your puppy thinks is traumatic can leave a lasting effect, possibly forever. The first period is from 8-11 weeks and the second is between 6-14 months of age. During these periods, you will want to keep your puppy clear of any frightening situations, but you will find that often difficult to determine.

A simple item like a chrome balloon on the floor could possibly scare the "bejeebers" out of your little pup. However, socialization continues and overcoming fears is part of that process so remain aware of what frightens your pup and slowly work at overcoming it.

There is no one-size-fits-all in knowing what your puppy finds fearful. Becoming familiar with canine body language can help you diagnose your pups fear factor. The second period often reflects the dog becoming more reactive or apprehensive about new things. Larger breeds sometimes have an extended second period.

The Importance of Play

When observing dogs in a pack or family, one will notice that dogs and puppies often enjoy playing with each other. During play, puppies learn proper play etiquette, such as how hard to bite or mouth and the degree to play rough. Their mother and littermates provide feedback for them to learn.

Play is instinctual, and as an innate dog, behavior is something that needs to be satisfied. Humans and dogs both play throughout their lifetime and many studies show that this social interaction is important for mental and physical health.

Providing your dog with ample amounts of play through games, such as fetch, tug or chase helps to satisfy their need for play and assists in strengthening the bond between dog and owner. When guided in play, your dog will not only acquire the rules of play, but his physical and mental needs will be met during the activity.

One terrific bi-product of play is that it burns off excess energy and as a result, it helps keep negative behaviors from surfacing. Dogs are naturally full of energy and they need an outlet to avoid potential negative behaviors, such as chewing, digging and barking. While these behaviors serve them well in the wild, when living with humans they can be a detriment to the harmony and success of the relationship.

Socialization Summary

- Proper socialization requires patience, kindness and consistency during teaching. You and your dog should both be having fun during this process. Allow your dog to proceed into new situations at his or her own pace, never force them into a situation that they are not comfortable.

If you think that your dog may have a socialization issue, seek professional advice from a qualified behavioral person. Because time is of the essence during their rapid growth period, do not delay.

- During the first few months of socialization, keep your puppy out of harm's way because he can easily pick up diseases from sniffing other dog's feces and urine. When you are first exposing your puppy to new people, places or cars, it is good practice to carry him to and from the car. Follow this practice both inside and outside when near dog clinics.

Keeping your pup protected from contaminated ground surfaces will help keep him healthy until he has had vaccines and is a bit older. Avoid areas where you suspect other dogs might have eliminated.

- Socializing your puppy, especially before the age of six months, is a very important step in preventing future behavioral problems. I will add that it is necessary for saving you a lot of future work.

- Socializing can and should continue throughout the lifetime of your dog. Socializing in a gentle and kind manner prevents aggressive, fearful and potential behaviors with possible litigious outcomes.

- A lack of socializing may lead to barking, shyness, destruction, territorialism or hyperactivity, and the risk of *wearing Goth make up and smoking clove cigarettes alone behind his doghouse.*

The earlier you start socializing, the better. However, all puppies and dogs can gradually be brought into new and initially frightening situations, eventually learning to enjoy them. Canines can adapt to various and sometimes extreme situations, they just need your calm, guiding hand. Don't fret if you are late in the game because you receive a 14-week-old puppy, you are still able socialize them but you might have a lot more work to do that can't be rushed.

- If your puppy does not engage with other dogs for months or years at a time, you can expect his behavior to be different when he encounters them again. *I mean, how would you feel if your sixth grade math teacher who you haven't seen in 17 years, just walked up and sniffed you?* This is why it is a lifelong process. Try to keep this in mind so you have those moments when you realize Danzig hasn't been around construction work in ages and might need a reminder of the experience.

- Meeting new kinds of people, including but not limited to people wearing hats, disabled folks, people with facial hair, and people in local services, such as postal carriers, fire and police officers, and of course crowds of various types of people.

- Meeting new dogs is encouraged. Slowly expose your dog to other pets, such as cats, horses, birds, llamas, pigs, gerbils, lizards and all critters close to where you live. If they are used to seeing and smelling them, the familiarity helps curtail sudden barking or chasing.

- Your dog's crate is not a jail. Be sure and take the time to teach your puppy to enjoy the comfort and privacy of his own crate. You want your dog's crate to be a place that he or she feels safe, for more information go to the crate-training chapter.

- To avoid doggy boredom, make sure your toy bin has plenty of toys for your puppy to choose. A Nylabone®, Kong® chew-toys, ropes, balls and tugs are many of the popular things your dog can enjoy and their *favorites should always be available for them wherever you have them sequestered.*

Here are some methods you can use when exposing your dog to something new, or something he has previously been distrustful.

- Remain calm and upbeat. If he is leashed, keep it loose.

- Gradually expose him to the new stimulus and if he is wary or fearful never use force. Let him retreat if he needs to.

- Reward your dog using treats; give him a good scratch or an energetic run for being calm and exploring new situations. Additionally, add in vocal praise for accomplishments.

On a regular basis, expose your dog to the things in the world that he should be capable of coping, which is everything. His gained familiarity will allow him to calmly deal with such situations in the future.

Stay away from routine, such as walking the same route daily. Though dogs love routine, periodically expose your dog to new locations and situations. This allows you to assess his need for further socialization and it allows you to discover new things. I certainly love exploring, so whenever possible I take my dogs to different areas for walks.

Socialization Checklist for Puppies and Adult Dogs

Be sure your dog is comfortable with the following:

- Male and female human adults.

- Male and female human children.

- Other household pets and dogs.

- Meeting strange dogs.

- Your house and neighborhood.

- Mechanical noises, such as lawn mowers and vehicles.

- Special circumstance people, for example, those in wheel chairs, crutches and wearing braces, Tourette syndrome or even strange indefinable *Uncle Larry* who walks with a limp.

To assure that your dog is not selfish, make sure that he or she is comfortable sharing the following:

- His food bowl, toys, and bedding and those can all be touched by you and others without receiving aggression from your dog.

- The immediate space shared with strangers, especially with children. This is necessary for your puppy's socialization so that he does not get paranoid or freak out in small places, e.g. at the next-door neighbor's house or in an elevator.

- His best friend you, and all family members or friends, and is not overprotective or territorial towards others.

For road tripping with your dog, make sure he or she is:

- Comfortable in all types of vehicles, such as a car, truck, minivan, SUV and if applicable public transportation.

- Always properly and safely restrained.

- You regularly stop for elimination breaks and hydration.

- *He knows how to operate a stick shift as well as an automatic and wears eye protection if he is letting the wind pound his face.*

I have faith that you will do a terrific job in socializing your dog so that he can greet the world calmly and is able to enjoy the surprises it regularly delivers.

4 Navigating Problem Behaviors

How to deal with a problem behavior before it becomes a habit

Everyone likes his or her own space to feel comfortable, familiar and safe, and your dog is no different. A proper living area is a key factor to avoiding all kinds of potential problems. Think of all the things your puppy will encounter in his life with humans, such as appliances and mechanical noises that are not common in nature, and can be frightening to your dog. It is essential to use treats, toys and praise to assist you and your dog while in the midst of training and socializing.

Dogs are social creatures and it is essential to communicate with them. Communication is always the key to behavior reinforcement. Regularly rewarding calm behavior and showing that you control his favorite things acts as a pathway to thwarting problems that can surface later.

Keep your Mini Aussie's world happy. Make sure it is getting a proper amount of exercise and that he is being challenged mentally. Make sure he is receiving enough time in the company of other dogs and other people. Keep a close eye on his diet, offering him good, healthy, dog-appropriate foods. Avoid excessive helpings when treating.

It is important that you be a strong leader. Dogs are pack animals and your dog needs to know that you are the *alpha*. Do not let situations fall into questionable scenarios that your dog is uncertain about who is in charge. Your puppy will feel confident and strong if he works for his rewards and knows that he or she has a strong, confident leader to follow. Let your dog show you good behavior before you provide rewards.

Your dog's first step towards overcoming the challenges in life is in understanding what motivates his own behavior. Some behaviors your dog will exhibit are instinctual. Chewing, barking, digging, jumping, chasing and leash pulling are things that all dogs do because it is in their genetic make-up. These natural behaviors differ from the ones we have inadvertently trained into the domestic canine. Behaviors, such as nudging our hands to be petted or barking for attention are actually accidently reinforced by us humans and not innate and should never be rewarded.

What motivates your dog to do what he does or does not do? You may wonder why he does not come when you call him while he is playing with other dogs. Simply, this may be because coming to you is far less exciting than scrapping with the same species. When calling your dog you can change this behavior by offering him a highly coveted treat and after treating, allow him to continue playing for a while.

Start this training aspect slowly, and in short distances from where he is playing. Gradually increase the distances and distractions when you beckon your dog. After he is coming regularly to you then begin to diminish the frequency of treating and supplement verbal or physical praise.

Here are some helpful tips to use when trying to help your Miniature Australian Shepherd through challenging behavior.

- Are you accidentally rewarding bad behavior? Remember that your dog may see any response from you as a reward. You can ignore the bad behavior if you are patient enough, or you can give your puppy the equivalent of a human *time out* for a few minutes. Make sure the time out environment is in calm, quiet and safe, but a very dull place that is not his crate.

- Think about the quality of his diet and health. Is your dog getting enough playtime, mental and physical exercise, and sleep? Is this a medical problem? Do not ignore the range of possibilities that could be eliciting your dog's challenging behavior. An unseen physical or mental deformity or ailment could be the cause of a chronic negative behavior.

Be sure and practice replacement behavior. Reward him with something that is much more appealing than the perceived reward that he is getting when he is acting in an undesirable manner. It is important to reward his good behavior before he misbehaves. If done consistently and correctly, this will reinforce good behaviors, and reduce poor behaviors.

For example, in the hopes of receiving love, your dog is repeatedly nudging your hand; instead teach him to *sit* by only giving him love after he sits, and never if he nudges you. If you command, "Sit" and he complies, and then you pat him on the head or speak nicely to him, or both, your dog will associate the sitting compliance with nice things.

If your pooch nudges and you turn away never acknowledging him he will understand that behavior is not associated with nice things. In a scenario where your dog is continually nudging you for attention, catch him before he comes running into your room and begins nudging. When you see him approaching, immediately say, "Sit" to stop him in his tracks.

- While practicing the replacement behavior, be sure you reward the right response and ignore the mistakes. Remember, any response to the wrong action could be mistaken as a reward by your dog, so try to remain neutral in a state of ignoring; this includes sight, touch and verbal acknowledgement. Be sure to offer your dog a greater reward for the correct action than the joy he is getting from doing the wrong action.

- Your dog's bad behavior may be caused by something that causes him fear. If you decipher this as the problem, then change his mind about what he perceives frightening. Pair the scary thing with something he loves. For example, your dog has a problem with the local skateboarder. Pair the skateboarder's visit with a delicious treat and lots of attention. He will soon look forward to the daily arrival of the skateboarder.

- Always, remain patient with your dog and do not force changes. Work gradually and slowly. Forcing behavioral changes on your dog may lead to worsening the behavior. Training requires that you work as hard as your dog, and maybe harder, because you have to hone your observational skills, intuition, timing, patience, laughter and the understanding of your dog's body language and demeanor.

5 Rewarding Instead of Punishing

Eyes – Mini Aussies can have odd colored eyes with one or both eyes may be blue, brown, hazel, amber or any combination of colors, including marbling and flecks.

It is always better to reward your Mini Aussie instead of punishing him or her. Here are a few reasons why:

- If you punish your dog, it can make him distrust or cause fear, aggression and avoidance of you. If you rub your dog's nose in his poop or pee, he may avoid going to the bathroom in front of you. This is going to make his public life difficult.

- Physical punishment has the tendency to escalate in severity. If you get your dog's attention by a light tap on the nose, he will soon get used to that and ignore it. Shortly the contact will become more and more violent. As we know, violence is *not* the answer.

- Punishing your dog may have some bad side effects. For example, if you are using a pinch collar, it may tighten when he encounters other dogs. Dogs are very smart, but they are not always logical. When your dog encounters another dog, the pinching of the collar may lead him to thinking erroneously that the other dog is the reason for the pinch. Pinch collars have been linked to the reinforcement of aggressive behaviors between dogs.

- Electric fences will make him avoid the yard.

- Choke collars can cause injuries to a dog's throat as well as cause back and neck misalignment.

- You may inadvertently develop and adversarial relationship with your dog if you punish your dog instead of working through a reward system and correctly leading. If you only look for the mistakes within your dog, this is all you will ever see. In your mind, you will see a problem dog. In your dog's mind, he will see anger and distrust of his master.

- You ultimately want to shape your dog's incorrect actions into acceptable actions. By punishing your dog, he will learn only to *avoid* punishment. He is not learning to change the behavior you want changed, instead he learns to be sneaky or to do the very minimum to avoid being punished. Your dog can become withdrawn and seemingly inactive. Permanent psychological damage can be done if a dog lives in fear of punishment.

- If you punish rather than reward neither you nor your dog will be having a very good time. It will be a constant, sometimes painful struggle. If you have children, they will not be able to participate in a punishment based training process because it is too difficult and truly no fun.

- Simply put, if you train your dog using rewards, you and your dog will have more fun and a better relationship. Rely on rewards to change his behavior by using treats, toys, playing, petting, affection or anything else you know your dog likes.

If your dog is doing something that you do not like, replace the habit with another by teaching your dog to do something different and then rewarding him or her for doing the replacement action. Then everyone can enjoy the outcome.

6 Clicker Training Your Mini Aussie

You can choose not to clicker train your dog and use this books rewards based training techniques without a clicker, however clicker training is proven to speed up puppy and dog training.

What the heck is that clicking noise? Well, it's a clicker, thus the name. If you are a product of a Catholic school, you might be very familiar with this device. You probably have nightmares of large, penguin like women clicking their way through your young life. Yes, it was annoying and at times terrifying, however, when it comes to training your dog, it will be helpful and fun.

A clicker is a small device that makes a sound that is easily distinguished and not common as a sound in nature, or one that humans normally produce. This unique sound keeps the dog that is being trained from becoming confused by accidently hearing a word used in conversation or another environmental noise. You click at the exact time when your dog does the correct action then immediately follow the click with a treat or reward.

The clicker is used to inform your dog that he did the right thing and that a treat is coming. When your dog does the right thing after you command, like drop your Chanel purse that is dangling from his mouth, you click and reward him with a nice treat.

Using the clicker system allows you to set your puppy up to succeed while you ignore or make efforts to prevent bad behavior. It is a very positive, humane system and punishment is *not* part of the process.

Here are some questions often asked about the clicker training:

- "Do you need to have the clicker on your person at all times?" *No.*

The clicker is a teaching device. Once your dog understands what you want your dog to do, you can then utilize verbal or hand cues, and if inclined verbal praise or affection instead of clicking and treating.

- "Can rewards be other things besides treats?" *Sure.*

Actually, you should mix it up. Use the clicker and a treat when you first start teaching. When your puppy has learned the behavior you want, then switch to other rewards, such as petting, play, toys or lottery tickets. Remember always to ask for the wanted target behavior, such as *sit, stay* or *come,* before you reward your dog. These verbal reinforcements can augment the clicker training and reward giving.

- "With all these treats, isn't my dog going to get fat?" *No.*

If you figure treats into your dog's daily intake and subtract from meals accordingly, your dog will be fine. The treats should be as small as a corn kernel, just a taste. Use food from his regular meals when you are training indoors, but when outdoors, use fresh treats like meat or cheese.

There are many distractions outside and a tasty fresh treat will help keep your puppy's attention. Dogs' finally honed senses will smell even the smallest of treats and this keeps them attentive.

- "What do I do if my dog doesn't act out the command?"

*Simpl*e, if your dog disobeys you, it is because he has not been properly trained yet. Do not C/T (Click and Treat), or verbally praise for any wrong actions, ignore the wrong action. Continue training because your dog has not yet learned the command and action you are teaching him to perform. He, after all, is just a dog.

If he is disobeying, he has been improperly or incompletely trained, perhaps the treats are not tasty enough. Try simplifying the task and attempt to make the reward equal to or better than what is distracting your dog. Eventually your dog will understand what action should be performed when the command word is spoken.

Helpful Hint

- *Conceal the treat! Do NOT* show your dog the treat before pressing the clicker and making the clicking sound. If you do this, he will be responding to the treat and not the click and this will *undermine* your training strategy.

Why and How Clicker Training Works

The important reason I put this information together is that it is essential to understand why timing and consistency is important, and why clicker training works. If any of this is confusing, do not worry, because I walk you through the training process step-by-step.

Clicker training started over seventy years ago and has become a tried and true method for training dogs and other animals. The outcome of using a clicker is an example of conditioned reinforcement. Rewarding the animal in combination with clicker use has proven highly effective as a positive reinforcement training method. It is a humane and effective way of training dogs without instilling fear for non-compliance.

In the 1950s, Keller Breland, a pioneer in animal training, used a clicker while training many different species of animals, including marine mammals. He met great success using this method training these animals. His system developed for clicker training marine mammals is still in use today.

Keller also trained dogs using the clicker. Because of its effectiveness, it was brought into use by others in the dog training community. Gradually, clicker training for dogs gained more and more popularity and by the early 1980's its use became widespread. The success of the clicker spans 7 decades and now is a widely accepted standard for dog training. Millions of dogs worldwide have been successfully trained using a clicker.

A trainer will use the clicker to mark desired actions as they occur. At the exact instant the animal performs the desired action, the trainer clicks and promptly delivers a food reward or other reinforcements. One key to clicker training is the trainer's timing, and *timing is crucial*.

For example, clicking and rewarding slightly too early or to late will reinforce the action that is occurring at that very instant rather than the action you were targeting the reward for. The saying goes, "you get what you click for."

Shaping

Clicker trainers often use the process of *shaping*. Shaping is the process of gradual transformation of a specific action into the desired action by rewarding each successive progression towards the desired action. This is done by gradually molding or training the dog to perform a specific response by first, reinforcing the small, successive responses that are similar to the desired response, instead of waiting for the perfect completion to occur.

The trainer looks for small progressions that are heading in the direction towards the total completion of the desired action and then clicks and treats. It is important to recognize and reward those tiny steps made in the target direction. During training, the objective is to create opportunities for your dog to earn frequent rewards.

In the beginning, it is acceptable to increase the frequency of a C/T to every 3-4 seconds or less. By gauging the dog's abilities and improvements, the trainer can gradually increase the length of time between C/T. It is necessary to assess the dog's progress from moment to moment, adjusting C/T to achieve the desired actionable outcome.

During training, and in conjunction with clicker use, the introduction of a cue word or hand signal can be applied. Eventually, the clicker can be phased out in favor of a cue or cues that have been reinforced during the training sessions. As a result, your dog will immediately respond by reacting, obeying and performing actions to your hand gestures and verbal commands.

Watching this unfold is a highly satisfying process that empowers your friend to be the best he can.

Why is clicking effective over using a word cue first?

The clicking sound is a unique sound that is not found in nature, and it is more precise than a verbal command. Verbal commands can be confusing because the human voice has many tonal variations, whereas the clicker consistently makes a sound that your dog will not confuse with any other noise. It is also effective because it is directed at your pup and followed by good things. Therefore, your dog completely understands which action is preferred and your dog will quickly understand that the click is followed by a reward.

The click sound is produced in a quick and accurate way that is in response to the slightest actions that your dog makes. This clarity of function of this tool increases the bond between you and resulting in making your dog more interested in the training sessions, and ultimately your relationship more engaging and entertaining. Dare I say fun?

On that note, do not forget to always have fun and add variety to your training sessions. Variety is the spice of life, mix up those treats, rewards and commands for each training session.

Clicker training works this way

At the *exact* instant the action occurs, the trainer clicks. If a dog begins to *sit*, the trainer recognizes that and *at the exact moment the dog's buttocks hits the ground the trainer clicks and offers the dog a reward*. Usually the reward is a small kernel sized food treat, but a reward can be a toy, play or affection. Whatever the dog enjoys is a reward worth giving.

Sometimes, after as little as 2-3 clicks have been issued a dog will associate the sound of the click with something it enjoys. Once the association is made, it will repeat the action it did when hearing the click and receiving the reward. Click = Reward, When this goes off in the dog's head, repeating the action makes sense.

The three steps are as follows:

1. *Get the action* you request

2. *Mark the action* with your clicker

3. *Reinforce the action* with a reward

How do you ask for actions when clicker training your dog?

During clicker training before adding a cue command such as *stay*, you wait until your dog completely understands the action. A cue is the names of the action, e.g. sit, stay or come, or it can be a hand signal that you are using when you ask your dog to perform a specific action. Your dog should know the action *stay* from the click and reward before you verbally name it. He or she has connected remaining in the same place to receiving a click and reward.

When training you do not want to add the *cue* until your dog has been clicked 5-10 times for the action, and is accurately responding in a manner that clearly shows he understands which action earns the click and reward. This is called introducing the cue.

Teaching your dog the name of the cue or action requires saying or signaling before your dog repeats the action. After several repetitions, begin to click and reward when your dog performs the action, be sure the cue is given before the reward. Your dog will learn to listen and watch for the cue, knowing that if he does the action a reward will follow.

Clicker Training Help

If your dog is not obeying the cue, answer the following questions and then revise your training process so that your dog knows the meaning of the clicker sound cue during all situations. Importantly, be sure that your dog is and feels rewarded for doing the correct action.

Trainers never assume a dog is intentionally disobeying without asking the questions below.

1. Does your dog understand the meaning of the cue?

2. Does your dog understand the meaning of the cue in the situation first taught, but *not* in the different situations that you gave the cue?

3. Is the *reward* for doing the action you want, satisfying your dog's needs? Is the treat or toy worth the effort?

Once you have answered these questions, change your training process to be certain that your dog understands the cue in all situations, including high distraction situations at a busy park.

Then be sure your dog is adequately rewarded and that it is clear your dog feels that he or she has been properly rewarded. This will help put you two back on the path of mutual understanding during your training sessions.

This will become clearer as you read how to teach commands.

7 Dog Treats

You are training your puppy and it is going well because your pup is the best dog in the world. *Oh yes he is, everyone knows this to be true.* Because of this fact, you want to make sure that you are giving your dog the right type of treats.

Treats are easy as long as you stay away from the things that aren't good for dogs, such as avocados, onions, garlic, coffee, tea, caffeinated drinks, grapes, raisins, macadamia nuts, peaches, plums, fruit pits, seeds, persimmons and chocolates.

Dog owners can make treats from many different foods. Treats should always be sized about the dimension of a kernel of corn. This makes them easy to grab from treat pouches and still flavorful enough for your hound to desire them.

All a dog needs is a little taste to keep them interested. The *kernel size* is something that is swiftly eaten and swallowed, thus not distracting from the training session. A treat is only to provide a quick taste, used for enticement and reinforcement, not as snack or meal.

When you are outdoors and there are many distractions, treats should be of a higher quality that is coveted by your pooch. Trainers call it a higher value treat because it is worthy of your dog breaking away from the activity they are engaged. Perhaps cubes of cheese or dried and cooked meats will qualify as your dog's high value treat.

Make sure you mix up the types of treats by keeping a variety of treats available. Nothing is worse during training than when your puppy turns his nose up at a treat because he has grown bored of it or holds it to be of lesser value than his interests hold.

Types of Treats

Human foods that are safe for dogs include most fruits and veggies, cut up meats that are raw or cooked, yogurt, peanut butter, kibble, and whatever else you discover that your dogs like. Be sure that it is good for them, in particular their digestive system. Be advised that not all human foods are good for dogs. Please read about human foods that are acceptable for dogs and observe your dog's stools when introducing new treat ideas.

How many times have you heard a friend or family member tell you about some crazy food that their dog loves? Dogs do love a massive variety of foods; unfortunately, not all of the foods that they think they want to eat are good for them. Dog treating is not rocket science but it does take a little research, common sense and paying attention to how your dog reacts after wolfing down a treat.

Many people like to make homemade treats and that is okay, just keep to the rules we just mentioned and watch what you are adding while having fun in the kitchen. Remember to research and read the list of vegetables dogs can and cannot eat, and understand that pits and seeds can cause choking and intestinal issues such as dreaded doggy flatulence.

When preparing treats, first remove any seeds and pits, and clean all fruits and veggies before slicing them into doggie size treats.

Before purchasing treats, look at the ingredients on the treat packaging and be sure there are no chemicals, fillers, additives, colors and things that are unhealthy. Some human foods that are tasty to us might not be so tasty to your dog and he will let you know. Almost all dogs love some type of raw or cooked meats. In tiny nibble sizes, these treats work great at directing their attention where you want it focused. In a high distraction area, a piece of liver might be exactly what you need to keep your dog's focus.

Here are some treat ideas:

- Whole grain cereals like cheerios without sugar added are a good choice.

- Kibble (dry foods). Put some in a paper bag and boost the aroma factor by tossing in some bacon or another meat product. Dogs are all about those yummy aroma sensations.

- Beef Jerky that has no pepper or heavy seasoning added.

- Carrots, apple pieces, and some dogs even enjoy melons.

- Meats that have been cubed and are not highly processed or salted, these are easy to make at home as well. You can use cooked left over foods.

- Shredded cheese, string cheese or cubed cheese. Dogs love cheese!

- Cream cheese, peanut butter or spray cheese. Give your dog a small dollop to lick for every proper behavior. These work well when training puppies to ring a bell to go outside for elimination.

- Baby food meat products, they certainly don't look yummy to us but dogs adore them.

- Ice Cubes, but if your dog has dental problems, proceed cautiously.

- Commercial dog treats, but use caution, there are loads of them on the market. Look for those that do not have preservatives, by products, or artificial colors. Additionally, take into consideration the country of origin.

Never feed or treat your four-legged friend from the dining table, because you do not want to teach that begging actions are acceptable. When treating, give treats far from the dinner table or from areas that people normally gather to eat such as by the BBQ.

Time to Treat

The best time to issue dog treats is between meals. Treating soon after a mealtime makes all treats less effective, so remember this when planning your training sessions. If during training you need to refocus your dog back into the training session, keep a high value treat in reserve.

Obviously, if your dog is full from mealtime he will be less likely to want a treat reward than if a bit hungry. If your dog is not hungry, your training sessions will likely be more difficult and far less effective. This is why it is a good idea to reward correct actions with praise, play or toys, and not to rely exclusively on treats.

- Love and attention are considered rewards and is certainly positive reinforcement that can be just as effective as an edible treat. Dog treating is comprised of edibles, praise and attention. Engaging in play or allowing some quality time with their favorite rope toy is also effective and at times, these rewards are crucial to dog training.

- Do not give your dog a treat without asking for an action first. Say, "Sit" and after your dog complies, deliver the treat. This reinforces your training and their obedience.

- Avoid treating your dog when he is over stimulated and running amuck in an unfocused state of mind. This can be counterproductive and might *reinforce a negative behavior* resulting in the inability to get your dog's attention.

- Due to their keen sense of smell, they will know long before you could ever know that there is a tasty snack nearby, but keep it out of sight. Issue your command and wait for your dog to obey before presenting the reward. Remember when dog treating, it is important to be patient and loving, but it is equally important not to give the treat until your dog obeys.

- Some dogs have a natural gentleness to them and always take from your hand gently, while other dogs need some guidance to achieve this.

If your dog is a bit rough during treat grabbing, go ahead and train the command "gentle!" when giving treats. Be firm from this point forward. Give no treats unless they are gently taken from your hand. Remain steadfast with your decision to implement this, and soon your pup will comply if he wants the tasty treat.

Bribery vs. Reward Dog Treating

The other day a friend of mine mentioned *bribing* for an action that he had commanded. I thought about it later and thought I would clarify for my readers. *Bribery* is the act of offering the food visually in advance so that the dog will act out a command or alter a behavior. *Reward* is giving your dog his favorite toy, treat, love or affection *after* he has performed the commanded action.

An example of bribery can happen when you want your dog to come, and *before* you call your dog, you hold a cube of steak for them to see. Reward would be giving your dog the steak after they have obeyed the *come* command. Never show the treats before issuing commands.

Bribed dogs learn to comply with your wishes *only when they see food*. The rewarded dog realizes that they only receive rewards after performing the desired actions. This also assists by introducing non-food items as rewards when training and treating.

8 Chewing Stuff

All puppies love and enjoy chewing, especially while teething, but a chewing Mini Aussie can do some serious damage, so be alert and diligent to thwart that behavior so it does not get out of hand. Keep many toys and doggy chews around so that you can redirect your puppy towards the dog specific toys and not your new black leather shoes.

Let your pup know that his or her toys are the only acceptable items to be chewed. Loneliness, boredom, fear, teething and separation anxiety are feelings that can motivate your puppy into chewing.

Until you have trained that *chewing only happens with their dog toys*, while you are away you should probably leave your pup in his crate or gated area. At all times be sure to throw some dog chew-toys in their crate, limiting your pups chewing to only those indestructible natural rubber chew-toys.

Lots of physical exercise, training, and mental challenges will assist in steering your dog away from destructive chewing. Until your puppy is over his "I'll chew anything phase," hide your shoes and other items that you do not want chewed. Before you bring your new puppy home, all areas where they will have access need to be properly puppy proofed. This protects your possessions and the pup's life.

Puppy proofing your home entails removing all harmful items that a puppy might chew or swallow, unfortunately, that means everything. Puppies love to put anything into their mouths. After all, they are kids learning about the world. It will be necessary to elevate electrical cords, remove floor debris, and all other random objects that a puppy can chew, eat or swallow.

Thoroughly inspect your entire house that is accessible to your puppy. Apply bitter spray to appropriate furniture and fixed objects that require protection. Take extra caution to remove from puppy reach all chemicals, pharmaceuticals and toxic liquids that might be accessed around the house.

The "Leave it!" and "Drop it!" commands should be trained early so that you can quickly steer your pup away from anything that is not his to chew. Avoid letting your dog mouth or chew on your fingers or hand, because that can lead to biting behaviors that can cause many problems for you and them.

Teething

Between the third and sixth week your puppy will begin to feel the notorious baby teeth eruption. Puppy teeth are not designed to grind heavy foods, and consist of predominantly small, razor sharp canines and incisors. These new teeth number about twenty-eight, and during this painful and frustrating teething period, puppies will attempt to seek relief on anything within reach that they can clamp their little mouths down on.

Later, when the baby teeth fall out and their adult teeth emerge, this will again cause discomfort, further increasing their drive to chew in search of relief. Usually by the end of six months, the intense chewing phase begins to wane. Although some variance exists by breed, adult dogs have forty-two teeth with the molars coming in last at around six to seven months of age.

Puppies are motivated to chew because of the discomfort that comes from teething, as well as to investigate new objects of interest. Chewing is a normal dog behavior that can be steered and directed toward owner approved toys and objects.

Dogs certainly love to chew on bones, and they can spend hours gnawing until they feel that they have successfully scoured it clean, sometimes burying it for a later chew session, or solely as a trophy. Wood, bones and toys are some of the objects that occupy a dog during the activity of chewing.

Chewing not only provides stimulation and fun, but it serves to reduce a dog's anxiety. It is our job to identify what our puppies can and cannot chew on, while gently establishing and enforcing the rules of chewing. This process begins by providing an ample amount of safe chew-toys for our puppy.

Chew-toys

A non-edible chew-toy is an object made for dogs to chew that is neither, consumable or destructible. Non-food items eaten by dogs are dangerous and can sometimes seriously harm your dog, so it is imperative to provide high quality and durable chew-toys.

Choosing the type of chew-toy will depend upon your dog's individual preferences and chewing ability, so you may have to go through several to find the most appropriate. Some *super chewer* dogs can destroy a rawhide chew in a fraction of the time as others, so your dog's prowess and jaw power will dictate the types of chews that you will want to provide.

Edible chews such as pig ears, rawhide bones, Nylabones® and other natural chew products are also available and appropriate for your puppy or adult dog. Beware that sometimes edibles can come apart in large chunks or pieces, thus having the potential to be swallowed, or possibly choke a dog.

For safety, keep an eye on your dog whenever he is working away on an edible chew. While your puppy is discovering the variety and joy of chewing, take notice of the chews that he enjoys most.

KONG® and Petsafe® make plenty of top quality chew-toys, including those can be stuffed with food, such as kibble or cheese that hold your dog's interest. KONG® products as well as the Petsafe® Busy Buddy® line are made from natural rubber and have a stellar reputation for durability.

Many other brands are available to choose. When choosing chew-toys, take into consideration whether or not you are purchasing a natural or synthetic product, as well as keep in mind what your pal's preferences are. Usually, anything that you stuff with food will begin a puppy craving for that particular toy, but be aware that is not always the case.

Stuffing Chew-Toys

There are some basic guidelines to follow when using a stuffable chew toy. First, kibble is the recommended foodstuff when filling your puppy's chew-toy. Kibble assists in keeping your puppy at a normal weight, and if this is a concern, you can simply exclude the amount you used in the toy from his normal feeding portion. Secondly, you can use tastier treats, such as cooked meat or freeze-dried liver, but these should be reserved for special rewards. There are plenty of stuffing recipes available, but be cautious about the frequency you treat your puppy with special stuffing.

Be conscious of when you reward your puppy, and avoid doing so when bad behaviors are exhibited. For example, if your puppy has been incessantly barking all afternoon, then if you provide a stuffed chew-toy do not reward him with something utterly delectable.

The art to stuffing chew-toys is that the toy holds your puppy's interest, and keeps him occupied. For your success, you will want to stuff the toy in a way that a small portion of food comes out easily, thus quickly rewarding your puppy. After this initial jackpot, the goal is to keep your puppy chewing while gradually being rewarded with small bits of food that he actively extracts. You can use a high value treat, such as a piece of meat stuffed deeply into the smallest hole that will keep your dog occupied for hours in search of this prized morsel.

With a little creativity and practice, the art of chew-toy stuffing will be acquired, benefitting you and your canine friend. After trial and error, you will begin to understand what fillings and arrangements will keep your puppy occupied for longer and longer times.

Why Feed Dinner from Stuffed Chew-Toys?

Here is some advice that I gleaned off a friend of mine, and it does seem to pack some merit. As you are probably aware, the current practice indicates that puppies should be fed two to three times daily, from their bowl. There is nothing wrong with this, but it does raise a question as to whether perhaps they think that they are being rewarded for the unacceptable behavior that was possibly acted just prior to eating time. *This should be taken into consideration, and feeding should be adjusted to avoid potential negative behavior reinforcement.

The other item that I was made aware is that if you feed your puppy by stuffing his chew-toy, it will occupy more of his time and keep him from negatively acting out of boredom, excessive curiosity or abundant adrenal stores.

The argument against bowl feeding is that it supplants the activity of searching for food as they would in the wild, and as a result of the quick gratification of the easy meal, there remains an over-abundance of time remaining to satisfy the dog's mental and physical stimulation.

To understand this better you have to put yourself into a puppy's paws. Besides sleeping and training, your dog has about twelve hours each day to fill with satisfying and rewarding activity. Resulting from an excess of unoccupied time, normal behaviors, such as grooming, barking, chewing, walking and playing can become repetitive and unfulfilling.

Sometimes an activity can lose its initial purpose and meaning, only to become a way to pass time instead of serving as a positive function of daily life. Obsessive and compulsive behaviors can come out of these long sessions of boredom. For example, vocalizing for alarm can become ceaseless barking, and grooming can turn into excessive licking or scratching likely resulting in harm to the skin.

It falls upon us to instruct our puppies on healthy, calm and relaxing ways to pass the time of day. This is a critical part of training and socialization. Remember, that by stuffing the chew-toy full of kibble you can successfully occupy hours of your puppy's time, helping to reduce the possibility of negative behaviors overtaking your puppy.

This can be accomplished by redirecting his attention to an activity that he enjoys, keeping his mind distracted from the potential of loneliness and boredom. Because of his time spent chewing the approved toy, he is kept calm and his time occupied, periodically rewarded by bits of kibble, and thus the possibility of developing any of the potential, aforementioned negative behaviors is minimized.

This feeding option is a method originally suggested by Dr. Ian Dunbar, a famed rewards-based trainer and SIRIUS® puppy-training pioneer. However, this method is not essential to maintain and train a healthy puppy; I felt it is worth mentioning since I was writing about chew-toys.

Many people refrain from feeding their dog's kibble, utilizing the optional diet of raw foods, thus modification in the feeding method would be required here. Other factors when utilizing this method should take into consideration your dog's individual personality, as well as ability to withdraw food from the toy. Whichever feeding method you choose to use, be certain to feed your puppy the healthiest, least processed, non-chemical laden foods that you can find.

Chew-toy Training

This is an option for controlling and shaping the chewing behavior. Something that I learned from other trainers is how to establish a chew-toy obsession for your puppy. When you bring your puppy home, you should immediately begin exposing him to chew-toys, always keeping them in close proximity, so you can effectively steer all of his chewing energies into these toys instead of your expensive leather shoes, flip-flops, or comfy slippers.

Puppies love to chew on just about anything that they can get their mouths on, but depending upon your puppy's personality, variance exists in the frequency and ferocity of the chewing. There is no reason to leave it to chance. By establishing an early obsession to chew-toys, you can be assured that all of your valuable human articles will be spared from the chewing machines we call *puppies*. Until he has completely learned that his toys are the only acceptable objects for him to chew, everything in your house should be considered *at risk*.

Chew-toys provide puppies a focal point in which to channel their energy, and serve to keep boredom from setting up shop. It is a necessity to teach your puppy early on that the chew-toys you provide are fun and delicious. A good way to do this is to take advantage of the hollow toys, and stuff them with kibble, or other tasty treats of your choice.

To bolster this training, you can keep your puppy's food bowl hidden for the first few weeks after his arrival, and serve all of your puppy's kibble from the stuffed toy, or a sterilized bone. Taking this action will support your puppy's quick understanding and connection between good things and his chew-toys. Remember, the goal here is to create an obsession to chew-toys, resulting in a dog that will leave all of the other non-chew toy items alone.

In order to reinforce his chew-toy obsession, you can use what is called, *the confinement program.* Through a process in which you narrow the choices of items your dog has available to chew, your puppy eventually will find a kind of solace in his own chew-toys. His association with his own chew-toys will grow as he grows, ultimately resulting in him craving to chew only his chew-toys and nothing else.

The confinement program training begins by securing your puppy behind his gated area and providing him with plenty of chew-toys to occupy his alone time. Whether you do this prior to leaving the house or while you are in the house, do not forget to leave fresh water for your puppy.

Additionally, every hour when you let your puppy out for elimination, begin to introduce chew-toy games.

There a variety of games you can play, such as find the *hidden chew-toy, chew-toy tug-o-war* and *fetch*. These games will reinforce his attachment to his chew-toys, and help create a positive obsession toward them. By providing your puppy with a singular choice that is stuffed with food, he will eventually develop a strong chew-toy obsession.

After your dog has formed his chew-toy habit, and has not had any other chewing mishaps, you can broaden his world by expanding his available confinement space to two rooms. As he proves his compliance as evidenced by not chewing items beyond his chew-toys, you can expand his roaming range of access to other rooms in the house, while gradually working up his access to the entire house.

If your puppy makes a chewing mistake, then return to the puppy confinement for 3-6 weeks, all depending upon his progress and the success of further confinement training. After a 3-week period, you will want to test the results of the behavioral modifications resulting from his confinement program (limited areas to roam).

Grant him more access and see if your puppy has reverted to chewing objects on your *no chew list,* or if the program has been a success and it is time move on and enlarge his range. If he reverts again to chewing on objects other than his chew-toys, continue the confinement for a couple of more weeks then test again.

Because this training will be concurrently trained with housetraining, you will also need to monitor when your puppy is having house-soiling accidents. Because your puppy is having accidents indoors, this may limit the house access that you can provide your puppy. It is recommended that in order for you to begin expanding his indoor range of access, your dog should be successfully housetrained and beyond the possibility of a soiling accident. *This training should not conflict with your house-training.

The benefits of making your dog's chew-toys and obsession are more than just for preventing household destruction. It also reduces barking and keeps him from running around the house, because while your puppy is chewing he is distracted, and thus unable to perform other activities.

Another potential behavior issue that has negative implications is the separation anxiety that can occur because of your absence. Because chewing occupies your puppies down time, it assists in the prevention and development of separation anxiety while you are away. It acts like a blanket or a teddy bear to a child.

Furthermore, it is pointed out that a chew-toy addiction is good for dogs that have Obsessive Compulsive Disorder. This addiction offers them an acceptable avenue to work out their obsessive compulsions. It is not a cure but instead a therapeutic device that can be used by them to obsess.

"Is this a good obsession for my puppy?"

Yes, it is, and additionally a good habit that is difficult to break. The benefits are that your puppy will not be chewing your personal items, and it works well towards keeping him away from compulsive behaviors, such as barking, digging, howling, anxiety from being alone and a list of other undesirable behaviors.

The action of chewing also has a calming benefit, thus acts as a stress reliever. It turns out that a simple rubber chew-toy is an effective tool for controlling and shaping behaviors, as well as a therapeutic tool to occupy and sooth.

PART II

Schooling Begins

9 Effective Mini Aussie Training

I have seen some Mini Aussies that spend a lot of time cuddling with their humans where as others only enjoy the occasional hello and show of affection. This depends upon your dog and your own personality. There are no absolutes in dog breed profiles; they are just an average based upon how the standard reads and what breeders try to attain for their Mini Aussie puppies. However, it is more common for Mini Aussies to pine to be near the family than apart and appreciate the family camaraderie.

Part of good training is learning your dog's personality, likes, dislikes and reactions to your actions. Dogs are amazingly tuned to every facial tick and physical action us humans do, so remember in your dog's presence to be aware of what you are doing. This is often forgotten by individuals who are in the process of shaping their dogs behavior.

Training is always happening when your dog is around, and the first year is when you set your dog's foundation for life. The first few months are crucial for you to be active and present in your dog's life, assisting them in knowing what it acceptable and regularly training your dog the basic obedience commands and appropriate behaviors.

When you begin early, puppies learn very quickly. This is because they are curious and unencumbered with any previous memories that are either good or bad.

This is why I stress making training enjoyable and fun, they don't know or think of it as work or negative unless you make it negative. Refraining from harsh vocal tones and physical actions works well and keeps fear or anxiety from creeping into what is supposed to be a fun time for bonding with your new best furry friend. Believe me, there will be plenty of laughs and head shaking moments during training.

To maintain your place in the family hierarchy, your new little furry friend must know that it is unacceptable to be aggressive towards other humans and animals, thus early proper socialization will assist in thwarting this type of aggressive behavior. Expose them to your household's inhabitants, environment, routine and rules of conduct.

Begin gradually socializing your puppy from the day you bring him home. Proper early socialization that continues throughout your puppy's lifetime will provide you with a well-adjusted dog that is able to handle almost any situation in a calm manner and look to you, the alpha, for guidance.

Early, thorough, and continual socialization is important for your Miniature Australian Shepherd. You do not want your dog acting territorial and wary of strangers, so it is important to expose them early to a variety of situations, animals, people and places. Socialization benefits you and your dog by providing you with a peace of mind and that you can expose your pup to different situations with the assurance that he will look to you for guidance in rules of etiquette for the indoor and outdoor world. Socialization is a foundation for all dogs throughout their lifetimes.

Before you begin your training sessions, it is a good idea to let your dog burn off some steam through exercise. He will be more focused and calm. Due to their intellect and willingness to obey, Mini Aussies are quick learners and love to perform. Be aware to use variety in training and treats. They do not respond well to repetitive training. It is common for a Mini Aussie to tear off running around the yard or house to burn excess energy.

Although intelligent, spunky and ready to work, sometimes Mini Aussie requires more repetitions and training sessions before regularly obeying commands at a high rate. You will discover that they have individual personalities and that some will learn and retain commands quickly, while others will take more time and training sessions before responding at an extremely high rate, but once they learn a command they don't forget it. I recommend regular lifetime practice of all commands to keep them sharp.

Focus on the basics first and spend a lot of time on *stay, come, no, leave it,* and *leash training.* These commands obeyed at a high percentage will help you to keep your Mini Aussie out of harm's way. They are fast and eager to engage in chasing prey or to round up animals and children.

The amount of herding ability that your Mini Aussie will display depends upon its recent breeding and individual personality. If you notice it early then spend extra time on shaping their behavior so that they understand nipping and bumping of humans is not allowed. If you require their herding abilities then begin teaching them in their youth to approach their animal charges calmly.

When training the *come* command outside, use a long check chord leash about 20 feet (six meters) or more, especially when you leave the yard and head to an open field or park. These leashes are also handy for fieldwork, sports and tracking.

Although very intelligent, don't be surprised if your Aussie decides not to obey every time you issue a command. This is where rewarding them with what they desire helps you in training. It might be chasing a disc or a ball that is a huge pleasure to them and thus a reward. Of course, it could be a simple "Atta girl" that allows them to feel special. You will figure it out and then use it to your advantage. Don't be afraid to keep their favorite pleasure from them when they are acting out in anyway or not obeying your commands.

This is where your rewarding them with what they most desire helps you in training. It might be playing Frisbee or chasing a ball that is a huge pleasure to them and thus a reward. Of course, it could be a simple "Atta girl" that makes them feel special. You will figure it out and then use it to your advantage. Don't be afraid to keep their favorite pleasure from them when they are acting out in anyway or not obeying your commands.

Knowing what you want to train your Mini Aussie to do is as important as training your dog. You can begin training almost immediately, at around six weeks of age. A puppy is a blank slate and does not know any rules, therefore it is a wise idea to make a list and have an understanding of how you would like your puppy to behave.

What are the household rules and proper dog etiquette? As he grows, the same principle applies and you may adjust training from the basics to more specialized behaviors, such as making your dog a good travel, hiking, agility or simply a companion dog. Know what conditions and circumstances you plan to expose your dog or puppy to outside of the household and strategize to be prepared for those encounters by slowly introducing your dog to those situations.

Establish yourself as the pack leader from the time you first bring your new dog or puppy home. Being the alpha leader assists in the training process, and your dog's relationship with you and your family. Life is much easier for your dog if you are in charge, leading and providing for his needs.

Leading as the alpha assists in the act of working together with your dog towards the goal of understanding the rules of conduct and obedience. Your dog will be at ease when the rules are understood. Training should be an enjoyable bonding time between you and your dog.

Remember that there is no set time limit defining when your dog should learn, retain and then obey commands. Use short training sessions and be aware that if either of you are tired, it is recommended that you stop and try again later. If something does not seem quite right with your dog, in any way, have him checked out by a veterinarian. An unseen mental or physical illness could be impeding your dog's training progress.

An effective incentive is to make everything you do seem fun. This is done with cheerful voice, praise, and all around lighthearted demeanor. Always refrain from forcing your puppy to do anything they do not want to do. Highly prized treats are usually a great incentive to do something, and you will find that a fun, pleasant, friendly, happy, vocal tone combined with the treats will be ample reward for good behaviors and command compliance. Begin training all new commands indoors. This includes silencing all of your audio-visual devices that act as distractions to dog's sensitive ears and your attention.

If you notice any negative behavioral issues and are not quite sure if you are offering your dog proper socialization and necessary training, do not hesitate to enter your puppy into a puppy kindergarten class to assist you with training and socialization.

Behavioral issues do not have to be present to enroll your dog into a puppy kindergarten; this assistance will benefit the both of you. Properly research the available classes so that their approach matches your own. The time to enroll your puppy is usually around eight to ten weeks of age, and after their first round of shots, although some kindergarten classes will not accept puppies until they are three to four months of age.

Reward good behaviors, but do not reward for being cute, sweet, loveable, or huggable. If you wish to reward your dog, always reward after you issue a command and your dog obeys the command. During your training sessions, be sure to mix it up by adding a variety of toys and treats and never forgetting to have fun.

An easy way to avoid the onset of many different behavioral problems is to give your dog's ample daily exercise to keep them fit healthy and keep destructive behavioral problems at bay. Always provide consistent structure, firm but fair authority, rule enforcement, and importantly, love and affection. By maintaining and balancing these things, you will help to create a loyal companion and friend.

- *Timing is crucial* when rewarding for good behaviors and making corrections for bad. Rewarding and correcting must be done right when the action occurs, otherwise the dog is confused why it is being rewarded or corrected.

- *Patience* and *Consistency* are your allies in the training game.

- Only train one command per session. Puppies only have the attention span to go about 5 - 10 minutes per session, and never exceed 15 minutes. Training a command once per day is enough for your dog to begin to learn and retain. You can train different commands in the different sessions. It is easy to perform at least 3-5 training sessions in a day, but whenever the opportunity presents itself you should reinforce the training sessions throughout the day.

For example, when opening a door or putting down a food bowl, first command *sit*, *down* or *stay* and be sure not to reward your dog unless your dog obeys. The most important thing to remember is to remain relaxed, keep it fun, and enjoy this time of bonding and training your puppy.

Five to ten minutes per session is a good time limit for young puppies. Some remain puppies longer than others remain and may not fully develop until year two; however, as dogs mature they will begin to remain focused for longer periods. Use a variety and an abundance of different treats and rewards. Rewards are play, toys, praise, affection, treats, and anything that you know that your dog enjoys. The simplest thing like a scratch in a preferred place can be a reward.

- All dogs have their own personalities and therefore respond to training differently. You need to account for individual personality and adjust accordingly. If needed, do not hesitate to solicit professional help and advice, but by carefully observing your dog, you should be able to adjust your training.

- We all love treats, and so does your dog. Giving your dog a treat is the best way to reinforce good behavior, to help change his behavior or just to make your dog does that insanely funny dance-like-thing. Make the treats small enough only to get a taste, around kernel sized. Remember, you do not want you pup filling up on treats as it might spoil dinner and interfere with his attention span, and large treats take time to chew and swallow, thus interrupting the session.

- Keep a container of treats handy with you at all times. You do not want to miss a chance to reward a good behavior or reinforce a changed behavior. Always carry treats when you go on a walk.

Remember what treats your dog likes most and save those for special times, like the big break-through. In addition, what you consider a treat and what your dog considers a treat are two vastly different worlds. A single malt scotch or chicken wings might be a treat in your mind, but dried liver bits or beef jerky in your dogs.

- Ask for something before you give the treat. Tell your dog to sit, stay, or lie down, print two copies of your resume, anything, before you reward your dog with treats, petting or play. By asking for good behavior, before you give your dog a reward, you demonstrate you are in charge, in an easy fun manner.

There is a common misconception that dogs are selfless and wanting to behave only to please out of respect for you. This is horse pucky. This line of thinking is incorrect and detrimental to your success with the training. You have to make sure that your dog knows exactly why he should be listening to you, and exactly what action you want from him. You are the alpha, the keeper of the treats, the provider of the scratching and the purveyor of toys. Keep this balance of power and the results will be your reward.

- Be positive. Think about what you want your dog to do, instead of what you don't want him to do. Do not send mixed messages. Simply, ignore the bad behaviors and reward your dog when he does the action you request. Begin with the basics, teach your dog some simple commands to communicate what you want, such as Sit, Come, Stay, Drop it and Leave it.

- There will be times that before a training session begins you will need to use a little exercise to release some of your dog's energy; this can increase his ability to focus during the session. Toy and many small dogs do not require excessive exercise but still require daily walks and play sessions.

- It is very important that you make sure your dog is comfortable in all sorts of situations. All dogs, even your sweet tempered pup, have the potential to bite. Making sure, he is comfortable in various situations and teaching your dog to be gentle with his mouth will reduce the risk of unwanted bites. Mouthing should not be acceptable behavior because it leads to potentially harmful actions.

- Kids are great, are they not? However, the notion that kids and dogs are as natural a pairing as chocolate and peanut butter is simply not true. Kids are often bitten by dogs because they unintentionally do things that frighten dogs. Sometimes a child's behavior appears like prey to a dog.

Never leave a dog and a child together unsupervised, even if the dog is good with children. Teach children not to approach dogs that are unfamiliar to them.

The way a child behaves with the familiar family dog may not be appropriate with another dog that they meet for the first time. Instruct children that tail pulling, hugging their necks tightly, leg pulling and hard head pats are unacceptable.

There exists many different ways to train puppies. Using clicker and rewards based training is an effective and humane way to train dogs and treat them with kindness.

Lying ahead of you will be the task of navigating your dog's unique personality, which will affect your training and relationship. Although, you have no doubt read and watched much about training, spoken with friends and breeders, your dog's personality is why it is imperative to keep an open mind and use your intuition to guide you while training, be flexible.

Your consent as the owner is the one thing that will allow your dog to become disobedient, out of control and possibly a danger to your family and the outside world.

Therefore, arming yourself with knowledge about dog behaviors, and understanding your own dog's personality will greatly assist you throughout the process of training and companionship alongside your dog. It is your responsibility to guide and train your dog to be a socially adjusted obedient dog so that the two of you have a fruitful relationship. Well-behaved dogs are welcomed anywhere and your goal should be to train your dog to be well behaved and obedient.

Training Landmarks

A. Avoid future problems by correcting issues early and stopping bad behaviors before they escalate. This is accomplished through a lot of supervised time spent together.

B. Begin training on the first day that your puppy arrives home. Do not force anything but as the trainer keep all of this in mind.

- Immediately begin establishing the household rules.
- Begin house-training.
- Begin chew toy training.
- Begin minimal socialization.

C. Common achievement timelines that should be set up for completion. Note on your training calendar and keep track of your puppy's progress. These milestones and your training progress will let you know if you need to solicit help in any of the following.

1. Socialization to humans by 12 weeks.

2. Biting/Nipping training successful by 18 weeks.

3. *Well socialized* by 5 months of age. At this stage your dog can meet and greet other humans and animals in a calm friendly manner. Your dog handles transportation well and is understanding all basic etiquette for strange encounters. Meeting this goal will set the precedence for your adult dog to have good manners and be trustworthy. Keep in mind that socialization is a lifetime endeavor.

4. *Housetraining* completion ranges from six months to twelve months. Dog size and personality contributes to the training length of time. By four months most puppies often know to wait, but might still have issues. Many puppies are housetrained by six to eight months, or mostly trained by six months with occasional accidents.

Examples of mentally stimulating activities for your Mini Aussie

- Retrieval games are physically and mentally stimulating.

- Agility games that are physical, but primarily mental, you can turn your household items into a course.

-Tracking, this uses dog's natural scenting abilities to find hidden objects.

- Herding trials or tests allow dogs to use their natural or trained herding abilities.

- Free play with other familiar dogs assists in socialization, energy release, and stimulation.

- Trick performance that is rewarded with access to your dog's highly valued items.

- Obedience classes.

- Flyball for physical activity.

- Hide and Seek with family members is good physical exercise for all.

- Working livestock is challenging both mentally and physically.

- Treibball is a relatively new dog sport where dogs gather and move large balls that represent a flock of animals.

Herding Breed Traits

I am including information on herding dogs to offer you the owner and trainer further insight into the characteristics these types of dog carry with them in their pedigree. The more information known about your Mini Aussie heritage, the better you will be equipped to train and understand him.

Herding dogs were originally bred for working or herding stock. They are referred to as working, stock, or herding dogs. The characteristics of this breed features heightened herding instincts derived from ancient hunting capabilities. Early in human history, dogs and humans began living and working with one another, relying on each other for survival. Humans began developing the herding breeds to manage domesticated animals, while simultaneously developing other breeds as guardians to protect the flocks from all types of predators. Herding and guarding dogs work together to keep the livestock together and safe.

For example, the Great Pyrenees Mountain Dogs steadfastly handle the guarding duties while the Pyrenean Shepherds diligently take care of the herding duties. Herders are known for their abilities to obey vocal and whistle commands, as well as think and act independently while performing their jobs.

Depending upon the different recognitions and classifications, I uncovered eighty-eight herding breeds in the world. The Herding Group is made up of sheep and cattle dogs that were, and are still bred to round up livestock and retrieve all stragglers.

Herding dogs use a variety of techniques, such as nipping, barking, running, and engaging in intense eye contact with their animal charges. Australian Kelpies and Aussies are known to run atop sheep (backing sheep) to move them along, and Border Collies are known for their staring and crouching style that enables them to mesmerize and herd almost any animal. Australian Cattle Dogs (Blue/Red Heelers) will nip at heels, or if necessary jump up to nip under a cows neck. The Mini Aussie's herding style is more upright than a Border Collie who crouches and stares down its herd. Mini Aussies also tend to move in towards the stock at a quicker rate than Border Collies.

Fearless, intelligent, alert, independent, and blessed with stamina and intense energy levels, these herding breeds possess the natural traits necessary to accomplish their jobs proficiently. Beyond their herding abilities, some in this group are used as police, guide and therapy dogs.

Versatility allows many of these breeds to herd cattle, ducks, geese, sheep, and goats, and the Mini Aussie is part of this group. Additionally, they will herd children, household pets, other dogs, and if not tethered they will even attempt to round up motor vehicles.

Because of their natural instincts, herding breeds that do not have a job and are to be household pets will need to be vigorously exercised and given opportunities to complete tasks. This can be accomplished through agility training, tracking games, herding trials, daily accompaniment with their humans on bike rides, jogs, hikes, runs, brisk walks or anything that will help deplete their seemingly endless energy reserves.

A herder that is not having their exercise needs met can become destructive, aggressive or display other negative behaviors. Before bringing home a herding dog, you must be certain that you can provide the proper amount of exercise and stimulation for these breeds. Most herding breeds need a few exercise outings per day, which should include a minimum of two hours of rigorous exercise.

Herding dogs come in a variety of coat types, heights, and weights. For example, the little Corgi's stand only 10 - 12 inches (25 - 30 cm) tall, while the French Beauceron stands 26–28 in (66–71 cm) tall. Most herders reside in the medium to large size classification. Amazingly, the little Corgi's are wonderfully efficient herding dogs that have been around since the Vikings brought them to Wales almost two thousand years ago. Since at least the 10th century, the little Pembroke Welsh Corgi has been herding cattle, ducks, geese, horses, and sheep. In recent times, herding dogs have been employed to keep ducks and geese clear of golf courses and airports.

Many in this group, including Mini Aussie, tend to be wary of strangers, but form tight loyal bonds with their handlers and family. They make a great addition as a family companion and enjoy being in the company of their humans. Nipping is something that needs to be addressed early when they are puppies. Always supervise your dog around small children. When children are running around playing, your herding dog immediately recognizes this as a herd to be tended, and they will begin nipping at the children's heels. You can sometimes observe them instinctually circling a group of children, in classic herding behavior. They do not intend to do harm, but a nip or hard bump can be painful and should not be allowed.

Early and ongoing socialization will help with aggression, possessiveness, territorialism and other potential negative behaviors that can surface. Herders are happiest when they have a purpose. These are some of the most intelligent and active dog breeds, and they have a strong predisposition for work.

The AKC created The Herding Group in 1983, and it is the newest American Kennel Club classification. Before the creation of their own group, these breeds were classified in the Working Group. In fact, this group has some of the most intelligent of all dog breeds. The Border Collie has been ranked as one of the most intelligent of all breeds. Other herding breeds ranked inside the top ten of some lists include the Australian Cattle Dog, German Shepherd, Shetland Sheepdog (Sheltie), and the Rottweiler.

10 Dog Communication

Training your Mini Aussie seems like a daunting task, but it is a unique and rewarding experience. It is the foundation of a healthy and long relationship with your new dog or puppy. You must be the one in charge of the relationship and lead with the pack leader mentality, all the while showing patience and love. Whether you choose to enroll your dog in an obedience school such as the Sirius® reward training system or go it alone at home, you will the need assistance of quality books like this one, videos, and articles to help guide you through the process and find solutions to obstacles along the way.

Without a doubt, it is nice to have an obedient friend by your side through good times and bad. Owning a dog is a relationship that needs tending throughout the years. Once you begin training, it will continue throughout the life of your dog friend.

An obedient dog is easier to care for and causes less household problems and expense. You know what needs to be done, but what about your dog. How do you read his messages in regards to what you are attempting to accomplish? I am going to cover dog's body language and vocal language to provide insight into what it is your dog is attempting to communicate. This should prove to be an asset while training your dog.

The art of *dogmanship* has been described as a partnership of species in which instinct and intuition are utilized over logical thought to enable work in collaboration. Humans need to be flexible and responsive, and able to not only to lead, but also to follow. Humans need to open their sensory awareness and place high importance upon nonverbal communications.

It is further defined as the understanding of how dogs communicate with one another in their own canine language and being able to communicate with dogs in their language. When you understand some or most of the techniques dogs use to communicate with each other, you can then apply it when communicating with dogs.

To do this you have to be able to isolate your human emotions and put the needs of the dog at the forefront. When a dog is born into this world, environmental and genetic factors will affect that dog's behavior. Additionally they have behaviors coded into their DNA that dictates their inherent canine behaviors. In dog-to-dog communication, every gesture and vocalized sound has meaning. This can be exceptionally subtle in action and difficult for humans to see and interpret.

Although dogs are intelligent and can learn human communication methods, it is not always the most efficient way to communicate with a dog. Dogs are simpler than humans are and it is more challenging to teach a dog to understand human communication than it is to use dog communication methods to communicate with your dog.

If a person is able to be open up to the idea, then they can learn the language dogs use to communicate with each other and incorporate that into their communication with dogs. Using this method, you begin to work in harmony with the dog and their natural instincts, instead of against them.

Commonly humans forget to address or never consider what a dog's natural instincts are. Embedded in their genetic code is the thirst for rules, boundaries and structure. Dogs enjoy knowing what the rules of etiquette for all situations are, and having the structure of a daily schedule for walks, playtimes, exercises and feedings. They also crave consistency in actions, and this is something that some humans regularly struggle with providing.

Therefore, it is essential to provide your dog with the things that they need, such as physical and mental exercises, leadership, play, toys, rule establishment and enforcement, and the essentials that are food, water, shelter, love, kindness and all the other things that dogs need to live a fruitful life.

The entire family should understand the rules of etiquette for your dog so that rule enforcement is always the same. An example of failed consistency is if your daughter is reprimanding your dog for an action that you let happen, there will be a conflict in your dog's brain. Your dog will not know which way to act and this will cause your dog distress and possibly anxiety that can lead to further dysfunctional idiosyncrasies.

Human behavior can have an entirely different meaning to a dog, and this is why commonly a dog-owner may be perplexed by his dog's behavior. The owner is thinking in human terms and not in dog terms. Negative dog behaviors are mostly a result from something missing from their life, and instead of blaming our dog for its behavior, we must figure out the root cause of this negative behavior and remedy it for our dogs, thus showing our leadership abilities and doing our job as their leader.

A dog's temperament is shaped by the owner's ability to provide him with what he instinctually needs. Educating yourself about dog communication and behaviors is your first step to achieving *understanding of natural canine communications* (dogmanship). Owning and properly caring for a dog requires a knowledge base that has been diagramed and written about to help you learn through personal observation. Studying your dog's behaviors and allowing your intuition to guide you will enable you to learn dog communication techniques

Using Human Body Language to Communicate

There are a couple of important things to keep in the forefront of your mind regarding human movements around dogs. The first is a tough one to master. *Stay calm even when you are not. Avoid fast erratic movements such as jumping back, making a loud noise when surprised or frightened, and flinging your arms into the air. These types of movements mimic prey or the dog can mistake these movements for a type of game that they want to play.

The dog's reaction might be that it attempts to put his mouth upon your fast moving limbs, jumps up or gives chase. The difficult part when you are surprised or nervous is to freeze in place and to avoid eye contact while simultaneously slightly turning your head away. If you feel it is necessary, fold your arms to your chest. If you need to move away from a dog then use slow fluid movements while backing away from the dog.

As a startled human we sometimes hold our breath, so do not forget to breathe and calm yourself. A dog may perceive your held breath as a sign that you are tense and going to react. This could escalate tensions.

Eye contact is very important to dogs and assists you in conveying to your dog that you are serious and in command. Always use direct eye contact when issuing commands or calling your dog by name.

If a dog jumps up on to you the best method of reaction is to *not* engage with your eyes, fold your arms across your chest and freeze in place. In essence, you are to avoid to the best of your ability any physical or eye engagement with the dog.

Jumping dogs usually want attention but when they continually do not get that attention, they begin to catch onto the fact that jumping is an unwanted and undesirable behavior.

I realize that their claws might hurt you, and some dogs are large enough to move you, so do the best that you can to ignore the dog and not make any sudden movements. This is covered further in the training chapter on jumping.

Dogs can sense our inner feelings by the way we use our tone of voice, body language and facial expressions. They are able to read us humans much better than most people can read a dog's body language. Their keen abilities to observe us intensely are used by them to interpret and anticipate what we want from them. Using the correct body language helps you when meeting unfamiliar dogs, and in controlling your own dog.

The following is an example of how a dog interprets human action. If you approach a *submissive dog* by leaning forward towards him and then move your hand towards his head, it will usually cause a negative reaction because you are acting out a dominate behavior and is therefore intimidated by you. Since the dog has already taken the submissive posture, the dog is not expecting a dominate action.

Conversely, if you approach the same dog by first crouching down beside him and then bring your hand from his chest up to his head this should produce a much different reaction. Our instinct is to pet dogs on their head, but when interacting with a submissive dog it is better to pet their chest to avoid intimidation.

"How do I identify a submissive dog?" That is a good question and the answer will help in many ways. A submissive dog will commonly lower its head and tail making its body smaller, while simultaneously avoiding eye contact. Sometimes owners mistake this for a dog feeling sad, when in fact he is submitting to the alpha owner and stating that they are the leader.

If your dog is showing this submissive posture, this means that you have achieved the alpha position and your dog is following your lead. Your dog is happy because he is comforted in knowing that he has a leader that is taking good care of him. A happy and secure submissive dog that lowers itself is not a dog that is recklessly jumping around vying for attention and trying to control its owner. Realizing what the submissive posture is and not confusing it with false thinking that your dog is upset or sad will help you from sending your dog confusing signals. The fact that your dog is showing this posture instead of jumping on you and trying to steer you is a good sign and does not mean that you need to cheer your dog up or act differently to address the posture.

Body Language in Training

Have you ever had trouble with your dog obeying your *come* command? Try this body movement. Instead of becoming angry, yelling, or begging, turn your back and crouch down. This position tells your dog that he is not in trouble and that you are not a threat to him. Do not repeatedly say the *come* command. This body position is an invitation instead of a demand. Often this position works, and when your dog comes to join you, always reward him.

As a last resort, you can try running away from your dog. This will commonly be perceived as play and often your dog will come running. If your dog is not obeying, continue to work on training your dog to obey the all-important *come* command so that you do not have to resort to these physical cues.

Maybe you have not been offering a good enough reason for your dog to come and need to improve your rewards, he has not retained the command, or you are still earning the dogs respect. Whichever the case, practice until your dog comes to you upon command at least 90% of the time. The *come* command is extremely important for the safety of your dog and your peace of mind.

In leash training, body language plays an important role. Every time your dog is pulling, you should change directions and walk the other way. Using this body language, you are teaching him that you are the one in control and decide the direction and speed of walking.

In addition, when you are walking your dog on the leash, you want him to maintain a close distance but never impede your walking and direction changes. If your dog is not keeping the proper distance and moving with you, but instead crowding, slightly bumping him while changing directions will stop him from crowding or impeding your walk. This can be practiced during training sessions that include many direction changes and serpentine walking. Your dog must know that you are in charge and you make the rules. Soon he will learn not to crowd or impede you so that the two of you can harmoniously walk with a loose leash.

Body language is equally important to communicating with dogs as it is with humans, but the difference is that communicating with humans comes naturally to us. Standing upright, remaining calm, confident, and consistent is how all alphas should act when directing their dogs, and if you notice, many powerful people do the same when interacting with humans. Keep this in the forefront of your mind, and the more you practice, the more natural and easy it will become.

It takes practice to be able to control our reactions, facial expressions and tones. Having this type of control helps some people to be better trainers than others. Remember that you are under constant observation from your dog and they respect their confident leader. Whenever you act less confident, your dog will immediately *notice* it.

Enjoying the dog training process and having a good time with your dog is also important, so do not be afraid to laugh and smile. You don't have to be unemotional or act like a statue while learning about dogs and yourself.

Learning Natural Dog Behaviors

Remember that we cannot always read a dog's body language accurately. All dogs have their own unique personality; therefore will express themselves in their individual way. It is possible that a dog's happy wagging tail could be another dog's way of conveying that it is nervous or anxious. A dog's breed, size, or appearances are not proper indicators of whether a dog will bite, but his body language is. Keep in in your thoughts when reading a dog's body language that it is difficult to be 100% accurate in our interpretations and to use caution around strange dogs.

In my book's, I cover some frequent dog positions and body language, but I realized more visual clues are needed. I found two handy free downloads at the ASPCA and American Humane websites with photographs of dog postures. The diagrams and descriptions will assist you in identifying what a dog's body language and postures are usually stating.

Use the information to observe your dog and verify if he is consistently using a body posture or movement that illustrates his mood and whether it corresponds with the diagrams. It is a good idea to keep a journal and log your observations so that you know what your dog is saying to you with his body movements.

Some dogs have curly spitz type tails and therefore it will take a keen eye to see and denote what their tail position might be conveying so you will have to rely more on facial, ear, mouth and body postures. Breeds with docked tails, flat faces and are black in color make it more difficult to read what they are trying express. From distance black colored dogs facial expressions can be difficult to see. Creating further difficulties are breeds that have puffy hair, long hair, or extensive hair that hides their physical features.

Observing your dog's ears, eyes, lips, mouth, body postures and tail movements, then matching them to your dog's emotional state will take some time, but when you begin to easily identify and understand your dog's emotions and intentions from his body language, you are well on your way to a better long-lasting relationship. Additionally, you will improve your training and communication skills with your dog and other people's dogs. This is your first step to mastering *dogmanship*. This skill can only be learned through the observation of dogs, trusting in your intuition, and in tandem with studying about dog communication.

Using daily focused observations, you will gradually become aware of your dog's communications and their meanings. Some dogs body language is easy to see and define so do not feel overwhelmed or intimidated by the process that I have outlined. Previous dog owners will attest that the more time spent with dogs the more you glean from their behaviors. Gradually you will become more aware of dog behavior and then subtle changes will occur in the way that you interact with dogs. The process is enjoyable because you are spending time with your dog companion. All dog trainers are continuously honing their dog language skills.

Body Language

What is body language? Body language is all of the non-verbal communication we exhibit when engaged into an exchange with another entity. Every one of those little tics, spasms, and movements that we act out comprise non-verbal body language. Studies state that over 50% of how people judge us is based on our use of body language. Apparently, the visual interpretation of our message is equal to our verbal message.

It is interesting that some studies indicate that when body language disagrees with the verbal message, our verbal message accounts for as little as 7-10% of how others judge us. With that kind of statistic, I would say that body language is extremely important for communication.

Similar to humans, dogs use their bodies to communicate. Their audio and visual senses are especially acute. Observe how your dog tilts his head, moves his limbs and what actions his tail is making. They are continuously reading us in the same manner.

The Tail

A wagging tail does not mean that a dog is friendly. With most dogs that have tails it can convey many messages, some nice, some nasty. Specialists say a dog's wagging tail can mean the dog is scared, confused, preparing to fight, confident, concentrating, interested, or happy.

"How do you tell the difference?"

Look at the speed and range of motion in the tail. The wide-fast tail wag is usually the message of "Hey, I am so happy to see you!" wag. The tail that is not tight between the hind legs, but instead is sticking straight back horizontally means the dog is curious but unsure, and probably not going to bite but remain in a place of neutral regard. This dog will probably not be confrontational, yet the verdict is not in. The slow tail wag means the same; the dog's friendly meter is gauging the other as friend or foe.

The tail held high and stiff, or bristling (hair raised) is a WATCH OUT!-Red Flag warning humans to be cautious. This dog may not only be aggressive, but dangerous and ready to rumble. If you come across this dog, it is time to calculate your retreat and escape plan.

Not only should the speed and range of the wag be recognized while you are reading doggie body language, one must also take note of the tail position. A dog that is carrying its tail erect is a self-assured dog in control of itself. On the flip side of that, the dog with their tail between their legs, tucked in tight is the, "I surrender man, I surrender, please don't hurt me" posture.

The chill dog, a la Reggae special is the dog that has her tail lowered but not tucked in-between her legs. The tail that is down and relaxed in a neutral position stating the dog is relaxed.

While training your dog or simply playing, it is a good idea to take note of what his or her tail is doing and determine if your dog's tail posture is matching their moods. Your understanding of your dog's tail movements and body posture will be of great assistance throughout its lifetime.

Up Front

On the front end of the dog is the head and ears with their special motions. A dog that cocks her head or twitches her ears is giving the signal of interest and awareness, but sometimes it can indicate fear. The forward or ear up movements can show a dog's awareness of seeing or hearing something new. Due to the amazingly acute canine sense of hearing, this can occur long before we are aware. These senses are two of the assets that make dogs so special and make them fantastic guard and watchdogs.

"I give in, and will take my punishment" is conveyed with the head down and ears back. Take note of this submissive posture, observe the neck, and back fur for bristling. Sometimes this accompanies this posture. Even though a dog is giving off this submissive stance, if it is showing bristling it should be approached with caution because it may feel threatened and launch an attack thinking he needs to defend himself.

"Smile, you are on camera." Yep, you got it, dogs smile too. It is usually a subtle corner pull back to show the teeth. Do not confuse this with the obvious snarl that entails a raised upper lip and bared teeth, sometimes accompanied by a deep growling sound. The snarl is something to be extremely cautious of when encountered. A snarling dog is not joking around--*the snarl is serious*. This dog is ready to be physically aggressive.

The Whole Kit and Caboodle

Using the entire body, a dog that rolls over onto its back and exposes his belly, neck and genitals is conveying the message that you are in charge. A dog that is overly submissive sometimes urinates a small amount to express his obedience towards a human or another dog.

Front paws down, rear end up, tail is a waggin. This, "hut, hut, hut, C'mon Sparky hike the ball," posture is the ole K-9 position of choice for, "Hey! It is playtime, and I am ready to go!" This posture is sometimes accompanied with a playful bark and or pawing of the ground in an attempt to draw you into his playful state. I love it when a dog is in this mood, albeit they can be aloof to commands.

Whines, Growls, Howls, Barks and Yelps, the Sounds Dogs Make

We just had a look at the silent communication of body language. Now, I will look into the doggie noises we cherish, but sometimes find annoying.

"Just what is our dog trying to tell us?" Our canine friends often use vocal expressions to get their needs met. Whines and growls mean what they say, so when training your dog, listen carefully. As you become accustomed to the dogs vocal communication, and are able to begin understanding them, the happier you will both become. Some dog noises can be annoying and keep you awake, or wake you up. This may need your attention to be trained as inappropriate vocalizations.

Barking

"What does a dog bark say and why bark at all?" Dogs bark to say "Hey, what's up dude," "I am hungry," "Look at me!" or "Want to play?" A bark may warn of potential trouble, to convey that the dog is bored or lonely. I think we all know that stimulated and excited dogs also bark.

It is up to us to survey the surroundings and assess the reason. We need to educate ourselves about our dog's various barks so we can act appropriately. Not every bark is a put on your slippers, grab flashlight and patrol the house late at night.

Whining and Whimpering

Almost from the time they are freshly made and feeding upon their mother's milk, our little puppies begin to make their first little fur-ball noises. Whimpering or whining to get their mothers attention for feeding or comfort is innate, and as a result, they know mom will come to them. They also use these two W's on us to gain our attention.

Other reasons for whimpering or whining are from fear produced by loud noises such as thunderstorms or fireworks. I think most of us have experienced the 4th of July phenomenon where the entire dog population is barking excessively until the wee hours of the morning when the last fireworks are ignited, and the final "BOOM!" dies off. Whining can also come from separation anxiety, but if your dog is whining for attention, you should not indulge him.

Growling

Growling means that you had better beware of the dogs intentions. Be acutely aware of what this dog is doing and the dog's intentions. Usually a dog that is growling is seriously irritated and preparing to be further aggressive. However, this is not always true, sometimes a dog will issue a growl requesting for petting to continue. It is our job to learn the difference with our pooches.

Howling

Picture the dark silhouette of a howling dog with a full moon backdrop. A dog's howl is a distinct vocalization that most dogs use, and every wolf makes. Howling can mean loneliness, desire, warning or excitement. A lonely howl is a dog looking for a response. Dogs also howl after a long hunt when they have tracked and cornered their prey. Some Scent hounds use a distinct sound named bay.

11 Housetraining Your Mini Aussie

When you first bring your peeing and pooping machine home, clip on his leash and carry him to the predetermined waste elimination spot that you and your family have chosen. Let your pup eliminate his then take him inside the home. Now that you have established his elimination spot, remind the family that is where your pup should be taken each time he has to eliminate.

It is a fact that dogs are a bit particular about where they "relieve" themselves and will invariably build a strong habit. While housetraining your Mini Aussie, remember that whenever he *soils somewhere* in the house, a strong preference is being built towards that particular area. This is why preventing soiling accidents is very important; additionally thoroughly cleaning the area where the defecation or urination has occurred is tremendously important. When your puppy does relieve himself in the house, *blame yourself* not your pup.

Until your puppy has learned where to do his business, you should keep a constant, watchful eye on him, whether he is in his crate, on a mat, beside you or in his pen. During housetraining, some people will *tether* their puppies to their waist or to a nearby object. This allows them to keep their puppies in eyesight at all times and is very good idea.

- When your pup is indoors but out of the crate, watch for sniffing or circling, and as soon as you see this behavior immediately take him outdoors. *Do not hesitate.*

- If your pup is having accidents in the crate, the crate may be too big. The crate should be big enough for your puppy to stand up, turn around, and lie down in. If crate accidents occur, remove any soiled items from the crate and thoroughly clean it.

- Keep your puppy confined to their specific gated puppy area where accidents can be easily cleaned, such as his pen or section of bathroom, pantry, laundry or similar room. Do not leave your puppy confined to their crate for hours upon end. You want their crate to be an enjoyable place that they find safe and comforting.

- Set a timer to go off every forty-five minutes to an hour so that you remember to take your puppy out before nature calls. With progress, you can increase the time duration between elimination outings.

- A good rule of thumb for elimination outing frequencies is as follows

- Up to six weeks of age, elimination every 45 minutes - hour.

- Two months of age, around two to three hours.

- Three months, four hours.

- Four months and up - around five hours.

These times will vary with individual dogs.

- If your pup doesn't do his *duty* when taken outdoors, wait a few minutes and then bring your pup back indoors and keep a close eye on him. One option is to keep your pup tethered to your waist so that he is always in eyesight, then try again in 10-15 minutes.

- While you are away, if possible, arrange to have a person to take your puppy outside to eliminate because this will greatly speed up the housetraining process.

Establish a Schedule

- You should take your puppy out many times during the day, most importantly after eating, playing and sleeping.

Feed your puppy appropriate amounts of food three times per day and leave the food down for around fifteen-minutes at a time and then remove it. You can keep a pups water down until about eight at night, but then remove it from your puppy's reach. This will help with accidents and waking up less in the night to endure the elements while he does his business.

- When you hear him whining, take him out for elimination once during the night. Puppies can usually hold their bladders for about 4-5 hours during sleep. Dogs do not like to soil their own area and only as a last resort will they soil their crate or bedding.

- Gradually, your puppy will be able to hold his urine for increasingly longer lengths of time, but until then keep to the every hour schedule unless he is sleeping, but always take him out after waking. Having your puppy's excrement and urine outdoors puts your puppy's housetraining on the fast track.

Consistency Is the Mother of Prevention

Until your puppy is reliably housetrained, bring him outside to the same spot each time and always leaving a little bit of his waste there as a scent marker. This will be the designated relief spot and if you like can place a warning sign at that spot. Remember to use this spot for *relief* only and not for play. Bring your puppy to his spot and when you see him getting ready to eliminate waste, say something like "potty time," "hurry up," or "now."

As your pup is eliminating, do not speak because it will distract him and potentially interrupt full elimination. Instead, ponder how much fun it will be when he is playing fetch and running back to you. When your puppy finishes, praise, pet, give a top-notch treat and spend about five minutes playing with him.

If your puppy eliminates in the house, remember, that it is *your fault*. Maybe you went too quickly. If you see your puppy relieving himself indoors, quickly bring him outside to the designated elimination spot so that he can finish there and when he is done offer praise for finishing in the correct spot.

Each time you find a mess, clean it thoroughly without your puppy watching you do it. Use a cleaner made specifically for pet stains so that there is no smell or evidence that you have failed him. This way it will not become a regular spot for your puppy and a new regular clean up chore for you. Regular outings should keep this chore to a minimum.

This Question Rings a Bell:

"Can I teach my puppy when to tell me when he needs to go out?"

- Yes, you can! Hang a bell at dog level beside the door used to let your pup outdoors. Put a dab of easy cheese or peanut butter on the bell. When he touches the bell and it rings, immediately open the door. Repeat this every time and take him to the elimination spot. Eventually, he will ring the bell without the food on it and this will tell you when he needs to go outside.

Be careful here, your puppy may start to ring the bell when he wants to go outside to play, explore or for other non-elimination reasons. To avoid this, each time he rings the bell, *only* take him out to the elimination spot. If he starts to play, immediately bring him in the house reinforcing that the bell means elimination only.

Now that the schedule has been established and you know what you are supposed to do, keep in mind that puppies can generally hold for a good one-hour stretch. Adult larger breeds of dogs can hold their bladders longer than smaller dog breeds and some small dogs cannot last the night before needing to go outside. Most adult dogs generally do not last longer than 8-10 hours between needing to urinate.

Housetraining completion ranges from six months to twelve months. A dogs personality contributes to the training length of time. By four months most puppies often know to wait, but might still have issues. Many puppies are housetrained by six to eight months, or mostly trained by six months with occasional accidents lasting a further few months.

All dog owners are much happier after this training is completed but keep in mind that scolding your dog for doing a natural thing *is not going to help you* in housetraining. Rewarding him for the outdoor eliminations and avoiding indoor accidents is your gateway to success.

Of course, when you see your pup about to pee or poop indoors, a quick "No" as you sweep him up to take him outside might temporarily cease the activity so that you can whisk them outside before any waste hits the ground or possibly your hand and arm. Then as previously mentioned, praise at the beginning of the outdoor elimination then remain quiet.

It isn't as difficult as it might read. Being active in housetraining will definitely speed up the process, but it does take a few months for puppies to increase their bladder abilities and to learn the rules.

Far to often new puppy owners are not around enough to follow the protocol efficiently and this regularly leads to housetraining taking longer. Some dogs learn suprisingly fast that outdoors is the only acceptable place to eliminate waste, but their bodies haven't matured to catch up to their brain function, so please practice patience and understanding.

I am certain you will do a great job.

12 Teaching Your Dog to Enjoy Handling

Teaching your Mini Aussie to be still, calm and patient while being handled is a very important step in your relationship. When you master this one, it makes life easier for both of you when at home, groomer or vet. Handling also helps when there is unwanted or accidental touching and especially when dealing with small children who love to handle dogs in all sorts of unusual and not so regular ways. This one will take patience and a few tricks to get started. Remember, that it is important to begin handling your new puppy immediately after you find each other and are living together.

The sooner your puppy accepts your touches and manipulations the easier life will be for the both of you because handling is needed for grooming, bathing, lifting, and affection, medical procedures, inspecting for ticks, fleas and caring for injuries.

Recognize that muzzles are not bad and do not hurt dogs. They can be an effective device and a great safety feature when your dog is learning to be handled. Easy cheese or peanut butter spread on the floor or on the refrigerator door can keep your puppy in place while he learns to be handled. If your puppy does not like to be handled, he will slowly learn to accept it.

You must practice this with your puppy for at least one to three minutes each day so that he becomes comfortable with being touched everywhere.

All dogs are unique and therefore some will accept this easier and quicker than others will. Handling training will be a life-long process but it is an enjoyable procedure.

With all of the following exercises, follow these steps

- Begin with short, non-intrusive gentle touching. *If your puppy is calm* and not trying to squirm away, use a word such as "good," "nice," or "yes," and give your pup a treat.

- If your puppy squirms, keep touching him but do not fight his movements, keeping your hand lightly on him while moving your hand with his squirms. Use your hand as though it were a suction cup and stuck to the place that you are touching. When he settles, treat him and remove your hand.

- Work from one second to ten seconds or more, gradually working your way up to touching for longer durations, such as 2,4,6,8 to 10 seconds.

- Do not go forward to another step until your puppy adapts, and enjoys the current step.

- *Do not* work these exercises more than a couple of minutes at a time. Overstimulation can cause your puppy stress. Continue slowly at your puppy's preferred pace.

Handling the Body

Paws

It is a fact that most puppies do not like to have their paws touched. Proceed slowly with this exercise. The eventual goal is for your puppy to adore his paws being fondled.

In the following exercises, any time your puppy does not squirm and try to get away, *click and treat* your pup. If he does squirm, stay with him using gentle contact, when your pup ceases wiggling, then *click and treat*, and release when he calms down. Each one of these steps will take a few days to complete and will require at least a dozen repetitions.

Confirm that you successfully complete each step and your puppy is at least tolerant of the contact before you go on to the next one. Continue to regularly practice.

- *Do each step with all four paws, and remember to pause a minute between paws, allowing your pup to regain his composure.*

- Pick up your puppy's paw and immediately click and treat. Repeat this five times and then continue forward by adding an additional one second each time you pick up his paw until ten seconds is reached.

Hold the paw for ten to twelve seconds with no struggling from your dog. Begin with two seconds then in different sessions work your way to twelve.

During holding the paw, begin adding the following.

- Hold the paw and move it around.

- Massage the paw.

- Pretend to trim the nails.

Side Note: Do not trim your dog's nails unless you are positively sure you know what you are doing. It is not easy and if you are not properly trained can cause extreme pain to your dog.

The Collar

Find a quiet, low distraction place to practice, grab treats, and put your puppy's collar on him.

1. While gently restrained, touch your dog's collar underneath his chin, and then release right away simultaneously clicking and treating him. Do this about ten times or until your puppy seems comfortable and relaxed with the process.

2. Grab and hold the collar where it is under his chin and hold it for about 2 seconds, C/T, and repeat. Increase the amount of time until you have achieved about ten seconds of holding and your puppy remains calm. Click and treat after each elapsed amount of time. By increasing the hold time by 2 seconds, gradually work your way up to ten seconds of holding. This may take several days and sessions.

3. Hold the collar under his chin and now give it a little tug. If he accepts this and does not resist, click and treat, and repeat. If he squirms, keep a gentle hold on the collar until he calms down, and then C/T and release him. Repeat this step until he is content with the procedure.

4. Now, switch to the top of the collar and repeat the whole progression again. Remember slowly increase the time held and the intensity of the tug.

You can pull or tug, but *do not jerk* your puppy's neck or head because this can cause injury and interfere with your outcome objectives of the training exercise. You can practice touching the collar while you are treating during training other tricks. Gently hold the bottom or top of the collar when you are giving your dog a treat reward for successfully completing a commanded behavior.

Mouth

1. Gently touch your puppy's mouth, *click and treat*, and repeat ten times.

2. Touch the side of your puppy's mouth and lift a lip to expose a tooth, *click and treat*, then release only after he stops resisting.

3. Gently and slowly, lift the lip to expose more and more teeth on both sides of the mouth, and then open the mouth. Then release when he does not resist, *click and treat*. Be cautious with this one.

4. Touch a tooth with a toothbrush, then work up to brushing your puppy's teeth for one to ten-seconds, and then later increase the time. Brushing your puppy's teeth is something you will be doing a few times weekly for the lifetime of your dog.

Ears

1. Reach around the side of your puppy's head and then briefly and gently touch his ear. Click and treat, repeat ten times.

2. When your puppy is comfortable with this, continue and practice holding the ear for one-second. If he is calm, click and treat. If he squirms, stay with him until he is calm. When your puppy calms down, click and treat, then release the ear. Do this until ten seconds is completed with no wiggling.

3. Maneuver your pup's ear and pretend that you are cleaning it. Do this gently and slowly so that your puppy learns to enjoy it. It will take a few days of practice until your puppy is calm enough for the real ear cleaning. If your puppy is already sensitive about his ears being touched, it will take longer. See ear cleaning in the Basic Care section.

Proceed slowly at your puppy's comfortable pace. There is no rush just the end goal of your pup enjoying being handled in all sorts of ways that are beneficial to him.

Tail

Many puppies are sensitive about having their tails handled, and rightly so. Think about if someone grabs you by the arm and you are not fully ready. That is similar to the reaction a puppy feels when grabbed, especially when their tails are handled.

1. Start by briefly touching the tail. When moving to touch your puppy's tail move slowly and let your hand be seen moving towards his tail. This keeps him from being startled. Repeat this

ten times with clicking and treating, until you notice your puppy is comfortable with his tail being touched.

2. Increase the duration of time you hold his tail until you achieve the ten-second mark.

3. Tenderly and cautiously pull the tail up, brush the tail and then tenderly pull on it until your dog allows you to do this without reacting by jerking, wiggling or whimpering.

Your Dog needs to be comfortable being touched on paws, ears, tail, mouth, entire body and this should be practiced daily.

Brushing

- Get your puppy's brush and lightly touch him with it all over his body. If he remains unmoving, give him a click and treat and then repeat. Repeat this until you can brush every part of his body without him moving.

Children

You must prepare your poor pup to deal with the strange unwelcome touching that is often exacted on them by children. Alternatively, you could just put a sign around his neck that says; "You must be at least 16 to touch this puppy." However, it is very likely that your puppy will encounter children that are touchy, grabby or pokey.

- Prepare your puppy for the strange touches that children may perpetrate by practicing while clicking and treating him for accepting these odd bits of contact, such as ear tugs, tail tugs, and perhaps a little harder than usual head pats, kisses and hugs. Keep in mind, as previously mentioned, puppies and kids are not a natural pairing, *but cheese and wine are*. Even a puppy that is good with kids can be pushed to a breaking point and then things can get ugly, and nobody wants that.

Always supervise children around your dog. ALWAYS! – It is a dog ownership law.

Lifting Dogs

In most cases, you have been carrying your dog around since a pup, but maybe you rescued a Mini Aussie or saved teenage dog that isn't quite used to your touches.

An emergency may arise that requires you to pick up your dog. As you do these maneuvers, move and proceed slowly and cautiously. First, briefly put your arms around your dog and if he stays still then give him a click and treat.

Increase the time duration with successive repetitions. Your dog should be comfortable for ten to fifteen seconds with your arms around him.

Next, slowly proceed lifting your dog off the ground just a few inches or centimeters, and then back down. Each time he does not wriggle, click and treat. Increase the time and the distance that you lift him from the ground and then move your dog from one place to another. Calculate the time it might take to lift and carry your dog from the house and place him into your vehicle. This is a good time goal to set for carrying your dog.

Eventually, by lifting your dog up and placing him on a table, you will be able to prepare your dog for trips to the groomer, open spaces or the vet.

You never know if you might have to lift a big dog. If you own an extra-large dog, or dog that is too heavy for you to lift, solicit help for this training from family or a friend. *Gigantor* may take two to lift safely and properly, or use one of the methods below.

Once up on the table you can practice handling in ways a groomer or veterinarian might handle your dog. This is good preparation for a day at the dog spa or veterinary procedures.

Your puppy will become comfortable with all varieties of touching and handling if you work slowly, patiently and with plenty of good treats. Handling training is a very important step in your dog's socialization.

13 Crate Training

Dogs need their own safe place to call home and relax. An owner's house might be a place to roam but it's not the den dogs crave. The crate satisfies a dog's longing for a den, and along with its many other uses provides comfort to them. All puppies should be taught to enjoy residing in their crate and know that it is a safe haven for them; therefore, it is important *never* to use it for punishment.

Before you begin crate training give your dog a couple of days to adjust to his new home and surroundings. Crate training can be trained for a dog of any age. A dog's love for their crate is healthy and assists you in taking care of him or her throughout their lifetime.

Try to limit your puppy's time in the crate to around one hour per session. Never leave your adult dog in a crate for longer than five hours without providing them time outside of the crate. As your puppy matures and has learned proper dog etiquette (not chewing everything in sight), is housetrained, and can be trusted to run freely around your house, you can then leave the door open so that they can use it for their private bungalow to come and go as they choose.

I have listed below the benefits of the crate, things to avoid, types, furnishings, the steps to crate train your dog, and troubleshooting, Godspeed.

Benefits of the Crate

- It aids in housetraining because dogs are reluctant to soil their own sleeping area.

- Acts as a mobile doghouse for trips via car, airplane, train and then to be used at destinations such as motels and foreign houses.

- The mobility can be utilized inside your own home by being moved throughout the house. *Especially beneficial during housetraining when you want your puppy near you.

- Can reduce separation anxiety.

- Keep your dog out of harm's way.

- Assists in chew-toy addiction.

- Aids your puppy in calming and quieting down.

Until he or she has learned that chewing, tearing, ripping of household and human items is forbidden, the crate keeps your dog shortly separated from destruction of those items.

Things to Avoid

- *Do not use the crate as punishment*. If used in this manner it will defeat the purpose and cause your dog to fear the crate instead of love it.

- *Avoid lengthy crating sessions*. Long periods in the crate defer socialization, exercise, and lend to doggy depression, anxiousness and anxiety.

- Puppies have an issue holding their need to eliminate waste. Young puppies tend to go hourly, but as they mature, the time between elimination lengthens. Keep this in mind for puppies and adult dogs, and always schedule elimination breaks. Set a timer to remind you to free your pooch from the crate and go outdoors.

A good rule of thumb for elimination intervals is as follows, up to six weeks of age - elimination every hour, at two months of age - around two to three hours, at three months - four hours, four months and up - around five hours. These times will vary with individual dogs.

If you are housetraining an adult dog, he or she might be able to hold their bowels longer, but have not yet learned that they are required to wait and go outdoors.

- *Soiled items*. Quickly remove and clean any soiled items inside the crate, and thoroughly clean the crate with a non-toxic cleaner that will erase any signs of elimination.

- Avoid crating your dog when your dog has not recently eliminated waste.

- Avoid continued involuntary crating after your puppy is housetrained and he or she understands that damaging human property is forbidden; instead only use the crate when necessary.

Buying, Furnishing, and Preparing the Crate

The time has come for you to go crate shopping and you notice that they come in many sizes and design options. Let the shopper in you compare the advantages and disadvantages of the different styles to figure out which will be best suited for your usage and dog. A few types are as follows, collapsible metal, metal with fabric, wire, solid plastic, fixed and folding aluminum, and soft-sided collapsible crates that conveniently fold up easily for travel.

Regarding traveling always have your dog safely secured when in a motor vehicle. There are crates specially designed and tested for vehicle transportation.

"What size crate do I purchase?"

The crate should be big enough for your puppy to stand up, turn around, and lie down in. If you wish to hedge your bet, instead of purchasing multiple crates you can purchase a crate that will accommodate your puppy when full size, but this will require blocking off the end so that they are unable to eliminate waste in a section and then move to another that is apart from where they soiled.

In summary, per the criteria mentioned above, you need to cordon off the crate to accommodate your puppy's smaller size and then expand as he or she grows.

"What do I put into the crate?"

Toys, treats, blanket or mat, and the entire home furnishings a young puppy needs and desires to be entertained. Avoid televisions, tablets, and radios.

Seriously, you should provide an ample supply of natural material indestructible chew-toys, and things such as indestructible balls. All of the chews and toys should be large enough not to be swallowed, and tough enough to withstand tearing apart a portion that could be swallowed by your puppy. Treats will be occasionally required, and stuffing them into the chew-toys will occupy the young pup for hours.

Clean water is another essential item that all dogs must have regular access. You can utilize a small rodent type water dispenser attached to the side of the crate. If you know that your dog will only be in the crate under two hours, then he or she will probably be able to go without water.

"Where do I place the crate?"

It is a good idea to place the crate close to where you are located in the house. This keeps a puppy from feeling lonely and you able to keep an eye out for signs that he or she needs to eliminate waste. As housetraining is successful, the crate does not have to be located beside you, only near you or in central location to where you are working or relaxing. Eventually the crate can be located at further distances, but you never want your dog to feel isolated.

Introducing Your Dog to the Crate

These steps will help your dog to adjust to his crate and associate it with good things such as security, comfort, and a quiet place to ponder the meaning of life, things such as why he or she walks on four legs and humans on two, and how does my food magically appear.

Never force your dog into the crate by using physical means of persuasion. Crate training should be a natural process that takes place on your dog's time schedule. Curious dogs might immediately begin to explore the inner domain while others take some time, and possibly some coaxing by using lures such as toys and food. Let the process proceed in small steps and gradually your dog will want to spend more time in his new five-star luxury crate. This training can proceed very quickly or take days to complete.

Phase I

1. Set the crate in a common area and confirm that all of the crate's goodies are inside. Open and secure the door. If your dog does not mosey on over in his or her own accord, then place them near the crate entrance and give him a pep talk using your happy-go-lucky fun voice. Wait a bit and see if his curiosity kicks in and he begins to explore the inner domain.

2. If your pep talk and shining personality are not sparking his curiosity then go to plan B, food lures. To begin, you don't have to use anything fancy, just use his normal puppy food. Drop some in the back of the crate and a couple closer to the front door, and see if that gets his little tail wagging and paws moving. After you place the food inside step away and give him some room to make his own decisions. Do not force anything. Just observe throughout the day and see if your dog is venturing inside or near the crate. Do this a few times throughout the day.

3. If this does not work, try it again. If he is still disinterested, you can also drop a favorite chew-toy into the crate and ask him to find his toy and see if that lures him into the crate.

4. Continue doing this process until your dog will walk all of the way into the crate to retrieve the food or toy. This step is sometimes accomplished in minutes, but it can take a couple of days. Be sure to praise your dog for successfully entering. Do not shut the door. Observe whether they are calm, timid, or frightened.

5. Once your dog is regularly entering his crate without fear, you can move onto phase II

Phase II

Phase II will help if your dog is not acting as though his crate is a place that he wants to enter and remain, and might be showing signs of fear or anxiety when inside. This phase will help warm him up to his crate.

By using feeding time, you can reinforce that the crate is a place that your dog should enjoy. During Phase II training, remain in the presence of your dog's crate or at least in the same room. Later you will begin leaving the room where he is crated.

1. Start by feeding your dog in front of his crate door. Feeding your dog near his crate will create a nice association with the crate. *If your dog already enters his crate freely, set the food bowl inside so that he has to enter the crate to eat.

2. Next, place his food bowl far enough into the crate that your dog has to step inside to eat. Then each following time that you feed him place the bowl further inside.

3. When your dog will stand and eat inside his crate, and you know that he is calm and relaxed, then you can close the crate door while he eats his meal.

The first time, immediately upon meal completion, open the door. Then after each successive meal, leave the door closed for longer durations. For example, after meals gradually increase to two, three, four minutes and then incrementally increase until you reach ten to fifteen minutes. Stay diligent and if you notice your dog begins frantically whining or is acting anxious, back up and then slow down on the time increases.

4. If your dog continues whining the next time, then leave him in there until he calms. *This is important*, because you cannot reinforce that whining is a way out of the crate, or a way always to get your attention or manipulate you.

5. Now that he is comfortable entering, eating, and spending some time in his crate, move onto Phase III, which explains about training your dog to enjoy spending more time in the crate with you around and out of the house.

Phase III

This is where you will continue increasing the time duration that your dog is crated. First, be certain that he is not displaying signs of fear or anxiety. Whining and whimpering does not always signify that anxiety is present. It is often a tool used when they want some attention from their mom or humans. It is a sympathy tool honed sharp when they were weaning on mothers milk.

If you choose at this point, you can begin issuing a command that goes with your crating action. For example, say "crate," "home," "cage," "cave," or whatever is simple and natural for you. Maybe cage sounds negative to us, but your dog does not know the difference.

1. Stand next to the crate with his favorite toy and then call him over to you and give the command "cave," while placing the toy inside. A hand signal that you choose can also be used along with this command, but make sure that you do not use the same hand signal for another command. As an option, you can use a favored treat instead of a toy.

When he enters, praise him, shut the door, and let him stay inside for duration of ten to fifteen minutes. You should remain close to the crate. Do this a few times separated by an hour or two. During dog training, gradually proceeding is always a good rule to follow.

2. Repeat the step above, but this time only stay nearby for about five minutes, and then leave the room for an additional ten to fifteen minutes. When you return, do not rush over to the crate, instead remain in the room for a few more minutes and then let your dog out of the crate. It is not necessary to physically remove him, just open the door.

Repeat this five to seven times per day and gradually increase the duration that your dog remains in the crate. Work your way up to 30-40 minutes when you are completely out of sight.

Do not forget to use your vocal command and physical cue every time that you want your dog to enter his crate.

3. Continue increasing the time that he is crated while you are home. Work up to one hour.

4. Next, place the crate near your room and let him sleep the night inside the crate near where you are sleeping such as in the doorway or just outside your bedroom. At this time, if your dog is able to go two hours

without needing to eliminate, then you can also begin to leave your dog crated when you need to leave the house for short durations of under two hours.

A good way to begin is to leave your dog in his crate while you are outdoors doing yard work. Remember that when your return inside, to act casual and normal. Do what you need upon returning inside, and then open the crate door and then secure the opened door.

*Puppies usually need to eliminate waste during the night, thus you will need to make some late night trips outdoors.

As your dog becomes accustomed to his crate and surroundings, you can begin gradually to move the crate to your preferred locations, but not to an isolated place.

Tips & Troubleshooting

In the beginning, especially with puppies, keep the crate close to where you are in the house and sleeping at night. As mentioned, you want to avoid any negative associations such as isolation that can result in depression or contribute to separation anxiety. This also strengthens your bond, and allows easy access for late night elimination trips.

Due to bladder and bowel control, puppies under six months should be kept crated for periods *under* four hours.

Ignore whining unless your dog responds to your elimination command or phrase that you have been using when taking him to his elimination spot. If he does respond, then you know that the whining was for that and not simply for attention.

I know it is difficult to ignore whining, but it must be done so that your new dog or puppy understands that you are not at their disposal every time they seek attention. If you are bonding, socializing and practicing the other suggested items, then your puppy or dog should not need the extra attention.

- Before crating, take your dog outdoors to eliminate. There should be only 5-15 minutes between elimination and crating. *Best chance for success for your dog not to soil his crate.

- Don't forget to leave plenty of fresh water, chew-toys and items that require problem solving. Food stuffed toys are a good choice.

- Don't place your dog into the crate for long periods before your departure from the house. Try to keep it under fifteen minutes or less.

- Fluctuate the time between crating and departure.

- When soiling accidents occur inside the crate, thoroughly clean the crate and its contents with a *pet odor neutralizer*. Warning, do not use ammonia.

- *A couple of warnings* regarding crating - Avoid crating in direct sunlight or excessive heat, if your dog is sick with diarrhea or vomiting, or is having bowel and urine control issues. You can resume training once these are resolved.

- Always provide sufficient exercise and socialization.

- Never use the crate as a form of punishment.

- Quick review of approximate crating times per age, are as follows, 9-10 weeks 30-60 minutes, 11-14 weeks 1-3 hrs. 15-16 weeks 3-4 hrs. 17 + weeks 4-6 hrs.

- *To thwart separation anxiety issues, never make a big emotional showing when you leave the house. Always act normal, because it is a normal thing for you to come and go. Do the same when you return, do not over dramatize your return, first do what you need to do then casually go over to his crate and open the door without making a big show of it. This aids your dog in understanding that all of this coming and going is a *normal* part of his life.

- After your dog is housetrained and is no longer destructive, do not forcibly crate your dog except when you absolutely need them crated. During other times, leave the door securely open and allow them to voluntarily come and go as they choose.

- Some reasons that your dog continues to soil his own crate are as follows. The crate is to large; there is a diet issue, health issue, is too young to have control, suffering severe separation anxiety, or has drunk to much water prior to crating.

- Another contributing factor could be the manner that your dog was housed prior to your acquiring him. If he was confined continuously to a small enclosure with no other outlet for elimination this will cause issues with housetraining and crating. If this is true for your dog, training will require more time and patience.

- Separation anxiety is an issue that cannot be solved using a crate. Consult the diagnosing and solving separation anxiety guidelines.

That wraps up crate training. I wish you well in crate and housetraining. I am sure that you will do wonderfully in shaping your dog's behaviors.

14 Teaching Clicker Response

Important - *Conceal the treat! <u>Do not</u> show your puppy the treat before depressing the clicker button,* and never deliver the treat prior to the clicker emitting a clicking sound. If you do this, your puppy will be responding to the treat and not the click, and this will undermine your training strategy.

Training should begin by simply observing your Mini Aussie puppy. What you are looking for is a desired behavior to reward. In other words, if your puppy is doing anything considered an undesirable behavior, then do not reward.

As long as your puppy is relaxed and behaving well, you can begin to train using this clicker response training. What you are doing here is training your puppy to associate the clicker sound with doing something good. Whenever you click, your puppy will associate the sound with an acceptable performance, and will know that he or she has a reward coming.

Timing is crucial when training your puppy. The essential technique when training your puppy with the clicker is by clicking precisely as the correct action takes place, followed by treating. It does not take long for your puppy to associate their behavior with the clicking sound, and subsequently receiving a treat. Make sure that the treat is produced *immediately* following the clicking sound.

Note: Throughout this training guide, *Click and Treat is sometimes written as C/T.* In addition, for ease of writing, I mostly refer to the gender of your dog in the male form, even though I know many people have female dogs. Please take no offense to this.

Crucial – Never click without treating, and never treat without clicking. This maintains the connection and continuity between clicking and treating, which is the framework for achieving your desired outcomes.

Steps

1. When your puppy is relaxed, you should stand, or kneel down at about an arm's length away and then click and give your puppy a treat.

2. Repeat this clicking and treating about 5-15 times. Pause a several seconds between clicks to allow your puppy to resume whatever he was doing. Do not click and treat if he seems to be begging for another treat. Find times throughout the day when he is performing any desired behavior, then click and treat. This teaches your puppy to associate the click with what you want him to do, and a tasty food treat.

When you click and your puppy's head swings around in anticipation of a treat, then you know that your puppy has made the association between the clicking sound and a reward.

4. Repeat steps one and two the day following the introduction of clicker training. When your puppy quickly responds to the click, then you can begin using the clicker to train commands.

Teaching puppies to respond to this method can take several training sessions, but most commonly after about a dozen click and treats, they begin to connect the clicking sound with a treat. Usually, at the end of the first 5-minute session, puppies tend to swing their head around when they hear the clicker sound.

Helpful Hint

After some dedicated training sessions, puppies tend to stop in their tracks and instantly come to you for a treat. At this time refrain from using this clicker technique to get your dog to come to you, but instead follow the instructions for teaching the *come command*.

15 Name Recognition

After your puppy responds to the clicking sound, and he knows very well that treats follow the clicking sound, you can now begin teaching him commands and tricks.

Now, we are going to teach your puppy some specific things. Let's start with the base exercise that is teaching your puppy to respond to his or her *name*. I assume that you have already gone through the painstaking process of naming your puppy, and now when his or her name is spoken you want your puppy to respond when you say their name. This can be easy, fun and gratifying when you finally achieve positive results.

Teaching your puppy his name is a basic and necessary objective that must be accomplished in order to gain and keep your puppies attention during further training.

Before beginning training, be sure to gather an ample variety of treats. Put these treats in your pockets, treat pouch or on a tabletop out of sight, and out of your puppy's reach.

1. Ignore your puppy until he looks directly at you, when he does, *click and treat* him. Repeat this 10-15 times. This teaches your puppy to associate the click with a treat when he looks in your direction.

2. Next, when your puppy looks at you, begin adding your puppy's name, spoken right before you *click and treat.*

3. Continue doing this until your puppy will look at you when you say his or her name.

4. Gradually phase out clicking and treating your puppy every time that he or she looks at you. Gradually decrease C/T incrementally; one out of two times, then one out of three, four, and then not at all. Do not phase out the C/T too quickly.

After successful name recognition training, you should C/T on occasion, to refresh your puppy's memory and reinforce the association to hearing his name and receiving a treat. Observe your puppy's abilities and pace during this training process, and when needed adjust appropriately. The ultimate goal is to have your puppy obey all the commands via vocal or physical cue, *without a reward*.

Responding to his or her name is the most important learned behavior, because it is the base skill of all future training. Therefore, you will want to give this training a considerable amount of attention, and thoroughly complete before moving on. Saying your puppy's name to gain his attention will always prelude issuing commands, e.g. "Axel Come."

I advise that you repeat this exercise in various locations inside and outside your home, while he is out on the leash, in the yard or in the park.

Eventually, make sure that you practice this while there are distractions, such as when there are guests present, when his favorite toys are visible, when there is food around and when he is among other dogs.

- Always maintain *good eye contact* when you are calling your puppy's name. Keep on practicing this name recognition exercise until there is no doubt that when you speak your puppy's name, he or she knows whom you are referring to and they respond appropriately.

It may sound odd, but also try the training when you are in different physical positions, such as sitting, standing, kneeling or lying down. Mix it up so that he gets used to hearing his name in a variety of areas and situations, and repeat this process frequently. No matter the situation, this command *must* be obeyed.

Name recognition will avoid trouble later on down the line. For example, if your puppy gets into something that he should not, such as a scrap with another dog, chasing a cat or squirrel, or far worse, getting involved in a time-share pyramid scheme, you can simply call your puppy's name to gain his attention and then redirect him.

You invariably want your puppy to come no matter what the distraction, so training "come" is also a crucial command to teach, and regularly practice throughout the lifetime of your dog. Remember, your puppy first needs to know his or her name so that you can teach these other commands such as *come*.

To be certain that you are able to grab your dog's attention in any circumstance or situation, continue to practice this training into adulthood to reinforce the behavior. When your puppy is appropriately responding to his or her name, I recommend moving forward to the *come* and *sit* commands.

16 "Come"

After your puppy recognizes, and begins responding to his name being called, then the "Come" command takes priority as the first command to teach. *Why?* Because this one could save his life, save your sanity and avoid you the embarrassment of running through the neighborhood in the middle of the night wearing little more than a robe and slippers while pleading for your dog to return.

There are quite a few drills and instructions for properly teaching this command but if you follow through completely your dog will obey the come command at least 90% of the time.

If by chance, he is checking out the olfactory magic of the trash bin, the best way to redirect your dog is firmly command him to "Come," followed immediately by a reward when he complies. Petting, verbal praise or play is an appropriate reinforcement and an effective redirecting incentive during this type of situation.

In order to grab your dog's attention no matter what activity he is engaged in, it is necessary to implement an effective verbal command. Unfortunately, the word "Come" is a commonly used word that is spoken regularly during daily life, thus making it difficult to isolate as a special command word, so I suggest that a unique and infrequently used word be chosen for this.

With my dog Axel, I use "jax" as my replacement word for *come*. For example, I say "Axel *jax*," which replaces the standard, "Axel come," or

"Axel here." When your dog hears this special cue word, he will recognize it as the word associated with the command to return to you and receive a special treat. However, if you find it effective and natural there is nothing wrong with simply using *come* as your command word.

Note: Choose a command word with one or two syllables, and one that you can easily say, because it will be difficult to change the substituted "Come" command word later. Examples are cane, cork and here.

When training the come command outside, use a long check chord leash about 20 feet (six meters) or more, especially when you leave the yard and head to an open field or park. These leashes are also handy for fieldwork, sports and tracking.

Here's what to do-

- If you have chosen to use a unique come command, you can begin here. We will not use the clicker at this time. First, gather your assortment of treats, such as bits of steak, bacon or whatever your dog most covets.

Begin with the tastiest treat in hand, and speak the new command word, immediately followed by a treat. When your dog hears this new word, he will begin to associate it with a special treat. Keep repeating this exercise, and mix up the treats that you provide. Remember to conclude each training session by providing a lot of praise to your dog. Repeat for about ten repetitions then proceed onto the next step.

- Gather your clicker and treats, and then find a quiet low distraction place so that both of you can focus. First, place a treat on the floor and walk to the other side of the room. Next, hold out a hand with a visible treat in it. Now, say your dog's name to get his attention, followed by the command "Come" using a pleasant happy tone when you do it.

When your dog begins to move towards you, press the clicker and praise him all the way to the treat in your hand. The objective of this is for him to ignore the treat on the ground and come to you. When he gets to you, *treat* him from your hand and offer some more praise and affection. Be sure and not click again and only give the treat.

Each time your dog comes to you, pet or touch his head and grab a hold of his collar before treating. Sometimes do this on top of the collar, and sometimes beneath his head on the bottom of the collar. This action gets your dog used to being held, so when you need to grab a hold of him by the collar he will not shy away or fight you. This was covered earlier in the Handling chapter.

Do this 10-12 times, and then take a break. Make sure that your dog accomplishes the task by walking the complete distance across the room to you, while wholly ignoring the treat that you placed on the floor.

Help

If your dog is stopping at the treat on the floor and not coming to you, do not use the clicker or any body movements that can be mistaken for a reward, ignore him.

If your dog can't quite seem to 'get it,' then reward him when he takes the first few steps toward you and before he gets to the treat. This is shaping your dog's behavior by rewarding partial completion. Next, you want to make sure he comes closer and closer to you before rewarding until he finally makes it all the way to you. When he does, give him a barnbuster triple sized reward.

- For the next session, you will need the assistance of a family member. First, situate yourselves at a distance of about 5-6 paces opposite each other, and place a treat on the floor between the two of you. Each of you show your dog a treat when you say his name followed by "Come."

Now, take turns calling your dog back and forth between the two of you. Treat and praise your dog each time he successfully comes all of the way to either of you, *while ignoring the treat*. Repeat this about a dozen times. The objective of this exercise is to reinforce the idea that coming when commanded is not only for you, but is beneficial to him as well.

- This time, grab your clicker. As before, put a treat on the ground, move across the room, and then call your dog's name to get his attention, but this time hold out an empty hand and give the command. This will mess with him a little, but that's okay, he's learning.

As soon as he starts to come to you, give him praise and when he reaches you, *click and treat* by using the opposite hand that you were luring him. If your dog is not completing the distance to you, press the clicker as he begins to move closer to you, and the first time he completes the distance, give him a supersized treat serving (7-10 treats). Each additional time your dog comes all of the way to you; reward your dog with a regular sized treat serving. Do this about a dozen times, and then take a break.

- Keep practicing this exercise, but now call your dog using an empty hand. Using this technique over several sessions and days should eventually result in a successful hand signal command. Following your dog's consistent compliance with this hand signal training, you can then take the training to the next step by phasing out the hand signal by using only a verbal cue. When shifting to the verbal cue training, reduce treating incrementally, first by treating one out of two times, then one out three times, followed by one out of four, five, six and lastly without treating at all.

Note: It is important to treat your dog periodically in order to reinforce the desired behavior that he is exhibiting as well as complying with the command you are issuing. Make sure your dog is coming when commanded, including when all family members and friends issue the command.

By the end of this section, your dog should consistently be obeying the hand signal and the verbal *come* commands successfully.

Let's get complex

- Now, by adding distractions we will begin to make obeying commands a more difficult task for your dog. The outcome of this training should result in better control over your pooch in times when there is distracting stimulus.

First, find somewhere where there are sights, sounds and even smells that might distract your dog. Almost anything will serve as a distraction. You can intentionally implement distractions, such as having his favorite toy in hand, by having another person present, or even doing this training beside the half of roast ox that is on the backyard rotisserie.

Indoors, distractive aspects of daily home life, such as cooking, the noise of the television, doorbell or friends and family coming and going can serve as distractions. Even move to calling your dog from different rooms of the house, meanwhile gradually introducing other distractions, such as music from the stereo, groups of people and combinations of the sort.

Of course, the outdoor world is a megamall of potential interruptions, commotions and interferences for your pal to be tantalized and diverted by.

Hint - During this training exercise, you will find it helpful to keep a log of not only how your dog is progressing, but also accounting for the different kinds and levels of distractions your dog is encountering.

Now, in the high stimulus setting, resume training using the previous set of learned commands. As before, begin with treats in hand, because in this instance, when necessary the snacks will act as a lure for your dog to follow rather than a reward. This will help him focus. The goal is to dispense with the treats by gradually phasing them out, eventually only using the vocal command.

When outdoors with your dog, practice calling the command "Come" when you and your dog are in the yard with another animal or person, followed by increasing and more complex distractions. Distractions, such as a combination of a person and animal together, then with multiple people conversing or while children are running around and then you can even throw some toys or balls into the distraction mix.

Eventually, move out onto the streets and sidewalks while introducing increasingly busier locations, remembering to keep track of your dog's progress as the situations become more and more distracting. The goal is that you want your dog to come every time you call "come," no matter how much noise and movement is happening around him.

If your dog consistently begins to return to you seven or eight times out of each ten commands, regardless of the distractions, this shows that the two of you are making very good progress, and that you are well on your way to the ideal goal of nine out of ten times compliant. If your dog is sporting ten out of ten times, you may consider enrolling him at an Ivy League university or paying a visit to NASA, because you've got yourself one special canine there.

We all want a dog that comes when you use the "Come" command. Whether he is seven houses down the road, or just in the next room, a dog that comes to you no matter what he is engaged in, is a dog worth spending the time training.

Interrupting Fetch Exercises, Hide & Seek, and the Decoy Exercise

Practice all of the following exercises with increasing distractions, both indoors and outdoors. Focus on practicing one of these exercises per session, eventually mixing up the order of the exercises as your dog masters each. Remember it is always important to train in safe areas.

Interrupting Fetch Exercises

Get an ample-sized handful of your Mini Aussies favorite treat. Then, lob a ball or a piece of food at a reasonable distance, and as your dog is in the process of chasing it, call him by issuing the *come* command. If he comes *after* he gets the ball/food, give your dog a little reward of one piece of treat. If he comes *before* he gets the ball/food, give your dog a supersized (7-10) serving of treats.

If your dog is not responding to your *come* command, then throw the ball and quickly place a treat down towards his nose height while at the same time saying, "Come", when he comes to you click and supersize treat your dog. Then, begin phasing out the treat lure.

After you have thrown the ball/food over several sessions, it is time to change it up. Like the exercise prior, this time you will fake throwing something and then call your dog. If your dog goes looking for the ball/food before he comes back to you, give a small treat. If he comes immediately after you say, "Come," give the supersized treat portion. Repeat this exercise 7-10 times per session.

Hide & Seek

While you are both outside, and your dog is distracted and does not seem to know you exist, quickly *hide* from him. When your dog comes looking for you, and eventually finds you, *click and treat* your dog in addition with lots of love and praise. By adding a little drama, make it seem like an extremely big deal that your dog has found you. This is something that you can regularly practice and reward.

The Decoy

One person calls the dog; we call this person the *trainer*. One person tries to distract the dog with food and toys; we call this person the *decoy*. After the trainer calls the dog, if the dog goes toward the decoy, the decoy person should turn away from the dog and neither of you offer rewards. When the dog goes towards the trainer, he should be rewarded by *both* the trainer and the decoy. Repeat 7-10 times per session.

Helpful Hints

- Let your dog know that his coming to you is always the best thing ever, sometimes offering him supersized treat rewards for this behavior. Always reward by treating or praising, and when appropriate you can add play with a favorite toy or ball.

- Never, call your Mini Aussie for something he might find unpleasant. To avoid this, disguise the real purpose. If you are leaving the field where he has been running, call your dog, put on the leash and play a little more before leaving. If you are calling your dog to get him into the bath, provide a few minutes of affection or play instead of leading him straight into the bath. This will pacify and distract from any negative association with coming to you. *This is worth noting and something many people forget to remain diligent.

- You are calling, and your puppy is not responding. What do you do now? Try running backwards away from your dog, crouch, and clap or show your dog a toy or food. When he comes, still reward him even if he has stressed you out. Avoid running *towards* your dog because it signals play *catch me*.

- If your dog has been enjoying some unabated freedom off lead, remember to give him a C/T when he checks in with you. Later you can phase out the C/T and only use praise.

- You should practice the *come* command five to ten times daily, ongoing for life. This command is one of those potentially life-saving commands that help with all daily activities and interactions. The goal is that your dog will come running to you, whether you are in or out of sight, and from any audible distance. As dog owners, we know that having a dog that obeys this command makes dog things less stressful.

17 "Drop it"

Teaching your Mini Aussie pup to *drop it* is a very important step in protecting your dog. *Why?* Well, if you have ever owned a young puppy, you know that it is one giant mouth gobbling up whatever is in sight. Rumor has it that Stephen Hawking actually got the idea of the black hole from his puppy's ever-consuming mouth.

Joking aside, sometimes valuable and dangerous things go into that all-consuming mouth, and the command to *drop it* may save a family heirloom, over even perhaps your dog's life.

If you teach your dog correctly, each time you command, "Drop it," your pup will open his mouth and drop whatever is in it. Most importantly, he will not only drop the item, but will allow you to retrieve it without protesting. When teaching the *drop it* command you must offer a good trade for what your dog has in his mouth. You need to out-treat your dog by offering a better treat of higher value in exchange for what is in his mouth at the time you issue the command.

Importantly, it is a good idea to stay calm and not chase your puppy because this elicits a play behavior that can work against your desired training outcomes.

If this command is successfully taught, your puppy will actually enjoy hearing "Drop it." This command will also build trust between the two of you. In example, if you say, "Drop it," then you retrieve the item, and afterward you give a treat, he will understand that you are not there simply to steal the thing he has found and enjoying. This will develop trust and the pup will not guard his favorite toys, food and items such as his dog bowl.

Negative behaviors such as *guarding*, can be avoided with this and other socialization training. Guarding is an aggressive behavior and something that can be avoided by early proper training practices.

Teach "Drop it" Like This

- Gather a variety of good treats, and a few items your dog might like to chew on, such as a favorite toy or a rawhide chew. With a few treats in hand, encourage your dog to chew on one of the toys. When the item is in his mouth, put a treat close to his nose and say, "Drop it" As soon as he opens his mouth, *click and treat* him as you pick up the item. Then, return the item to your dog.

At this point, your dog may not want to continue to chew on the item because there are treats in the area and his mouth is now free to consume. If he appears now to be distracted by the treats you possess, rather than the chew-toy, you can take this as an opportunity to pause the training.

Be sure and keep the treats handy though, because throughout the day when you see him pick something up, you both can practice the *drop it* command. Do this at least ten times per day or until this command is mastered.

In the event that he picks up a forbidden item (running shoes) you may not want to give back to your pooch, instead, give your puppy an extra tasty treat or a supersized serving as an equitable exchange for the item that you confiscate. You want your puppy to be redirected, and he should be properly rewarded for his compliance.

- Once you have done the treat-to-the-nose *drop it* command ten times, try doing it *without* holding the treat to his nose. Continue to use your hand, but this time it should be empty. Say the command, and when he drops the item, *click and treat*.

Make sure the first time he drops it when you are not holding a treat to his nose, that you give him a supersized treat serving from a different hand.

Practice this over a few days and training sessions. Do not rush to the next step until his response is consistently compliant, and training is successful at a high rate of 85%+.

- This next part of the *drop it* training will further reinforce the command, in particular during situations where a tug-of-war between you may ensue. This time you will want to use a treat that your dog might find extra special, like a hard chew-toy pig ear or rawhide, making sure that it is something that cannot be quickly consumed.

100

Next, hold this new chew-toy in your hand and offer it to your dog, but this time *do not let it go*. When your dog has the chew-toy in his mouth, say, "Drop it." When your dog drops it for the *first time*, C/T, being sure to give your dog extra treats, and then offer the chew-toy back to keep.

Because better treats are available, he may not take the chew-toy back. Recognize this as a good sign, but it also signals a time for a break. Later, repeat this training about a dozen times before you move on to the next phase of teaching *drop it*. If your dog is not dropping the chew-toy after clicking, then the next time use a higher value treat.

For the next phase training, repeat the exercise above, but this time do not hold onto the chew, just let him have it. As soon as your dog has it in his mouth, give the command "Drop it." When your dog drops the chew-toy, C/T a supersized portion, then be sure to give the chew-toy back to him to keep. Your dog will be thrilled by this exchange. Once you have successfully done this a dozen times, move onto the next step.

During this phase, if your dog does not drop the chewy, it will be necessary to show the treat first, as incentive. Once he realizes that you hold treats, you will want to work up to having him drop it before the treat is given. This in actuality is *bribery*, and I do not suggest utilizing this action as a short cut elsewhere during training. *Remember*, only use this method as a last resort, and discontinue it quickly.

- Now, try this command with the things around the house that he is not supposed to chew on, pens, chip bags, socks, gloves, tissues, shoes, or that 15th century priceless Guttenberg bible.

After you and your dog have achieved success indoors with this command, try the exercise outside where there are plenty of distractions. To hold his attention when you are moving into further distracting situations, be sure and have with you the best of treats.

Keep in mind that your goal is to have the *drop it* commands obeyed in any situation, so keep increasing the distractions when training.

- Practice the *drop it* command when playing fetch, and other games. For example, when your dog returns to you with his ball, command "Drop it," and when he complies, offer up the magic duo of praise plus a treat.

- Gradually phase out the clicking and treating of your dog every time that he drops something on command. Progressively reduce treating by first treating one out of two times, then one out three times, followed by one out of four, five, six, and finally not at all.

Always remain aware of your dog's abilities, and his individual pace, being sure not to decrease treating to rapidly. The desired outcome of this training is that your dog will obey *all* commands by a vocal or physical cue, without a reward. As a reminder, then occasionally offer a tasty reward to let him know your pup know how much you appreciate his obedience.

Know These Things

- If your Mini Aussie already likes to incite games of grab and chase with you, it is best to curb this behavior from the onset by teaching your dog that you *will never* chase after him if he thieves and bolts. If your dog grabs and runs, <u>completely</u> ignore him. For you to be effective here, it means that you do not indicate your disapproval with any sort of eye contact, body language, or vocalization. He will quickly get bored, and drop the item on his own.

- If your dog refuses to drop an item, you may have to retrieve it manually. You can do this by placing your hand over the top of your dog's muzzle, and with your index finger and thumb placed on either side of the upper lip, firmly pinch into the teeth.

Before utilizing this technique, it is best to attempt to calm your dog's excitement as much as possible. In most cases, your dog will open its mouth to avoid the discomfort, at that that time you can retrieve the item, whatever it may be. This may take a couple of practices to get the correct pressure and the most effective location to apply it, but it works well.

In the rare instance that this fails, you can simply use both hands and try to separate the jaws by slowly pulling, *not jerking*, the upper and lower jaws apart. Think crocodile handler, minus the severed limbs.

-Another trick for distracting your puppy's attention is rapping your knuckles on a hard surface to emulate a knock at the door. Often, a puppy will want to investigate what he perceives as a guests arrival, thus dropping whatever is in its mouth to greet the nonexistent visitor.

18 Time to Sit

Sit is one of the basic commands that you will use regularly during life with your dog. Teaching your Mini Aussie to *sit* establishes human leadership by shaping your dog's understanding of who the leader is. This command can also help curb problem behaviors such as jumping up on people. It can also assist in teaching polite doggy etiquette, particularly, patiently waiting for you, the trusted alpha leader. Teaching your dog to sit is easy, and a great way for you to work on your catalog of essential leadership skills touched upon in previous chapters.

- Preparation, gather treats and then find a quiet place to begin training. Wait until your puppy sits down by his own will, and soon as his fuzzy rump hits the floor, *click and treat*. Treat your pup while he is still sitting, then promptly get him up and standing again. Continue doing this until your pup immediately sits back down in anticipation of the treat. Each time he complies, be sure to click and treat.

- Next, integrate the verbal command of "Sit." Each time he begins to sit on his own, say, "Sit," then reinforce it with a C/T. From here forward, only treat your pup when he sits after being commanded to do so. Practice for 10-15 repetitions then take a break.

Do These Variations

- Continue the training by adding the distraction of people, animals and noises to the sessions. As with the come command, you want your dog to sit during any situation that may take place. Practice for at least five minutes each day in places with increasingly more distractions and locations.

- Run around with your dog while you are sharing play with one of his favorite toys. After getting him worked up and excited, command your dog to "Sit." When he complies, click and treat your dog.

- Before going outside, delivering food, playing with toys, giving verbal praise, petting or getting into the car, ask your dog to *sit*. Having your dog sit before setting his food bowl down is something you can practice every day to help bolster his compliance to the sit command.

- Other situations where you can practice the sit command can be when there are strangers present or before opening doors for visitors. Having your dog sit before opening the door to guests is a great way to avoid jumping onto them. Later, add sit-stay.

Other excellent opportunities to practice the sit command is when there is food on the table, when you are barbequing or when you are together in the park.

Keep practicing this command in all situations that you may encounter throughout the day with your dog. I recommend a gradual increase to the level of distractions you expose the pup to during this training. Sit is a powerful and indispensable command that you will utilize throughout the life of your dog. Later, we will add the command of sit-stay in order to keep your dog in place until you release him.

How are things going for you? Are you seeing results and understanding the power of rewards training? I hope that you are and that both you and your dog are enjoying the training and bonding process.

-It is important eventually to phase out the clicking and treating every time your pup obeys the *sit* command. After his consistent obedience to the command, begin gradually to reduce C/T by treating every other compliance, then once out three times, followed by once out of four, five, six, and then finally cease.

Be sure to observe your dog's abilities and pace, making sure not to decrease C/T too rapidly. The overall goal of this training is to have your dog obey all commands without a reward, and only by a vocal or physical cue.

-Take advantage of each day, and the multiple opportunities you have to practice the sit command.

19 "Leave it"

Keep in mind that leave it and drop it are distinctly different commands. The goal of the *leave it* command is to steer your Mini Aussie's attention away from any object before it ends up in his mouth, thus making it a proactive command.

A proficiency in this command will help to keep him safe from dangerous items, for example objects like dropped medications, broken glass, trash, wires, chemical tainted rags or that treasured item you spy your dog about to place into his mouth.

A simple "Leave it" command can thwart those especially smelly, frequently dead things that dogs find irresistible and often choose to bring us as offerings of love and affection. We all know that our dogs love to inspect, smell, taste and in some cases roll in what they find. You can begin to teach the leave it command as soon as your dog recognizes his own name, e.g. "Axel, Leave it!"

- Start with a treat in each fisted hand. Let puppy have a sniff of one of your fists. When he eventually looks away from the fist and has stopped trying to get the treat, click and treat, but treat your dog from the opposite hand that he sniffed. Repeat this exercise until he completely refrains from trying to get the treat from you, as evidenced by showing no interest in your fist.

- Next, open your hand with the treat, and show him the treat. Close your hand if he tries to get the treat. Do this until he simply ignores the treat in the open hand, known as the decoy hand. When he ignores it, click and give your dog the treat from the other hand. Keep doing this until from the start of the exercise he ignores the treat in the open hand.

When you have reached this point, add the command "Leave it." Now, open the decoy hand, say "Leave it" just once for each repetition, and when your dog does, click and treat him using the other hand.

- Now, put the treat on the floor and say, "Leave it." If he tries to get it, cover it with your hand. When your dog looks away from the treat that is lying on the floor, click and treat your dog using the other hand. Continue issuing the command *leave it* until your dog no longer tries to get the treat that is on the floor.

-For the next exercise, put the treat on the floor and say, "Leave it," and then stand up. Click and treat if he obeys. Now, while on leash, walk your dog by the treat and say, "Leave it." If he goes for it, prevent this by restraining him with the leash. C/T him only when he ignores the treat. *Increase the length of time between the *leave it* command and the C/T. This is strengthens your pups dedication to obeying your instructions.

Teaching your dog to leave it using a treat first, will allow you to work up to objects such as toys, animals, pills, spills and even people. Once he gets the idea in his head that leave it means rewards for him, you both can eventually work towards more complex situations involving more difficult to resist items. Begin with a low value item such as a piece of kibble, and then move to a piece of hard to resist meat, his favorite toy, another animal and then people.

- After your dog is successful at leaving alone the treat and other items, take the training outside into the yard, gradually adding people, toys, animals and other hard to resist distractions. Next, head to the dog park or any other place with ever more distractions.

- Remember to keep your puppy clear of dog parks until at least after his seventh week, preferably no sooner than his tenth week, and certainly only after his first round of vaccines. Some veterinarians and experts suggest even waiting until after the second round of vaccinations before your dog is exposed to other animals.

Continue practicing daily until your dog has this command down pat. This is another potential lifesaving command that you will use regularly during the life of your dog and allows you peace of mind.

- At this point, you both can have some real fun. Try placing a dog biscuit on your pups paw, snout, or head and say, "Leave it." Gradually increase the time that your pup must leave the biscuit in place. Try this when he is in the sitting and other down positions. Have some fun and be sure to reward your dog the biscuit after he leaves it undisturbed. ~ Enjoy!

- Gradually phase out clicking and treating your dog every time that on command he obeys "Leave it." As with prior commands, begin gradually reducing treating by one out of two times, one out three times, then one out of four, five, six, and finally none.

Remember not to decrease too quickly or it will undermine your training. Keenly observe your dog's abilities and pace at all times. The goal is that your pooch will obey all the commands without a reward, eventually with only a vocal or physical cue.

20 "Down"

Teaching your Miniature Australian Shepherd to lie down not only helps to keep him in one spot, but also offers a calming timeout and is a useful intervention to curtail and even prevent barking. When paired with the stay command, you can keep your dog comfortably in one place for long periods.

Down not only protects your dog in potentially hazardous situations, but it also provides you with peace of mind that your dog will remain in the place that you commanded him to stay. This is yet another essential command that you will utilize daily throughout the lifetime of your dog.

Basics

- Begin training in a quiet place with few distractions and bring plenty of treats. Wait for your dog to lie down of his own will, and then *click and treat* while he is in the lying down position. If he does not pop up afterwards, toss a treat to get him up again.

Repeat rewarding the down posture with C/T's until he begins to lie down immediately after he gets the treat. His compliance means that he is starting to understand that good things come to him when he lies down, so in anticipation of this, he lies right back down.

- Now, augment the training with the addition of the verbal command *down*. As soon as your dog starts to lie down, say "Down," and click and treat. From here on, only C/T your dog when he lies down after your command.

- Next, practice this in a variety of areas and in situations of various distractions. Begin the practice indoors, then take it outside into your yard, and then wander into the neighborhood, and beyond. Remain patient in the more distracting locations.

Situations to command your dog to lie down could be times when there are strangers present, when there is food nearby, or when the stereo or television is on. Anytime you are outdoors barbequing, having a party, in the park and during walking together are excellent opportunities to practice this command.

Maintain diligence with this training, and attempt to find situations of increasing levels of distraction where you might need to use the command *down*. Remember that consistent compliance is what you are looking for. The power and importance of the down command will prove to be one of the most useful of all to train and maintain during the life of your dog.

After your success with the training of down, you can then move to the combination command of "Down-stay," which should be trained in order to keep your dog in place until you release him. Imagine the ease and joy when your pooch accompanies you to the local café and lies quietly and obediently at your feet while you drink your morning coffee.

Having an obedient companion is a very attractive and respected attribute of any responsible dog owner.

It is important to monitor and track your partner's progress by taking notes during training, especially as you increase the distractions, highlight where and when more work and attention is needed.

- Gradually phase out clicking and treating your dog every time that he obeys the "Down" command. Reduce the treats to one time out of two compliances, followed by one out of three, then one out of four, five, six, and finally stop altogether. Do not decrease the treats too rapidly and be sure to observe closely, your dog's abilities and pace. The goal of the training is to have your dog obey all commands with only a vocal or physical cue, without a reward.

Problems Solved

- If your dog will not comply with the *down* command, you need to return the training to a low distraction area like a bathroom. Unless your dog likes decorative bath soaps or vanity mirrors, there is not much to distract him in the bathroom. Continue the training there until your pup is regularly obeying and then move out into other rooms.

- If your dog does lies down but pops right back up, be sure that you are only treating him when in the lying down position. In this way, your dog will sooner understand the correlation between the command, action and the subsequent treat.

21 "Stay"

Stay is perhaps a command that you have looked forward to teaching, after all, it is up there on top of the list as one of the most useful and used essential commands. This command can be effectively paired with *sit* and *down*. With these combination commands under your belt, daily life with your companion will be made easier for the entire family.

Teaching your dog restraint has many practical uses. By reinforcing the wanted behavior of remaining in place, your dog will not end up in potentially dangerous situations such as running out the door and into the street.

This command also limits the possibility of your dog putting you in embarrassing or inconvenient situations, such as jumping up on people, or chasing the neighbor's pet kangaroo. Furthermore, it is a valuable command that teaches compliance, which facilitates better control of your dog.

Stay not only teaches your dog patience, but also reinforces his understanding of who is in charge of the decision-making. After you have taught your dog *sit* and *down*, the stay command should be next on your training agenda because they make for natural pairings.

- To begin with, find yourselves a quiet low distraction place, and bring plenty of treats. Give the sit command, and after he obeys, wait two-seconds before you *click and treat*. Continue practicing while gradually extending the duration of time between his compliance and his receiving the click and treat, thus reinforcing the length of time he is in the sit position. Work up to 10-15 seconds of sitting before clicking and treating.

- Next, you can begin to issue the combination *sit-stay* command, and this time you can add a hand signal to the mix. While you issue the command, the signal can simply be your flat hand directed towards his fuzzy little face at a distance of about 12 inches/30 centimeters.

You can also choose a unique hand signal of your own to use in conjunction with sit-stay, being careful to avoid the use of the middle finger, as not to offend the neighbors or passersby. Continue practicing while increasing the time your pup is in the sit position. Gradually increase the sit-stay time to one minute before you C/T.

- If your dog gets up during this training, it means you are moving too quickly. Try again with a shorter stay time goal, and then slowly increase the time your dog is to remain completely still. Continue practicing until your dog will stay for longer intervals.

*A good way to keep track of your dog's progress through each training session is always to utilize your training log. This is helpful for many reasons, including monitoring his compliance, goals, outcomes and unwanted behaviors.

Now it is time to test your progress.

Say "Sit-stay," and take one big step away from your dog and then C/T him for his obedience. Keep practicing this until you can take two big steps in any direction away from your dog without him moving. *It is essential that you return to treat your dog at the exact spot in which he stayed in place. Refrain from treating him if he rises or if he comes to you.

Keep progressing with this exercise until you can take several steps away, eventually moving completely out of sight from your dog while he stays stationary. Work towards the goal of him staying motionless for two full minutes while you are in his sight, followed by an additional two minutes that you remain out of his sight.

By gradually increasing the stay-time interval during this training, you reinforce the stay-response behavior to the point that your dog will stay put *no matter what is going on.* Often dogs will simply lie down after a number of minutes in the stay position. Usually, after about five minutes my dog just lies down until I release him.

- Lastly, begin increasing the distractions while practicing all that has been trained up to this point. As previously instructed, begin the practice indoors, outside into the yard, and then move away from the familiarity of your house and neighborhood.

For obvious reasons, be patient in the more distracting locations. It is important to maintain a practice routine of at least five minutes per day, particularly in places with increasing distraction. During your training sessions, continue to add other people and animals, all in a variety of noisy and increasingly distracting environments.

The desired outcome of this training is to have a dog that remains in place in any situation you both may encounter during your life together.

Now, repeat the above steps chronologically using the command "*Down*" and "Down-stay."

- Gradually phase out clicking and treating your dog every time that on command he obeys a command. As previously instructed, phase out treating by reducing it gradually, first by treating one out of two times, then once out three times, followed by once out of four, five, six, and then finally refrain all together. Be sure not decrease the treats too quickly. Observe and take notes of your dog's abilities and pace.

When finished with this section you should have the commands "Sit-stay" and "Down-stay" regularly obeyed by your dog. Take care not to train both commands in the same training sessions.

Helpful Hints

- *Always,* reward your dog in the location where he has remained in place.

- It is important to refrain from releasing him with a C/T while using the *come* command. This will invariably confuse the outcome of the training, and diminish the importance of the come command. Keep it clear and simple

- Note when your dog decides not to participate. It could be that the training is getting to difficult, too quickly. When giving commands to your dog, put variation in the stay times and locations. Give the little fella a chance to learn at his own pace.

- Practice the command of *stay,* particularly before he meets a new person. Practice this also before he follows you out the door, into the car or in the course of feeding before you put down his food bowl.

- If you encounter any difficulties, back up a step or calmly resume later. Be aware that each dog has his own pace of learning, so your ongoing patience is crucial. It is best to simply laugh, smile and roll with your dog's natural abilities while enjoying the process of teaching and learning together. After all, this is all quality time spent while hanging out with your new best friend.

22 Leash Training

Training your Mini Aussie pup to the leash will probably be one of the hardest tasks you will do. Leash training is one of those items that take a bit more time and effort from both of you. However, in the end it is very rewarding and serves to strengthen the trust and bond between you and your canine.

A leash or lead, is simply the rope that tethers you to your companion. Though a strong good quality and adjustable leash is mandatory, a feature of greater significance is the collar or harness. There is a variety of collars to choose from and it is up to you to do some research to determine which one is the best fit for your dog. Head collars and front attachment harnesses are a couple of choices. Make sure it fits properly, is sized correctly and that your dog is comfortable wearing it.

Keep in mind some general guidelines suggested when choosing a collar. If you are small and your dog is large, or if your dog tends to be aggressive or powerful, you will need to exert the greatest control, so the sensible choice should be a head collar.

Front attachment collars are an excellent choice for any dog or activity. Head and frontal attached collars should be used with leashes with a length of six feet (1.82 meters) or less. The reason for maintaining a shorter leash is that a longer lead length could allow your bolting dog to gain enough speed to injure him when the lead runs out and becomes suddenly taut.

The main goal of leash training is to get your dog to walk beside you without pulling against the leash. An effective method during training is simply to stop moving forward when your dog pulls on the lead, turn, walk the opposite direction, and then when he obediently walks beside you, reward with treats, praise and affection to reinforce the wanted behavior. The following steps will help you train your dog to have excellent leash manners. Remember, *loose leash walking is the goal!*

Before moving forward to the next instructional step below, please make sure that your dog consistently performs the target action of the training step that you are teaching. His consistent compliance is necessary for the success of this training, so do not be inclined to hurry or rush this training.

Walking With You Is A Treat (The beginning)

Start by donning your dog with a standard harness fastened with a non-retractable leash that is about ten to twenty feet (3-6 meters) in length. Before starting the training session, remember to load up your pouch or pockets with top-notch treats and head out to the back yard or another familiar and quiet low distraction outdoor spot. It is best if there are no other animals or people present during this initial phase. You need all of your dog's attention towards you.

First, decide whether you want your dog to walk on your left or right side. The side you choose is the side that you will treat your dog. When you deliver treats, deliver from your thigh level. Eventually, your dog will automatically come to that side because that is where the goodies can be found. Later, you can train your dog to walk on either side of you, but for now, stick with one side.

Training from both sides allows you the flexibility to maneuver your dog anywhere, such as out of harm's way or more practical applications like walking on either side of the street.

- Place a harness on your dog and attach the leash. Begin the training by randomly walking about the yard. When your dog decides to walk along with you, *click and treat* on the chosen side, at the level of your thigh. To "walk along with you" specifically refers to an action where your dog willingly joins you in full compliance when you move along, and in a manner without applying any resistance to the lead.

If he continues to calmly walk on the correct side, give him a *click and treat* with every step or two that you take together, thus reinforcing the desired behavior. Keep practicing this until your dog remains by your side more often than not.

At this time, do not worry about over-treating your trainee; you will eventually reduce the frequency of delivery and then eventually phase out treats completely upon his successful mastering of this skill. You can deduct the training treats from the next meal.

- Repeat ambling around the yard with your pal in tow, but this time walk at a faster pace than your prior sessions together. As before, when your dog decides to walk with you, give him a *click and treat* at thigh level of the chosen side. Keep practicing this until your dog consistently remains by your side, at this new pace. This leash training should occur over multiple sessions and days.

There is no need to rush any aspects of training. Remember to be patient with all training exercises, and proceed at a pace dictated by your dog's energy level and his willingness to participate.

Eyes on the THIGHS (Second act)

If you are here, then your next task is to train your dog to consistently walk beside you and not pull you around your yard or explore the end of his lead.

Keeping your dog focused on the training at hand. Teaching him that you are in control of the leash is crucial.

This time, start walking around the yard and wait for a moment when your dog lags behind or gets distracted by something. If he is distracted, say, "Let's go," followed by a non-violent slap to your thigh to get his attention. Make sure you use a cheerful voice when issuing this command

and refrain from any harsh tactics that will intimidate your pooch, because that can certainly undermine any training.

When he pays attention to you, simply walk away. By doing this, it isolates the cue connected to this specific behavior, thus moving closer to your dog's grasp of the command.

- If your dog catches up with you *before* there is tension on the leash, *click and treat* him from the level of your thigh. *Click and treat* him again after he takes a couple of steps with you, and then continue to reinforce this with a C/T for the next few steps while he continues walking beside you. Remember, the outcome of this training is 'loose leash walking.'

If your dog catches up *after* the leash has become taut, *do not treat him.* Begin again by saying, "Let's go," then treat him after he takes a couple of steps with you. Only reinforce with C/T when he is compliant.

- If he does not come when you say, "Let's go," continue moving until there is tension on the lead. At this point, stop walking and apply firm but gentle pressure to the leash. When he begins to come toward you, praise him as he proceeds. When he gets to you, *do not treat him,* instead say, "Let's go," and begin walking again. Click and treat your dog if he stays with you and continue to C/T your dog for every step or two that he stays with you.

Keep practicing this step until he remains at your side while you both walk around the yard. If he moves away from you, redirect him with pressure to the lead and the command cue of "Let's go," followed up by a C/T when he returns to the appropriate position of walking obediently in tandem with you.

Do not proceed forward to subsequent steps of the training until your dog is consistently walking beside you with a loose leash, and is appropriately responding to the "Let's go" command. It can sometimes take many days and sessions for your dog to develop this skill, so it is important for you to remain patient and diligent during this time. The outcome of this training is well worth your time and effort.

Oh! The things to smell and pee on (Third act)

Just like you, your dog is going to want to sniff things and eliminate. During these times, you should be in control. While your dog is on the leash, and when he is in anticipation of his regular treating, or at about each five-minute interval, say something like, "Go sniff," "Go play," "Free time," or some other verbal cue that you feel comfortable saying, followed by some free time on the leash.

Keep in mind that this is a form of reward, but if he pulls on the leash, you will need to redirect with a "Let's go" cue, followed by your walking in the opposite direction, quickly ending his free time. If your dog remains compliant, and does not pull on the leash before the allotted free time has elapsed, you are still the one that needs to direct the conclusion of free leash time, by saying, "Let's go," coupled with you *walking in the opposite direction*.

Where's is my human? (Fourth act)

Using steps one through three, continue practicing leash walking in the yard. During the course of the training session, gradually shorten the lead until 6-foot (1.8meter) length remains. Now, change the direction and speed of your movements, being sure to *click and treat* your dog every time he is able to stay coordinated with the changes you implement.

As loose leashed walking becomes routine and second nature for your companion, you can start phasing out the click and treats. Reserve the C/T for situations involving new or difficult training points, such as keeping up with direction changes or ignoring potential distractions.

Out in the Streets (Fifth act)

Now, it is time for the big step, taking your dog out of the yard and onto the sidewalk for his daily walk. You will use the same techniques you used in your yard, only now you have to deal with more distractions.

Distractions can come in all forms, including other dogs, friendly strangers, traffic, alarming noises, sausage vendors, feral chickens, taunting cats and a host of other potential interruptions and disturbances. At this time, you might want to consider alternate gear, such as a front attachment harness or a halter collar that fits over the head offering ultimate control over your companion.

Arm yourself with your dog's favorite treats, apply the utmost patience, and go about your walk together in a deliberate and calm manner. Remember to utilize the "Let's go," command cue when he pulls against his leash or forgets that you exist.

In this new setting, be sure to treat him when he walks beside you and then supersize the portions if your dog is obedient and does not pull on the lead during a stressful moment or an excitable situation. Lastly, do not forget to reward with periodic breaks for sniffing and exploring. The free time rewards reinforce his willingness to comply.

Stop and Go exercise (Sixth act)

Attach a 6-foot lead to the collar. With a firm hold on the leash, toss a treat or toy at about twenty feet (6 meters) ahead of you and your dog, then start walking toward it. If your dog pulls the leash and tries to get at the treat, use the "Let's go" command and immediately walk in the opposite direction of the treat. If he stays beside you without struggle while you walk toward the treat, allow him to have it as a reward.

Practice this several times until your dog no longer pulls toward the treat and stays at your side waiting for you to make the first move. The other underlying goal is that your dog should always look to you for direction and follow your lead before taking an action such as running after a toy while still leashed.

Switching Sides (Seventh Act)

After your dog is completely trained to the specific side and with a few months of successful loose leash walking practice under your belt, then you can begin the training again. This time you will target the opposing side that the two of you have previously trained.

There is no need rush, so proceed with the training of the opposite side when you know the time is right, and you are both comfortable with changing it up a bit. As previously mentioned, the desired target is a dog that is able to walk loose leashed on either side of you. This skill is essential for navigating your dog with ease and safety while in the outside world.

Troubleshooting

- If your dog happens to cross in front of you during your time together, he may be distracted, so it is important to make your presence known to him with a gentle leash tug or an appropriate command.

- If your dog is lagging behind you, he might be frightened or not feeling well, instead of pulling your dog along, give him a lot of support and encouragement. If the lagging is due to normal behavioral distractions, such as scent sniffing or frequent territorial marking, keep walking along. In this case, it is appropriate to pull gently on the leash to encourage his attention to the task at hand.

- The reinforcement of wanted behaviors necessitates you delivering numerous rewards when your dog walks beside you or properly executes what it is you are training at that time. During your time together, pay close attention to your dog's moods, patterns and behaviors. You want to pay close attention to these things so that you can anticipate his responses, modify your training sessions, or simply adapt whatever it is you are doing to assure that his needs are being met and you are both on the same page.

Being conscious of your dog's needs assists in maintaining a healthy respectful bond between the two of you. Make an effort to use playful tones in your voice with a frequent "Good dog," followed by some vigorous petting or some spirited play. Try to be aware of when your dog is beginning to tire and always attempt to end a training session on a high note, with plenty of treats, play and praise.

Heel

You will find this command indispensable when you are mobile, or perhaps when you encounter potentially dangerous situations. There will be times where you will need to issue a firm command in order to maintain control of your dog in order to keep the both of you out of harm's way. *Heel* is that command.

During your time together exploring the outside world, things such as another aggressive dog, busy traffic, construction sites, teasing cats or that irresistible squirrel may warrant keeping your dog close to you. If trained to the heel command, your dog will be an indispensable asset in helping to avert possible hazardous circumstances with these examples. The heel command is a clear instruction trained to assure that your dog remains close beside you *until you say otherwise*.

- Begin this training inside your back yard or in another low distraction area. First, place a treat in your fist on the side you've decided to train. Let him sniff your fist, then say "Heel," followed by a few steps forward leading him along with the fisted treat at thigh level. Click and treat him as he follows your fist with his nose. The fist is to keep your dog close to you. Practice for a few sessions.

- Next, begin the training as before, but now with an empty fist. With your fist held out in front of you, give the "Heel" command, and then encourage your dog to follow by your side. When he follows your fist for a couple of steps, *click and treat* him. For each subsequent session, repeat this practice a half dozen times or more.

- Continue to practice heel while you are moving around, but now begin to increase the length of time *before* you treat your dog. Introduce a new direction in your walking pattern or perhaps use a serpentine-like maneuver snaking your way around the yard. You will want to continuously, but progressively challenge him in order to advance his skills and to bolster his adaptability in various situations.

During all future outings together, this closed-empty-fist will now serve as your non-verbal physical hand cue instructing your dog to remain in the heel position. From here on out, remember to display your closed empty fist at your side when you issue your heel command.

- Now, move the training sessions outside of the security of your yard. The next level of teaching should augment his learning by exposing him to various locations with increasingly more distractions. The implementation of this new variation in training is done to challenge and to enhance your walking companion's adaptability to a variety of situations and stimulus.

Continue to repeat the *heel* command each time you take your dog out on the leash. Keeping his skills fresh with routine practice will ease your mind when out exploring new terrain. Knowing that your dog will be obedient and will comply with all of your commands, instructions and cues will be satisfying and keep you both safe and sane.

Out in the crazy, nutty world of ours there are plenty of instances when you will use this command to avoid unnecessary confrontations or circumstances with potentially dangerous outcomes. If by chance you choose to use a different verbal cue other than the commonly used *heel* command, pick a word that is unique and easy to say, and does not have a common use in everyday language. This way you avoid the possibility for confusion and misunderstanding.

23 Teaching "Touch"

Touch has an easy rating and requires no knowledge of other tricks, but your dog should know its name, and sitting on command is helpful. The supplies needed are a wooden dowel to be used as a touch-stick, your clicker, and some treats.

Touch training teaches your dog to touch, and in this lesson to touch the end of a stick. It can be any type of wooden dowel, cut broom handle, or similar that is around three feet (1 meter) in length. During training, add a plastic cap, rubber ball, or good ole duct tape to the end so that there are no sharp edges that can harm your dog. A good sanding job to dull all sharp edges will work as a good alternative.

Teaching "touch" using the touch-stick will enable you to train other tricks. You will discover that the touch-stick is useful in training, so take care that you correctly train your dog the *touch* command. Touch is used later to teach Learn Names, Ring Bell, Jump Over People, Spin, Jump, and more.

1. Begin training in a quiet place with few distractions, and bring plenty of treats.

2. Start with your dog in the sitting position or standing near you with his attention towards you. Hold your stick away from your body. Keep holding it while doing nothing else but holding the stick steady at a level that your dog can easily touch with his nose.

124

3. Luckily, a dog's natural curiosity will get the best of them and your dog should touch the stick. When your dog touches it with his nose or mouth, *click and treat*. Be sure to click immediately when your dog touches the end of the stick. Sometimes it is just a sniff, but those count for beginning to shape the command and require a C/T to let your dog understand what behavior you are seeking.

If your dog is not interested in the stick, then you will need to do the touching for him. Do this by gently touching your dog's nose while simultaneously clicking, and then treating. Keep doing this until your dog is regularly touching the stick when you hold it out.

4. The next time your dog touches the stick C/T while simultaneously saying the command, "Touch." Remember timing is important in all tricks. Your dog needs to know the exact correct action that he is being rewarded for performing. Repeat this a dozen times. Continue over multiple sessions until your dog is easily touching the end of the touch-stick when commanded. Feel free to add some "Good dog" praises.

Hands On

Teaching Axel this trick was an interesting outing. When I first held out the stick, Axel swiped it away with his paw. After a couple of more times, he finally smelled the end with his nose and I quickly clicked and treated. He responded to that, and after reinforcing that with several more click and treats, he started quickly touching the end of the stick.

After using the *touch* command a dozen times, he realized a treat came after he touched the end of the stick, and moving forward through a few training sessions, he started touching it each time I issued the *touch* command. I kept practicing and after a couple of more sessions, I locked it in. I was then able to use the *touch* command and touch-stick to train other tricks.

If your dog is touching the end of the stick with heavy force, then you can add some foam to the end of the stick to cushion his super-nose.

Troubleshooting

"What if my dog is touching the middle of the stick, or not touching the stick at all?"

I mentioned that Axel took a few swipes at the end of the stick before touching it. Each time he did this, I ignored this behavior even though he looked at me expecting a reward. He could smell the treats in my hand, but I did not click and reward the wrong action. Finally, as I held the stick out close to his snout, he smelled it with his nose and I quickly clicked and treated.

Do not reward until your dog is touching *only* the end of the stick. This allows you to use the touch command in training other tricks. If your dog will not touch it try gently touching the end of the stick to his nose and C/T, but quickly move away from that and let your dog begin to do the touching on his own.

24 Teaching to Learn Names

Learning names has an intermediate to difficult rating and requires knowledge of the touch command. The supplies needed are a toy, treats and your clicker.

Dog owners have known for years that dogs are smarter than many people give them credit. They are capable of learning the names of many different objects, such as their toys, people and places.

Dogs are capable of learning hundreds and even upwards to a thousand words. Furthermore, once your dog learns the name of something, he or she can find it, grab it and bring it to you.

Not all dogs are capable of learning the same number of words and some will learn and retain better than others, so do not get frustrated if it takes some time for your dog to recognize and remember what object, place, or person goes with the name you are speaking.

Using the steps in this exercise your dog can learn the names of all your family members, his personal items, such as his crate, collar, toys and leash. Beyond those items, your dog can learn the names of different rooms, which enable you to use the "Go" command to have your dog, go to a specific room.

Select a toy that you may already refer to by name. Chances are that you already often speak the names of dog-associated items when speaking to your dog and he recognizes that word. Be consistent in your name references to your dog's toys, such as Frisbee®, tug, ball, rope and squeaky. Changing the reference name will sabotage this training.

1. To begin, find a low distraction area, treats at the ready and one of your dog's favorite toys. I will use *tug* in this example.

2. Start by using *touch* and have your dog touch your empty hand, when he does, *click and treat* your dog. Repeat this five times.

3. Next, grab your dog's toy into your hand, say, "Touch," and if he touches the tug and not your hand, C/T your dog.

4. Repeat number three, but this time, add the toy name, say, "Touch tug." When your dog touches the *tug*, and nothing else, C/T at that exact moment he does this. Repeat this 6-10 times.

5. After a break, practice steps 1-4 over a few sessions and two days.

6. In the next phase warm up with numbers 1-4, then hold the tug out away from you and say "Touch tug," when he does C/T. Repeat this 6-10 times. Then extend the tug at full arm lengths from you and repeat 6-10 times. Practice this over a couple of sessions. Take note of your dog's progress and when he is ready proceed to number seven.

7. Now, place the tug onto the floor but keep your hand on it and say, "Touch tug," when he does, C/T. Repeat 6-10 times.

8. Place it on the floor without your hand upon it and say, "Touch tug," and when he does, treat a barnbuster sized treat serving. Feel free to throw in some verbal good boy/girls. If your dog is not moving to it, be patient, silent, and still to see if he can figure it out on his own. Remember that your dog wants his treat.

9. Moving forward with the same toy, place it around the room in different areas increasingly further from you. Place it on top of a small stool, on the ground, low-lying shelves and have your dog "Touch tug." Practice this over a few days and when your dog is regularly responding move onto number ten and a new toy.

10. Changing to another toy, use a toy such as Frisbee® or ball, that when spoken sounds much different from the previous toy name. Repeat the steps 4-9 with this next toy.

11. Time to test if your dog can tell the difference. Sit down on the couch or floor and place both the Frisbee® and the tug behind you. Take out the Frisbee® and practice five touches, C/T each time your dog correctly touches upon command. Next, do the same with the tug.

12. Now, hold one toy in each hand and say, "Touch Frisbee®" and see if your dog touches the correct toy. If your dog touches the Frisbee®, C/T, and then give a barnbuster sized reward. If your dog begins to move towards the Frisbee®, but you observe that he is unsure what to do, C/T for moving in the correct direction. If your dog goes to the tug or does nothing, remain neutral offering no C/T or verbal reward.

Keep working on this and practicing until your dog regularly goes to the correct toy that you command to be touched. Then following the same process continue adding toys. When you get to three and then four, toys/objects you can lay all four in front of you and command "Touch (object name)" and see if your dog can choose and recognize the correct toy/object.

13. Practice the "Touch tug, ball, Frisbee, chew" by placing the objects in different parts of the room and have him identify each correctly. Practice this often to keep the names fresh in your dog's mind.

14. Teaching names of people is done a little differently, because for obvious reasons you cannot hold them in your hand, if they are willing, you could however have them sit on the floor. You can use the training stick from teaching *touch* to help teach the names of rooms and things, such as crate, bed and mat. Also, use the training stick to introduce people and their names.

Alternative to #14 - Teaching a person's name to your dog can be taught like this.

1. Hold onto your dog's collar and have a family member show your dog a treat. Have the person walk into the other room. Then say, "Axel, find Michelle," or whatever the person's name is. Now let go of the collar and see if your dog will go into the other room and to that person. It is okay to follow your dog. If he does go to the person, give your dog a C/T and a huge barnbuster reward along with praise.

2. Repeat five times and take a break.

3. After number two, have the family member go into different rooms, and do five repetitions in each room.

4. It will take a few sessions for your dog to learn and retain the names. Do not forget to practice forever.

Hands On

I taught this to Axel, but my wife's Poodle Roxie knows many more names of objects, people and places, but Axel can respectably perform the trick. He is my pal and goes through all of these things willingly, but some days I have to give him a break because darn it he earns it.

Teaching Axel names while using the "Touch" command I started out by using the touch command with my empty hand and getting a peculiar look from him. He touched my hand and I C/T about a half dozen times.

Holding Axels attention while in the sitting position in front of me, I then I picked up the tug into my hand and repeated the exercise saying, "Touch tug," and only C/T when he touched the tug. I'll confess it took a few attempts and me adjusting my hand so that he had to touch the tug when he moved his nose towards my hand holding the tug.

I ran through exercises 1-4 over a few days and about six sessions.

Eventually, I felt confident to start moving the tug further from my body and then onto the floor, couch cushion, into the corner of the room and so forth. It took some time and patience for him quickly to understand that he was to go to the item being named.

Eventually, I was able to place it into different rooms inside the house and say, "Touch tug" and he would bolt off looking for it. From there I added further toys, such as Frisbee®, that I discovered by his ears and the way that he looked at me that he already recognized the word.

Troubleshooting

"I am scratching my head because my dog does not understand what I am trying to teach!"

In the beginning, you can try maneuvering your hand so that your dog will touch the toy and not your hand.

Watch your time when training. Keep your sessions short and if your dog is still a puppy or acting like one keep your sessions around 3-5 minutes, while older dogs can usually go about 10 minutes per training session. If you notice any signs of fatigue, end the session on a high happy note and stop for the day. Begin anew the following day.

Hint: After your dog recognizes, and is regularly touching objects in different locations, solicit other people to practice giving your dog the command. Combine this with "Take it" & "Bring it" and your dog will go find and bring to you any objects he has learned names. Have fun and enjoy adding objects and people.

25 Go West Young Mini Aussie

"Go" is a great cue to get your puppy into his crate or onto his mat or rug, and later his *stuffed goose down micro-fiber plush bed*. This is a very handy command to send your dog to a specific location and keep him there while you tend to your business. Before teaching *go*, your dog should know his name and already be performing to the commands *down* and *stay*.

While training the following steps, do not proceed to the next step until your dog is regularly performing the current step.

- Find a quiet low distraction location to place a towel or mat on the floor and grab your treats. Put a treat in your hand and use it to lure your dog onto the mat while saying, "Go." When all four paws are on the mat, *click and treat* your dog. Do this about ten to fifteen times.

- Start the same way as above, say "Go," but this time have an empty hand, act as though you have a treat in your fist while you are luring your dog onto the mat. When all fours are on the mat *click and treat* your dog. Do this ten to fifteen times.

- Keep practicing with an empty hand and eventually turning the empty hand into a pointed index finger. Point your finger towards the mat. If your dog does not understand, walk him to the mat and then click and treat. Do this about ten to fifteen times.

- Now, cue with "Go" *while pointing* to the mat, but do not walk to the mat with him. If your dog will not go to the mat when you point and say the command, then keep practicing the step above before trying this step again. Proceed practicing the command *go* while using the pointed finger and when your dog has all four paws on the mat, click and then walk over and treat him while he is on the mat. Do this about ten to fifteen times.

- Now, grab your mat and try this on different surfaces and other places, such as grass, tile, patio, carpet and in different rooms. Continue to practice this in more and more distracting situations and don't forget your towel or mat. Take the mat outdoors, to your friends and families houses, hotel rooms, the cabin and any other place that you have your trusted companion with you.

One Step Beyond – "Relax"

In accordance with "Go" This is an extra command you can teach. This is a single word command that encapsulates the command words *go, down,* and *stay* all into one word. The purpose is to teach your dog to go to a mat and lie on it until he is released. This is for when you need your dog out from under foot for extended lengths of time like when you are throwing a party.

Pair it with "Down and stay" so your dog will go the mat, lie down, and plan on staying put for an extended period of time. You can substitute your own command, such as "Settle," "Rest," or "Chill," but once you choose a command stick with it and remain consistent.

This command can be used anywhere that you are, informing your dog that he will be relaxing for a long period and to assume his relaxed posture. You can train this command when your pup is young and it will benefit you throughout your life together.

- Place your mat, rug, or what you plan using for your dog to lie down upon.

- Give the "Go" command and C/T your dog when he has all four paws on the mat. While your dog is on the mat, issue the command "Down stay," and after compliance go to him and C/T while your dog is still on the mat.

- Now, give the "Relax" command and repeat the above exercise with this relax command. Say, "Relax," "Go" and C/T your dog when he has all four paws on the mat. While your dog is on the mat, issue the command "Down stay," and C/T while your dog is still on the mat. When your dog understands the *relax* command it will incorporate go, down, and stay.

Practice 7-10 times per session until your dog is easily going to his mat, lying down, and staying in that position until you release him.

- Next, give only the "Relax" command and wait for your dog to go to the mat and lie down *before* you *click and treat* your dog. Do not use any other cues at this time. Continue practicing over multiple sessions, 7-10 repetitions per session until your dog is easily following your one word instruction of *relax*.

- Now begin making it more difficult; vary the distance, add distractions and increase the times in the relax mode. This is a wonderful command for keeping your dog out of your way for lengthy durations. You will love it when this command is flawlessly followed.

Helpful Hint

-While you are increasing the time that your dog maintains his relaxed position, click and treat every 3-10 seconds.

- You can also shape this command so that your dog assumes a more relaxed posture than when you issue "Down stay." When your dog realizes that the "Relax" command encompasses the super relaxed posture that he would normally use under relaxed conditions, he will understand that he will most likely be staying put for a lengthy period and your dog might as well get very comfortable.

Another obedience command that can and should be taught is the release command. Do not forget to teach a release command word to release your dog from any previous command. Release is command #14 in my 49 ½ Dog Tricks book that will soon, or is already for purchase. *Release* is easier to train if your dog already *sits* and *stays* on command.

This command informs your dog that they are free to move from whichever previous command you had issued and your dog complied, such as *sit or down*.

When released your dog should rise from the position but remain in place. This is an obedience command that can keep your dog safe and you from worrying about your dog bolting off or moving at the wrong time during a potentially dangerous situation. You can choose any command, such as "Move," or "Break." As a reminder, one or two syllable words work best when teaching dogs commands.

26 Jumping Issues

Your dog loves you and wants as much attention from you as possible. The reality is that you are the world to your dog. Often when your dog is sitting quietly, he is easily forgotten. When he is walking beside you, you are probably thinking about other things, such as work, dinner, the car, chores you need to accomplish or anything but your loyal companion walking next to you.

Sometimes your dog receives your full attention only when he jumps up on you. When your dog jumps up on you, then you look at him, physically react in astonishment, maybe shout at him and gently push him down until he is down on the floor. Then, you ignore him again, and make a mental note to teach your dog not to jump up onto you. What do you expect? He wants your attention. Teaching your dog not to jump is essentially teaching him that attention will come only if he has all four paws planted firmly on the ground.

It is important not to punish your dog when teaching him not to jump up on you and others. Do not shout "No!" or "Bad!" Do not knee your dog or push him down. The best way to handle the jumping is to turn your back and ignore your dog.

Remember, since he loves you very much, your dog or puppy may take any physical contact from you as a positive sign. You do not want to send mixed signals; instead, you want to practice complete ignoring that consists of no looking or audio. If you do use a vocal command, do not say, "Off," instead use "Sit," which your dog has probably already learned. Try not to use a command, and instead proceed with ignoring.

For jumping practice, it would be ideal if you could gather a group of people together who will participate in helping you train your dog that jumping is a no-no. You want to train your dog to understand that he will only get attention if he is on the ground. If groups of people are not available, then teach him to remain grounded using his family. When your dog encounters other people, use a strong "Sit stay" command to keep all four paws planted firmly on the ground. I covered "Sit stay" above, and now you understand how useful and versatile this command can be.

No Jumping On the Family

This is the easiest part, because the family and frequent visitors have more chances to help your dog or puppy to learn. When you come in from outside and your dog starts jumping up, say, "Oops!" or "Whoa," and immediately leave through the same door. Wait a few seconds after leaving and then do it again. When your dog finally stops jumping upon you as you enter, give him a lot of attention.

Ask the rest of the family to follow the same protocol when they come into the house. If you find that he is jumping up at other times as well, like when you sing karaoke, walking down the hallway or are cooking at the barbeque, just ignore your dog by turning your back and put energy into giving him attention when he is sitting.

No Jumping on Others

Prevention is of utmost importance and the primary focus in this exercise. You can prevent your dog from jumping by using a leash, a tieback, crate, or gate. Until you have had enough practice and your dog knows what you want him to do, you really should use one of these methods to prevent your dog from hurting someone or getting an inadvertent petting reward for jumping. To train, you will need to go out and solicit some dog training volunteers and infrequent visitors to help.

- Make what is called a *tieback*, which is a leash attached to something sturdy, within sight of the doorway but not blocking the entrance keeping your dog a couple of feet or about a meter away from the doorway. Keep this there for a few months during the training period until your dog is not accosting you or visitors. When the guest arrives, hook your dog to the secure leash and then let the guest in.

Guests Who Want to Help Train Your Dog (Thank you in advance)

All of these training sessions may take many sessions to complete, so remain patient and diligent in training and prevention until your dog complies with not jumping on people.

- Begin at home, and when a guest comes in through the door, and the dog jumps up, they are to say "oops" or "whoa," and leave immediately. Practice this with at least five or six different visitors, each making multiple entrances during the same visit. If your helpers are jumped, have them completely ignore your dog by not making any eye contact, physical or vocal actions other than the initial vocal word towards your dog, then have them turn their backs and immediately leave.

- When you go out onto the streets, have your dog leashed. Next, have your guest helper approach your dog. If he strains against the leash or jumps have the guest turn their back and walk away. When your dog calms himself and sits, have the guest approach again.

Repeat this until the guest can approach, pet and give attention to your dog without your dog jumping up. Have the volunteer repeat this at least five to seven times. Remember to go slowly and let your dog have breaks. Keep the sessions in the 5-7 minute range. For some dogs, this type of training can get frustrating. Eventually, your dog will understand that his jumping equals being ignored.

- Use the tie-back that you have placed near the door. Once your dog is calm, the visitor can greet your dog if they wish. If the guest does not wish to greet your dog, give your dog a treat to calm his behavior. If he barks, send your dog to his gated time out area.

The goal is that you always greet your guests first, *not your dog*. Afterward, your guests have the option to greet or not greet, instead of your dog always rushing in to greet every guest. If he is able to greet guests calmly while tied back, then he may be released. At first hold the leash to see how your dog reacts, then if he is calm release him.

A Caveat to These Two Methods

1) For those who are not volunteers to help teach your dog and are at your home visiting, there is another method. Keep treats by the door, and as you walk in throw them seven to nine feet (2.1 - 2.7 meters) away from you. Continue doing this until your dog begins to anticipate this.

Once your dog is anticipating treats every time someone comes through the door it will keep him from accosting you or visitors that walk through the doorway. After your dog eats his treat and has calmed down, ask him to sit, and then give him some good attention.

2) Teach your dog that a hand signal such as grabbing your left shoulder means the same as the command "Sit." By combining the word "Sit" with a hand on your left shoulder, he will learn this. If you want to use another physical cue, you can substitute your own gesture here, e.g. holding your left wrist or ear.

Ask the guests that have volunteered to help train your dog to place their right hand on their left shoulders and wait until your dog *sits* before they pet him or give any attention. Training people that meet your dog will help both you and your dog in preventing unwanted excitement and jumping up. Having your dog sit before he can let loose with jumps is proactive jumping prevention.

27 Excessive Barking

Any dog owner knows that dogs bark for many reasons, most commonly, for attention. Your Mini Aussie may bark for play, attention or because it is close to feeding time and he wants you to feed him. Dogs also bark to warn intruders and us, so we need to understand why our dog is barking. Not all barking is bad. Some dogs are short duration barkers while others can go on for hours, we do not want that and either do our neighbors so let's remedy that before it gets out of control.

Whatever the case *do not* give your dog attention for barking. Do not send the signals that your dogs barking gets an immediate reaction from you, such as you coming to see why he is barking or even moving towards him.

As I mentioned in the opening paragraph, they do sometimes bark to warn us, so we should not ignore all barking but instead we need to assess the barking situation before dismissing it as nonsense barking. With a bit of assessment you can diagnose your dogs barking and then take the proper action to shape his or her barking behavior.

When you know the cause is a negative behavior that needs correction, say, "Leave it" and ignore him. While not looking at your dog go to the other side of the room or into another room, you can even close the door behind you until your dog has calmed down. *Make it clear to your barking dog that his barking does not result in any rewards or attention.

In everyday life, make sure you are initiating activities that your dog enjoys and are always happening on *your* schedule. You are the alpha leader so regularly show your pup who is in charge and make sure that he earns what he is provided. Have your pup *sit* before he gets any reward.

I love dogs and I am sure that you do too, but an incessant barking dog can drive anyone to frustration and potentially anger. People would be surprised how many dogs have lethal action taken against them from neighbors that have been pushed to the breaking point by a neighbor's unstoppable barking dog. This is something I never want to happen to your family.

Your dog may bark when seeing or hearing something interesting. Below are a few ways to deal with this issue.

Prevention when you are at your residence

- *Teach your dog the command "Quiet."* When your dog barks, wave a piece of food in front of his nose at the same time you are saying, "Quiet." When he stops barking to sniff, *click and treat* him right away. Do this about four or five times and then the next time he barks, pretend you have a piece of food in your hand next to his nose and say, "Quiet." Always *click and treat* him as soon as he *stops* barking and continue to *click and treat* him again for every few seconds that he remains quiet after you issued the command.

Eventually, as you make your way to five or ten seconds, gradually increase the time duration between the command quiet, clicking *and treating*.

- *Prevent it.* Block the source of sound or sight so that your dog is unable to see or hear the catalyst that is sparking his barking. Use a fan, stereo, TV, curtains, blinds or simply put him in a different area of the house to block him from the stimulus.

- When your pup hears or sees something that would typically make him bark and he *does not bark*, reward him with attention, play or a treat. This is reinforcing and shaping good behaviors instead of negative behaviors. This is an important step in rewards based training and shaping non-barking behavior.

The Time Out

- Yes you can you can use a *time out* on your dog, but do not use it too often. When you give your dog a time out, it takes your dog out of his social circle and provides your dog what is known as a negative punishment.

This kind of punishment is powerful and can have side effects that you do not want. Your dog may begin to fear you when you walk towards him, especially if you have the irritated look on your face that he recognizes as the *time out face*. The *time out* should be used sparingly. Instead, focus on teaching your dog the behaviors that you prefer while preventing the bad behavior through blocking the stimulus.

Choose a place where you want the time out spot to be located. Make sure that this place is not the relief spot, crate or his play area. Ideally, it will be a boring place that is somewhere that is not scary, too comfortable but safe. A gated pantry or the bathroom works well.

- Secure a 2-foot piece of rope or a short leash to your puppy's collar. When your pup barks, use a calm voice and give the command, "Time out," then take the rope and walk him firmly but gently to the time out spot. Leave him there for about 5 minutes, and longer if necessary.

Release him when your dog is calm and not barking. You may need to do this two to a dozen times before he understands which behavior has put him into the time out place. Almost all dogs are social and love being around their humans, so this can have a strong impact.

Prevention when you are away from your residence

- Again, prevent barking by blocking the sounds or sights that are responsible for your dog or puppy going into barking mode. Use a fan, stereo, curtains or blinds, or keep him in another part of the house away from the stimulus.

- Use a Citronella Spray Collar. Only use this for when the barking has become intolerable. Do not use this when the barking is associated with fear or aggression. So that your dog understands how it works you will want to use this a few times when you are at home before using it when away.

Citronella collars work like this. The collar has a sensitive microphone that senses when your dog is barking, when this happens it triggers a small release of citronella spray into the area above a dog's nose. It surprises the dog and disrupts barking by emitting a smell that dogs dislike.

Out walking

While you are out walking your dog, out of shear excitement or from being startled, your pup might bark at other dogs, people, cars and critters. This can be a natural reaction or your dog may have sensitivities to certain tones, the goal is to try to limit the behavior and quickly cease the barking.

Here are some helpful tools to defuse that behavior.

- Teach your dog the *"Watch me"* command. Begin this training in the house in a low distraction area. While you hold a treat to your nose, say your dog's name and "Watch me." When your dog looks at the treat for at least one second give him a click and treat. Repeat this about 10-15 times. Then increase the time that your dog looks at you to 2-3 seconds and then repeat a dozen times.

- Next, repeat the process while pretending to have a treat on your nose. You will then want to incorporate this hand to your nose as your hand signal for *watch me*. Click and treat when your dog looks at you for at least one second, then increase to two or three seconds, and *click and treat* after each goal. Repeat this about 10-15 times.

- Increase the duration that your dog will continue to watch you while under the command *Click and treat as you progress*. Try to keep your dog's attention for 5-10 seconds. Holding your dog's attention for this length of time usually results in the catalyst for him to move away from the area or to lose interest in the barking stimulus.

- Now, practice the "Watch me" command while you are walking around inside the house. Then practice this again outside near something he finds interesting. Also, practice in a situation that he would normally bark. Continue practicing in different situations and around other catalysts that you know will produce your dog barking.

This is a great way to steer attention towards you and away from your dog's barking catalysts.

Other Solutions

- When you notice something that normally makes your dog bark and he has not begun to bark, use the "Quiet" command as a preemptive measure. For example, your dog regularly barks at the local skateboarder. When the trigger that provokes your dog's barking, the skateboarder comes zooming by, use the command "Quiet," and *click and treat*. Click and treat your dog for every few seconds that he remains quiet.

Teach your dog that his barking trigger gets him a *quiet* command. Your dog will begin to associate the skateboarder with treats and gradually it will diminish his barking outbursts at the skateboarder. Then continue with other barking catalysts.

- If he frequently barks while a car is passing by, put a treat by his nose and then bring it to your nose. When he looks at you, *click and treat* him. Repeat this until he voluntarily looks at you when a car goes by and does not bark, continuing to *treat* him appropriately.

- You can also reward your dog for calm behavior. When you see something or encounter something that he would normally bark at and he does not, *click and treat* your dog. *Instead of treats, sometimes offer praise and affection.* As a reminder, it is a good idea not to always use treats as rewards.

- If you are out walking and your dog has not yet learned the *quiet* cue or is not responding to it, turn around and walk away from whatever is causing your dog to bark. When he calms down, offer a reward.

- As a last resort use the citronella spray collar when your dogs barking cannot be controlled using the techniques that you have learned. Use this only when the barking is *not* associated with fear or aggression.

Your dog is Afraid, Aggressive, Lonely, Territorial or Hung-over

Your dog may have outbursts when he feels territorial, aggressive, lonely or afraid. All of these negative behaviors can be helped with proper and early socialization, but occasionally they surface.

Often rescue dogs have not been properly socialized and bring their negative behaviors into your home. Be patient while you are teaching your new dog proper etiquette. Some breeds, especially watch and guarding breeds are prone to territorialism and it can be a challenge to limit their barking.

- As a temporary solution, you should first try to prevent outbursts by crating, gating, blocking windows, using fans or music to hide sounds and avoid taking your dog places that can cause these barking outbursts.

This is not a permanent solution, but is a helpful solution while you are teaching your dog proper barking etiquette. To allow your dog a chance to find his center, relax his mind and body, do this for about seven to ten days before beginning to train against barking.

Some Tips

- If training is too stressful on you or your dog, or not going well, then you may want to hire a professional positive trainer for private sessions. When interviewing, tell him or her that you are using a clicker or rewards based training system and are looking for a trainer that uses the same type or similar methods.

- Always, remain calm, because a relaxed and composed alpha achieves great training outcomes. A confident, calm, cool and collected attitude that states you are unquestionably in charge goes a long way in training all commands.

It is important to help your dog to modify his thinking about what tends to upset him. Teach him that what he was upset about before now predicts his favorite things.

Here is how

- When the trigger appears in the distance, *click and treat* your dog. Keep clicking and treating your dog as the two of you proceed closer to the negative stimulus.

- If he is territorially aggressive, teach him that the doorbell or a knock on the door means that is his cue to get into his crate and wait for treats. You can do this by ringing the doorbell and luring your dog to his crate and once he is inside the crate giving him treats.

- You can also lure your dog through his fears. If you are out walking and encounter one of his triggers, put a treat to his nose and lead him out and away from the trigger zone.

- Use the "Watch me" command when you see him getting nervous or afraid. *Click and treat* him frequently for watching you.

- Reward *calm* behavior with praise, toys, play or treats.

- *For the hangover, I recommend lots of sleep and water.*

Your dog is frustrated, bored or both

All dogs including your dog or Mini Aussie may become bored or frustrated. At these times, your dog may lose focus, not pay attention to you and *spend time writing bad poetry in his journal*.

A few things that can help prevent boredom and frustration are as follows.

- Keep him busy and tire him out with chew-toys, exercise, play and training. These things are a cure for most negative behaviors. A tired dog is usually happy to relax and enjoy quiet time.

- Your pup should have at least 30 minutes of aerobic exercise per day. In addition to the aerobic exercise, each day he should have an hour of chewing and about 15 minutes of training. Keep it interesting for him with a variety of activities. It is, after all, the spice of life.

- Use the command "Quiet" or give your dog a time out.

- As a last resort, you can break out the citronella spray collar.

Excited to Play

- Like all of us, your puppy will get excited about play. Teach your dog that when he starts to bark, the playtime stops. Put a short leash on him and if he barks, use it to lead him out of play sessions. Put your dog in a time out or just stop playing with your dog. Reward him with more play when he calms down.

Armed with these many training tactics to curb and stop barking, you should be able to gradually reduce your dogs barking and help him to understand that some things are not worth barking. Gradually you will be able to limit the clicking and treating, but it is always good practice to reward your dog for not barking. Reward your dog with supersized treat servings for making the big breakthroughs.

28 Nipping

Friendly and feisty, little puppies nip for a few reasons such as when they are teething, playing or they want to get your attention. If you have acquired yourself a nipper, not to worry because in time most puppies will grow out of this behavior on their own. Other dogs, such as some bred for herding, nip as a herding instinct. They use this behavior to round up their animal charges, household animals and all human family members, especially children. Other dogs can acquire this annoying action by us allowing it to continue when they playfully nip at our heels.

You will want to avoid punishing or correcting your dog while he is working through the nipping stage, because this could eventually result in a strained relationship down the road. However, you will want to teach your puppy how delicate human skin is. Let your dog test it out and give him feedback. You can simply indicate your discomfort when he bites or nips, by using and exclamation, such as, *"Yipe!"*, *"Youch!"* or *"Bowie!"* in addition to a physical display of your pain by pulling back your hand, calf or ankle, will usually be enough for your dog to understand that it is not an acceptable behavior.

After this action, it is important to cease offering any further attention towards your dog, because this provides the possibility that the added attention will reinforce the negative behavior. If you act increasingly more sensitive to the nips, he will begin to understand that we humans are very sensitive and quickly respond with sudden vocal and physical displays of discomfort.

This is a very easy behavior to modify because we know the motivation behind it. The puppy wants to play and chew, and who is to blame him for this? Remember, it is important to give your dog access to a variety of chew-toys and when he nips, respond accordingly, then immediately walk away and ignore him. If he follows you, and nips at your heels, give your dog a time out. Afterward, when your dog is relaxed, calm and in a gentle disposition, stay and play with him. Use the utmost patience with your puppy during this time, and keep in mind that this behavior will eventually pass.

Preventing the Nippage

- Always have a chew-toy in your hand when you are playing with your puppy. This way he learns that the right thing to bite and chew is the toy and *not your hand or any other part of your body.*

- Get rid of your puppy's excess energy by exercising him *at least* an hour each day. As a result, he will have less energy to nip.

- Make sure he is getting adequate rest and that he is not cranky from lack of sleep. Twelve hours per day is good for dogs, and it seems for teenagers as well.

- Always have lots of interesting chew toys available to help your puppy to cope during the teething process.

- Teach your kids not to run away screaming from nipping puppies. They should walk away quietly or simply stay still. Children should never be left unsupervised around dogs.

- Play with your puppy in his gated puppy area. This makes it easier to walk away if he will not stop biting or mouthing you. This quickly reinforces his understanding that hard bites end play sessions.

- As a last resort, when the other interventions and methods discussed above are not working, you should increase the frequency of your use of a tieback to hold your dog in place within a gated or time out area. If your dog is out of control with nipping or biting, and you have not yet trained him that biting is an unacceptable behavior, you may have to use this method until he is fully trained.

For example, you may want to use this when guests are over or if you simply need a break. Always use a tieback while your dog is under supervision and never leave him tied up alone. The tieback is a useful method and can be utilized as a tool of intervention when addressing other attention getting behaviors like jumping, barking and the dreaded leg humping.

The best option during this time, early in his training, is to place him in a room with a baby gate blocking the doorway.

Instructing Around the "Nippage"

- Play with your dog and praise him for being gentle. When he nips say, "*Yipe!*" mimicking the sound of an injured puppy, and then immediately walk away. After the nipping, wait one minute and then return to give him another chance at play, or simply remain in your presence *without nipping*.

Practice this for two or three minutes, remembering to give everyone present or those who will have daily contact with your pup a chance to train him through play. It is crucial that puppies *do not receive any reward for nipping*. After an inappropriate bite or nip, all physical contact needs to be abruptly stopped, and quick and complete separation needs to take place so that your puppy receives a clear message.

- After your puppy begins to understand that bites hurt, and if he begins to give you a softer bite, *continue to act hurt even if it doesn't*. In time, your dog will understand that only the slightest pressures by mouth are permissible during play sessions. Continue practicing this until your puppy is only using the softest of mouths, and placing limited tension upon your skin.

- Next, the goal is to decrease the frequency of mouthing. You can use the verbal cues of *quit* or *off* to signal that his mouth needs to release your appendage. Insist that the amount of time your puppy uses his mouth on you needs to decrease in duration, as well as the severity of pressure needs to decrease. If you need incentive, use kibble or liver to *reward after you command and he obeys.* Another reward for your puppy when releasing you from his mouth grasp is to give him a chew or chew-toy stuffed with food.

- The desired outcome of this training is for your puppy to understand that mouthing any human, if done at all, should be executed with the utmost care, and in such a manner, that without question the pressure *will not inflict pain or damage.*

- Continue the training using the verbal cue of *quit,* until *quit* becomes a well-understood command, and your dog consistently complies when it is used. Interject breaks every 20-30 seconds when playing and any type of mouthing are occurring. The calm moments will allow excitement to wane and will help to reduce the chances of your dog excitably clamping down. Practice this frequently, and as a part of your regular training practice schedule. The result from successful training and knowing that your dog will release upon command will give you piece of mind.

- If you have children, or are worried about the potential for injury due to biting, you can continue training in a way that your dog knows that mouthing is *not permitted under any circumstance*. This level of training permits you from having to instruct a permissible mouthing pressure resulting in a reduction of your anxiety whenever your dog is engaged in playing with family or friends. This of course nearly eliminates the potential for biting accidents to occur.

Remain vigilant when visitors are playing with your dog. Monitor the play, and be especially attentive to the quality of the interaction, being alert that the session is not escalating into a rough and potentially forceful situation in which your dog might choose to use his mouth in an aggressive or harmful way.

You will need to decide the rules of engagement, and it will be your responsibility that others understand these rules. To avoid harm or injury it will be necessary for you to instruct visitors and family prior to play. Excessive biting also pertains to other dogs and animals; it should not be tolerated when used with pain inflicting force.

29 Digging Help

Some dogs are going to dig no matter what you do to stop it. For these diggers, this behavior is innate to them, so remember that these dogs have an urge to do what they do. Whether this behavioral trait is for hunting or foraging, it is deeply imbedded inside their DNA and it is something that cannot be easily turned off. Remember that when you have a digger for a dog, they tend to be excellent escape artists, so you will need to bury your perimeter fencing deep to keep them inside your yard or kennel.

Cold weather dogs, such as Huskies, Malamutes, Chows and other "Spitz" type dogs often dig a shallow hole in an area to lie down in, to either cool down or warm up. These dogs usually dig in a selected and distinct area, such as in the shade of a tree or shrub. Feral dogs mimic this to create sleeping spaces at night. I see this commonly with stray dogs living near beaches. In the mornings, you can see sleeping holes littering the beach where a number of dogs have slept.

Other natural diggers, such as Terriers and Dachshunds are natural hunters and dig to bolt or hold prey at bay for their hunting companions. These breeds have been genetically bred for the specific purpose of digging into holes to chase rabbits, hare, badgers, weasels, and other burrowing animals.

Scent hounds, such as Beagles, Bassets and Bloodhounds will dig under fences in pursuit of their quarry. This trait is not easily altered or trained away, but you can steer it into the direction of your choosing.

To combat dog escapes you will need to bury your fencing or chicken wire deep into the ground. It is suggested that 18-24 inches, or 46-61cm into the soil below the bottom edge of your fencing is sufficient, but we all know that a determined dog may even go deeper, when in pursuit of quarry. Some dog owners will affix chicken wire at about 12 inches (30.5cm) up onto the fence, and then bury the rest down deep into the soil. Usually, when the digging dog reaches the wire, its efforts will be thwarted and it will stop digging.

Some dogs dig as an instinctive impulse to forage for food to supplement their diet, this might be your dog's preference for digging up your garden. Because dogs are omnivorous, they will sometimes root out tubers, rhizomes, bulbs, or any other edible root vegetable that is buried in the soil. Even nuts buried by squirrels, newly sprouting grasses, the occasional rotting carcass or other attractive scents will be an irresistible aroma to their highly sensitive noses.

Other reasons dogs dig can be traced directly to boredom, lack of exercise, lack of mental and physical stimulation and improperly or under-socialized dogs. Improperly socialized dogs can suffer from separation anxiety and other behavioral issues. Non-neutered dogs may dig an escape to chase a female in heat. Working breeds, for instance Border Collies, Australian Cattle Dogs, Shelties and others can stir up all sorts of trouble if not kept busy. This trouble can include incessant digging.

It has been said that the smell of certain types of soil can also catch a dog's fancy. Fresh earth, moist earth, certain mulches, topsoil and even sand are all lures for the digger. If you have a digger, you should fence off the areas where you are using these alluring types of soils. These kinds of soils are often used in newly potted plants or when establishing a flowerbed or garden. The smell of dirt can sometimes attract a dog that does not have the strong digging gene, but when he finds out how joyful digging can be, beware; you can be responsible for the creation of your own "Frankendigger."

Proper socialization, along with plenty of mental and physical exercises will help you in your fight against digging, but as we know, some diggers are going to dig no matter what the situation. Just in case your dog or puppy is an earnest excavator, here are some options to help you curb that urge.

Create a Digging Pit

A simple and fun solution is to dig a pit specifically for him or her to dig to their little heart's content. Select an appropriate location, and use a spade turn over the soil a bit to loosen it up, mix in some sand to keep it loose as well as to improve drainage, then surround it with stones or bricks to make it obvious by sight that this is the designated digging spot.

To begin training your dog to dig inside the pit, you have to make it attractive and worth their while. First bury bones, chews, or a favorite toy, then coax your dog on over to the pit to dig up some treasures. Keep a watchful eye each time you bring your dog out and do not leave him or her unsupervised during this training time.

It is important immediately to halt any digging outside of the pit. When they dig inside of the designated pit, be sure to reward them with treats and praise. If they dig elsewhere, direct them back to the pit. Be sure to keep it full of the soil-sand mixture, and if necessary littered with their favorite doggie bootie. If your dog is not taking to the pit idea, an option is to make the other areas where they are digging temporarily less desirable, such as covering them with chicken wire and then making the pit look highly tantalizingly, imitating a doggie digging paradise.

Buried Surprises

Two other options are leaving undesirable surprises in the unwanted holes your dog has begun to dig. A great deterrent is to place your dog's own *doodie* into the holes that he has dug, and when your dog returns to complete his job, he will not enjoy the gift you have left him, thus deterring him from further digging.

Another excellent deterrent is to place an air-filled balloon inside the hole and then cover it with soil. When your dog returns to his undertaking and his little paws burst the balloon, the resulting loud "POP!" sound will startle him resulting in your dog reconsidering the importance of the digging mission. After a few of these shocking noises, you should have a dog that thinks twice before digging up your bed of Pansies.

Shake Can Method

This method requires a soda can or another container filled with rocks, bolts or coins, remembering to place tape or apply the cap over the open end to keep the objects inside.

Keep this "rattle" device nearby so that when you let your dog out into the yard you can take it with you to your clandestine hiding spot. While hidden out of sight, simply wait until our dog begins to dig. Immediately at the time of digging, take that can of coins and shake it vigorously, thereby startling your dog. Repeat the action each time your dog begins to dig, and after a few times your dog should refrain from further soil removal. Remember, the goal is to *startle* and to distract your dog at the time they initiate their digging and not to terrorize your little friend.

Shake can instructions

1. Shake it quickly once or twice then stop. The idea is to make a sudden and disconcerting noise that is unexpected by your dog who is in the process of digging. If you continue shaking the can, it will become an ineffective technique.

2. Beware not to overuse this method. Remember your dog *can become desensitized* to the sound, and thus ignore the prompt.

3. Sometimes, it is important to supplement this method by using commands, such as "No" or "Stop."

4. Focus these techniques, targeting only the behavior (e.g. digging) that you are trying to eliminate.

5. Sometimes, a noise made by a can with coins inside may not work, but perhaps using a different container filled with nuts and bolts or other metal items will. Dogs might find the tone/pitch of certain metals more disconcerting to their hearing.

Examples are soda or coffee cans that are filled with coins, nuts, bolts or other metal objects. You might have to experiment to get an effective and disruptive sound. If the noise you make sets off prolonged barking instead of a quick startled bark, then the sound is obviously not appropriate. If your dog does begin to bark after you make the noise, use the "Quiet" command immediately after and never forget to reward your dog when he stops the barking, thereby reinforcing the wanted behavior.

I hope that these methods will assist you in controlling or guiding your four-legged landscaper in your desired direction. Anyone that has had a digger for a dog knows it can be challenging. Just remember that tiring them out with exercise and games is often the easiest and most effective in curbing unwanted behaviors.

~ Paps

PART III

30 Basic Care for Miniature Australian Shepherds

Oral maintenance, nail clipping, and other grooming will depend upon you and your dog's activities. We all know our dogs love to roll and run through all sorts of ugly messes and put obscene things into their mouths and then afterward run up to lick us.

Below is a list of the basic grooming care your dog requires. Most basic care can easily be done at home by you, but if you are unsure or uncomfortable about something, seek tutelage and in no time you will be clipping, trimming and brushing like a professional.

It is vital that handling training begin at the onset of bringing your puppy home because this will aid in all grooming, training, socialization and potential medical procedures. Early handling of your dog is crucial for grooming because it will allow you or the groomer to perform grooming while manipulating all of your dog's body parts with little to no resistance. Most owners should be able to learn and perform some or all of the grooming techniques themselves.

If you are grooming your dog up on a table or slippery surface, first place a non-slip cloth or mat over that area so that your dog doesn't slip or move during the grooming process. This will avoid potential injury.

Coat Brushing

Daily brushing of your dog's coat can be done or at least a minimum of three to four times a week depending upon the condition of the coat. During heavy shedding twice yearly, daily brushing is recommended. Daily brushing is not required, but it is healthy for the coat and skin. Additionally, it aids in regularly inspecting your dog for ticks, fleas, lumps, or rashes.

Mini Aussies have a double coat that is not high maintenance and sheds dirt well. They are moderate to heavy shedders so regular brushing will keep your hair mess to a minimum and keep their skin and coat healthy. Shearing is not recommended or necessary, their double coat protects them during all climate conditions, so it is best to leave it long.

Brushing with a slicker brush 3-4 times per week is a good habit to get into, but at least brush twice weekly to keep tangles to a minimum and their coat healthy. Their coats do pick up burs and critters, which is why I recommend 3-4 times per week to brush and inspect. The goal is to keep tangles from turning into mats that are time consuming to remove and often require scissoring out of the coat.

Use a long tooth undercoat rake after brushing with the slicker brush. When you find tangles, gently work them with your fingers and slicker brush to untangle. The undercoat rake is to brush deep into the coat down to the skin but not scraping the skin but using a motion that is up and out from the skin. If your dog has tangle issues, a metal-toothed comb with wide and close spaced teeth helps work tangles out.

Mini Aussies do not require much trimming on their bodies but some trimming around the top and bottom of their paws can be done if the hair grows to long. Always use caution on the pad area, in this area many people use clippers instead of scissors. Additionally, if you choose you can trim some of the tail, ears and leg areas to create a uniform look.

When brushing, first place your dog into a position that is comfortable for both. You can either have your dog lie down on his side, or stand if he does not mind. I prefer standing as it allows easier access and better angles. Begin brushing at the head and brush in the direction that the coat flows all the way to the tail tip. If your dog is lying down, then roll them to the others side and repeat.

Always be patient and move slowly when grooming your dog's head and muzzle area, the eyes, ears, nose and mouth are all sensitive areas that can incur harm. Before you decide to groom your Mini Aussie yourself, learn the proper way to use shears and scissors when trimming around the head, muzzle and body. Depending upon the style you choose some of the grooming equipment can vary.

Bathing

Regular but not frequent bathing is essential. Much depends upon your dog's coat. Natural coat oils are needed to keep your dog's coat and skin moisturized. Never bathe your dog too frequently and brushing before bathing is recommended. Depending upon what your dog has been into, a bath once month or less is adequate.

- Supplies – Dog specific shampoo, 3-4 towels and a nonslip bathmat for inside the tub.

- Shampoo – Use a dog shampoo made specifically for sensitive skin. This helps avoid any type of potential skin allergy, eye discomfort and furthering pre-existing skin conditions.

- Coax your dog into the tub and shut the door (just in case he is not in the mood, or decides to bolt outside while still wet). We have all experienced this.

- Use warm water, never hot water. Hot water tends to irritate the skin and can cause your dog to itch and then scratch. Do not use cold water on your dog.

- Apply enough shampoo to create lather over the body, but take care not to use so much that rinsing is difficult and time consuming. Rub into lather while avoiding the eyes and ears.

- Bathe the head area last.

- Rinse repeatedly and thoroughly to avoid skin irritation.

- Thoroughly dry your dog by using a towel. If it is cold outside you will want to finish by using a low setting hair dryer. Additionally, a slicker brush can be used while drying, remembering to brush in the direction of the hair growth.

Nail trimming

For optimal foot health, your dog's nails should be kept short. There are special clippers that are needed for nail trimming that are designed to avoid injury. You can start trimming when your dog is a puppy, and you should have no problems. However, if your dog still runs for the hills or squirms like an eel at trimming time, then your local groomer or veterinarian can do this procedure.

Dog's nails are composed of a hard outer shell named the *horn* and a soft cuticle in the center known as the *quick*. The horn has no nerves and thus has no feeling. The quick is composed of blood vessels and nerves, and therefore needs to be avoided.

Black nails make the quick harder to identify. White nails allow the quick to be recognized by its pink coloring. Dogs that spend a lot of time walking and running on rough surfaces tend to have naturally shortened quicks. Furthermore, the quick grows with the nails, so diligent nail trimming will keep the quick receded.

- Identify where the quick is located in your dog's nails. The object will be to trim as close (2mm) to the quick as possible without nipping the quick and causing your dog pain and possibly bleeding.

- To identify the quick in black nails, begin cutting small pieces from the end of the nail and examine underneath the nail. When you see a uniform gray oval appear at the top of the cut surface, then stop further cutting. Behind the gray is where the quick is located, if you see pink then you have passed the gray and arrived at the quick. If you have done this, your dog is probably experiencing some discomfort. *The goal is to stop cutting when you see the gray.*

-File the cut end to smooth the surface.

- If you accidentally cut into the quick, apply styptic powder. If not available, cornstarch or flour can be substituted.

- If your dog challenges your cutting, be diligent and proceed without verbal or physical abuse, and reward after successful trimming is completed. If you encounter the occasional challenge, your diligence should curtail the objection. If you manage never to cut into your dog's quick, this helps prevent any negative associations with the process, but some dogs simply do not enjoy the handling of their paws or nail trimming.

Ear cleaning

You should clean your dog's ears at least once a month, but be sure to inspect them every few days for bugs such as mites and ticks and look for any odd discharge that can be an indication of infection, requiring a visit to the vet. Remember to clean the outer ear only, by using a damp cloth or a cotton swab doused with mineral oil.

Eye cleaning

Whenever you are grooming your dog, check their eyes for any signs of damage or irritation. Other dog signals for eye irritation are if your dog is squinting, scratching or pawing at their eyes. You should contact your veterinarian if you notice that the eyes are cloudy, red or have a yellow or green discharge.

Use a moist cotton ball to clean any discharge from the eye. Avoid putting anything irritating around or into your dog's eyes.

Brushing teeth

Pick up a specially designed canine tooth brush and cleaning paste. Clean your dog's teeth as frequently as daily. Try to brush your dog's teeth a minimum of a few times per week.

If your dog wants no part of having his or her teeth brushed, try rubbing his teeth and gums with your finger. After he is comfortable with this, you can now put some paste on your finger, allow him to smell and lick it, then repeat rubbing his teeth and gums with your finger. After he is comfortable with your finger, repeat with the brush. In addition, it is important to keep plenty of chews around to promote the oral health of your pooch. When your dog is 2-3 years old, he or she may need their first professional teeth cleaning.

Anal sacs

These sacs are located on each side of a dog's anus. If you notice your dog scooting his rear or frequently licking and biting at his anus, the anal sacs may be impacted. When you notice this, it is time to release some fluid from them using a controlled method. If you are not comfortable doing this, you can ask your veterinarian how to diagnose and treat this issue.

Both the male and female dogs have anal glands and they are found directly beneath the skin that surrounds the anal muscles. The other name for them is scent glands. These glands tell other dogs the mood of a dog, health and gender, which is why so much but sniffing goes on between dogs.

To release the fluid when they are enlarged it is good practice to place your Mini Aussie inside a bathtub. The fluid is pungent and brownish in color so a tub protects anything that might come into contact.

Place a finger on each side of the sac, then apply pressure upwards and inwards towards the rectum and this is when you should see the fluid come out. If for some reason fluid does not come out, then seek assistance because if they are enlarged they need to be emptied.

31 A Dog's Nutrition

As for nutrition, humans study it, practice it, complain about it, but usually give into the science and common sense of it. Like humans, dogs have their own nutritional needs and are subject to different theories and scientific studies.

In the beginning, there were wild packs of canines everywhere and they ate anything that they could get their claws and teeth into. Similar to human survival, dogs depended upon meat from kills, grasses, berries and other edibles that nature provided. Thankfully, nature is still providing all the food animals need.

In the mid to late 1800's a middle class blossomed out of the industrial revolution. This new class with its burgeoning wealth had extra money to spend and started taking on dogs as house pets. Unwittingly they created an enterprise out of feeding the suddenly abundant household pets.

Noting that the sailor's biscuits kept well for long periods, James Spratt began selling his own recipe of hard biscuits for dogs in London, and shortly thereafter took his new product to New York City. It is believed that he single-handedly started the American dog food business. This places the dog food and kibble industry at just over 150 years old, and is now an annual multi-billion dollar business.

All the while, we know that any farm, feral or other dog that can kill something and eat it will do just that. Nothing has changed throughout the centuries. Raw meat does not kill dogs, so it is safe to say that raw food diets will not either. If you are a bit tentative about the idea of raw foods, cooking the meats you serve your dog is a viable option.

Feeding Your Puppy and Adult Dog

We recommend feeding you Mini Aussie foods for active breeds and avoiding foods for small or toy dogs.

To check if your puppy has its proper dietary needs met, make sure that your puppy is active, alert and is showing good bone and muscle development. To understand the correct portion to feed your dog, ask the breeder to show you the portion that they feed their puppies. Then observe whether your puppy is quickly devouring their food and then acting as though he wants and needs more. If so, then increase the portion a little until you find the correct serving. If your puppy is eating quickly, then begins to nibble, and finally leaves foods in the bowl, then you are over-feeding.

As you adjust the food portion to less or more; observe whether your puppy is gaining or losing weight so that you can find the proper portion of food to serve during feeding times. Very active puppies tend to burn lots of energy and this is one reason that a puppy might need a little extra food in their bowl. The suggested portions are on the food containers, but this world is not a one-size-fits-all place. Observation and logging those observations is needed to determine the correct portions for your dog.

Most agree that puppies should not leave their mothers until they are at least eight weeks old. This allows their mother's milk to boost their immunity by supporting antibodies and nutrition that are needed to become a healthy dog. Around three to four weeks old puppies should begin eating some solid food in conjunction with their mother's milk because this helps their digestion process begin to adjust to solid foods making the transition from mother's milk to their new home and foods easier.

Puppies are going to eat four times a day up until about eight weeks. At eight weeks, they can still be fed four times a day or you can reduce to three times. Split the recommend daily feeding portion into thirds. Puppies' nutritional requirements differ from adult dogs so select a puppy food that has the appropriate balance of nutrients that puppies require. Puppy food should continue to support healthy growth, digestion and the immune system. Supplying your growing puppy with the correct amount of calories, protein and calcium is part of a well-balanced diet.

When choosing your puppy's feeding times, choose the times that you know will be the best for you to feed your puppy. Feeding on a regular schedule is one part of over-all *consistency* that you are establishing for your puppy to know that as the leader you are reliably satisfying their needs. After setting the feeding schedule, remain as close to those times as possible. For example, 7 am, noon, and again at 5pm are good times if that fits your schedule. An earlier dinnertime helps your puppy to digest then eliminate before their bedtime.

During the three to six month puppy stage, teething can alter your puppies eating habits. Some pups may not feel like eating due to pain, so it is your responsibility to remain diligent in your job to provide them all of their nutritional requirements and confirm that they are eating.

Hint: Soaking their dry food in water for 10-15 minutes before feeding will soften it and make it easier for your puppy to eat. This avoids suddenly introducing different softer foods to your puppy and avoids the unknown consequences such as diarrhea and gas.

At six months to a year old, your puppy still requires high quality nutritionally charged foods. Consult your breeder or veterinarian about the right time to switch to an adult food.

When you switch to an adult food, continue to choose the highest quality food that has a specified meat, and not only by-products. Avoid unnecessary artificial additives. In many cases, higher quality foods that you feed your dog allow you to serve smaller portions because more of the food is being used by your dog and not just flowing through. Fillers are often not digested and this requires feeding your dog larger portions.

Additionally, follow the alpha guideline that states that *humans always eat first*. This means that the humans finish their meal entirely and clear the table before feeding their dogs, or feed your dog a couple of hours before you and your family eat. This establishes and continues the precedence that all humans are above the dog in the pecking order.

Help Identifying Dog Food Quality

- The first ingredient, or at a minimum, the second should specify *meat* or *meat meal*, NOT by-product.

- *"What is a by-product?"* Unless specified on the label, a by-product can be left over parts from animals and contain parts of hooves, feet, skin, eyes or other animal body parts.

- Beware of ingredients that use wording such as *animal* and *meat* instead of specific words like beef or chicken.

- "Meal" when listed in ingredients is something that has been weighed after the water was taken out, an example would be *chicken meal*. This means it has been cooked with a great amount of water reduction occurring in the process, and thus it is providing more actual meat and protein per weight volume.

  As an example, if the dog food package only states "beef" in the ingredients, it refers to the pre-cooking weight. This means that after cooking, less meat will be present in the food.

- A label that states "beef" first then "corn meal" secondly, is stating that the food probably contains a lot more corn than beef.

  Corn is not easily digested nor does it offer much in the way of nutrients that are vital to a dog's health. Furthermore, it has been linked to other health issues, and dogs are not designed to eat corn and grains in high doses. Try your best to avoid corn, wheat and soy in your dog's food. The higher quality more expensive foods are often worth the cost to advance your dog's health.

- If you decide to change dog food formulas or brands, a gradual change over is recommended, especially if your dog has a sensitive stomach. This is done by mixing some of the old with the new, and then throughout the week gradually increasing the amount of new.

An example schedule of changing dog foods

Day 1-2 Mix ¼ new with ¾ old foods

Day 2-4 Mix ½ new with ½ old

Day 5-6 Mix ¾ new with ¼ old

Day 7 100% of the new dog food

The Switch - Moving From Puppy to Adult Food

When your puppy is ready to make the switch from puppy to adult dog food, you can follow the same procedure above or shorten it to a four to five day switch over. During the switch, be observant of your dog's stools and health.

If your dog appears not to handle the new food formula then your options are to change the current meat to a different meat, or try a different formula or brand. Avoid returning to the original puppy food. If you have any concerns or questions, consult your veterinarian or breeder.

Raw Foods

Let us first remember that our dogs, pals, best friends and comedic actors were meant to eat real foods such as meat. Their DNA does not dictate them to eat dry cereals that were concocted by humans in white lab coats. These cereals based and meat-by-products ingredients may have been keeping our pets alive, but in many cases not thriving at optimum levels.

There are many arguments for the benefits of real and raw foods. Sure it is more work, but isn't their health worth it? It is normal, not abnormal to be feeding your dog, a living food diet; it is believed that it will greatly boost their immune system and over all health. A raw food diet is based off pre dog food diets and is a return to their wild hunting and foraging days and pre-manmade biscuit foods.

I travel a lot throughout South East Asia and majorities of these dogs eat what their humans eat and are doing just fine.

There are different types of raw food diets. There are raw meats that you can prepare at home by freeze-drying or freezing that can then be easily thawed to feed your dog, commercially pre-packaged frozen raw foods, or offering up an entire whole animal.

All of these diets take research and careful attention so that you are offering your dog all that they need, and something that their bodies can easily tolerate. Correct preparation of raw foods diets needs to be understood, for example, it is suggested that vegetables are cut into very small pieces or even pureed.

Raw food diets amount to foods that are not cooked or sent through a processing plant. With some research, you can make a decision on what you think is the best type of diet for your dog. For your dog's health and for their optimal benefits it is worth the efforts of your research to read up on a raw foods diet, a mix of kibble and raw foods, or a raw and cooked foods diet mix. *All foods,* dry, wet or raw contain a risk, as they can all contain contaminants and parasites.

Known benefits are fewer preservatives, chemicals, hormones, steroids and the addition of fruits and vegetables into their diet. Physically your dog can have firmer stools, reduced allergies, improved digestion, healthier coat and skin, and over-all improved health.

Some of the negative attributes are the lack of convenience versus kibble and potential bacterial contamination. However, dogs are at a lowered risk for salmonella and E. coli than humans are. A dog's digestive system is more acidic and less prone to such diseases; the greater risk is to the preparer. Many experts state that the overall risk of a *properly prepared* raw food diet is minimal.

There is a process named HPP (High Pressure Pasteurization) which most pre-prepared raw food brands utilize in their processing that does not use heat but eliminates harmful bacteria without killing off good bacteria.

Rules of thumb to follow for a raw food diet

1. Before switching, make sure that your dog has a healthy gastro-intestinal track.

2. Be smart, and do not leave un-refrigerated meats for prolonged periods.

3. To be safe, simply follow human protocol for food safety. Toss out the smelly, slimy or the meat and other food items that just do not seem fit for consumption.

4. Keep it balanced. Correct amount of vitamins and minerals, fiber, antioxidants and fatty acids. Note any medical issues your dog has and possible diet correlations.

5. If switching from bag or can, a gradual switch over between foods is recommended to allow their GI track to adjust. Use new foods as a treat, and then watch stools to see how your dog is adjusting.

6. Take note of the size and type of bones you throw to your dog. Not all dogs do well with real raw bones because slivers, splinters and small parts can become lodged in their digestive tracks. Always provide the freshest bones possible to dogs. *Never give dogs cooked bones.*

7. Freezing meats for three days, similar to sushi protocol, can help kill unwanted pathogens or parasites.

8. Remember to be vigilant, and take note of your observations about what is working and not working with your dog's food changes. If your dog has a health issue, your veterinarian will thank you for your detailed note taking.

9. Like us humans, most dogs do well with a variety of foods. There is no one-size-fits-all diet.

10. Before switching over, please read about raw foods diets and their preparation and follow all veterinary guidelines.

"BARF®" is an acronym that means Biologically Appropriate Raw Food. It is a complete and carefully balanced blend of raw meat, fruits, vegetables and bone. The formula mimics what nature designed for our pet's to thrive in the wild. The result is a pet free of allergies, digestive problems and full of life!

In summary, the first line of defense against disease is feeding your dog a proper diet which includes feeding them *premium* dry food, canned food, Raw food or (BARF diet), home cooked food or any combination of these.

Vitamins – Nutrients - Minerals

According to nutritional scientists and veterinarian health professionals, your dog needs twenty Amino Acids, ten of which are essential. At least thirty-six nutrients and a couple of extra may be needed to combat certain afflictions. Your dog's health depends upon the intake of the following nutrients. Read labels and literature to take stock of the foods you provide your canine.

It may take time to understand what kind of diet your dog will thrive. Do your best to include in your dog's daily diet, all thirty-six nutrients mentioned here. All of which can come from fruits, veggies, kibble, raw foods, and yes, even good table scraps. You will soon discover that your dog has preferred foods.

For your dog to maintain optimum health, he needs a daily source of GI track healthy, well-rounded diet with a good balance of exercise, rest, socializing, care and love.

36 Nutrients for dogs:

1. 10 essential Amino Acids – Arginine, Histidine, Isoleucine, Leucine, Lysine, Methionine, additionally Phenylalanine, Threonine, Tryptophan, and Valine.

2. 11 vitamins – A, D, E, B1, B2, B3, B5, B6, B12, Folic Acid, and Choline.

3. 12 minerals – Calcium, Phosphorus, Potassium, Sodium, Chloride, Iron, Magnesium, Copper, Manganese, Zinc, Iodine, and Selenium.

4. Fat – Linoleic Acid

5. Omega 6 Fatty Acid

6. Protein

Please take the time to REVIEW this Miniature Australian Shepherd training guide and tell others about the positive information inside.

REVIEW NOW by going to the Amazon Page below and posting your

POSITIVE REVIEW

My family thanks you

Paul

32 Final Thoughts

Believe me, this is not everything that there is to know about dogs. Training your Miniature Australian Shepherd is a lifelong endeavor. There are a myriad of other methods, tricks, tools and things to teach and learn with your dog. You are never finished, but this is half of the fun of having a dog, as he or she is a constant work in progress. Your dog is living art.

If your training experience is anything similar to mine, there were days and times when you thought your dog would never catch on or interested in participating and learning. I hope that you were able to work through the difficult times and the result is that you and your dog now understand one another at a high level resulting that you are in command of your dog.

Owning and befriending our dogs is a lifetime adventurous commitment that is worthwhile and rewarding on every level. It seems as though many times Axel knows what I am thinking and acts or reacts accordingly, but he and I are together more than most of my family members. Through the good and bad times, he always makes me smile, sometimes when he is being the orneriest I smile the biggest. He is such a foolhardy, loveable, intelligent, and clownish dog, how could anyone be sad around him.

Remember, it is important to learn to think like your dog. Patience with your dog, as well as with yourself is vital. If you do this right, you will have a relationship and a bond that will last for years. The companionship of a dog can bring joy and friendship like none other. Keep this book handy and reference it often. In addition, look for other resources, such as training books, and utilizing like-minded experienced friends with dogs that can share their successes and failures. Never stop broadening your training skills. Your efforts will serve to keep you and your Miniature Australian Shepherd happy and healthy for a long, long time.

Thanks for reading! I hope that you enjoyed this as much as I have enjoyed writing it. If this training guide informed how to train your dog, please review this guide and tell others about the positive information in this guide. I am always striving to improve both my writing and training skills. I look forward to reading your comments.

About the Author

Paul Allen Pearce is the author of many breed specific "Think Like a Dog" dog-training books.

As a youth, a family trip to Australia forever changed the course Paul would take on his way to return home to South Carolina to begin a family, raise dogs, and eventually write. For a year in high school, Paul headed back to Australia to study, and then again, during college he did the same. After finishing college, he headed to Africa to work with the Peace Corps.

Paul's family is dog lovers and often took in strays. Paul and his siblings were taught how to care and train the family pets and dogs. Both his parents grew up with many animals and had generational knowledge to pass forth to their offspring. Being reared around all sorts of animals, his curiosity to work with animals grew. Upon returning back to the U.S. and purchasing his own dog he realized he didn't know as much as he could, thus began his journey into owning and full time dog training.

Paul states, "Dog training is my passion. I love dogs, animals, and the wonders of nature. It is easy to write about your passion and share what you have learned and discovered. I hope that my readers enjoy and learn from what I have learned and improve their dog relationships. My past explorations throughout twenty countries and states helped me to broaden my perspective regarding animal behavior and treatment. Let us all be kind to animals, not only dogs."

Other Books

"Don't Think BE Alpha Dog Secrets Revealed"

**"Puppy Training Stuff - The 14 Puppy
Essentials
*Your Puppy Needs Now"***

**"No Brainer Dog Trainer"
(Breed specific dog training series)**

Content Attributions

Photos: We wish to thank all of the photographers for sharing their photographs via Creative Commons Licensing.

COVER / BASIC CARE

https://upload.wikimedia.org/wikipedia/commons/a/a7/Miniature_Australian_Shepherd_red
_tricolour.JPG

By Jillian Schoenfeld (Jillian Schoenfeld) [Public domain], via Wikimedia Commons

BIO

pxhere.com / CC any use

PROBLEM BEHAVIORRS

pxhere.com / CC any use

EFFECTIVE MINI AUSTRALIAN TRAINING

Stimulating activities

pxhere.com / CC any use

DOWN

https://commons.wikimedia.org/wiki/File%3AMiniature_Australian_Shepherd_blue_merle.
jpg

https://upload.wikimedia.org/wikipedia/commons/5/5f/Miniature_Australian_Shepherd_blu
e_merle.jpg

By Mike from Baltimore, USA (How About Now?) [CC BY 2.0
(http://creativecommons.org/licenses/by/2.0)], via Wikimedia Commons

SIT

Pixabay.com CC any use

STAY

Pixabay.com CC any use

FINAL THOUGHTS

https://commons.wikimedia.org/wiki/File%3ABlue_Merle_Miniature_American_Shepherd
_with_Frisbee.jpg_https://upload.wikimedia.org/wikipedia/commons/2/2f/Blue_Merle_Min
iature_American_Shepherd_with_Frisbee.jpg_By Mullinspw (Own work) [CC0], via
Wikimedia Commons

Legal Disclaimer

The author of "Think Like a Dog" books, Paul Allen Pearce is in no way responsible at any time for the action of your pet, not now or in the future. Animals, without warning, may cause injury to humans and/or other animals. Paul Allen Pearce is not responsible for attacks, bites, mauling, nor any other viciousness or any and all other damages.

We strongly recommend that you exercise caution for the safety of self, the animal, and all around the animals while working with your dog. We are not liable for any animal or human medical conditions or results obtained from training.

While all attempts have been made to verify information provided in this publication, neither the author nor the publisher assume any responsibility for errors, omissions or contrary interpretation of the subject matter contained herein. The publisher and author assume no responsibility or liability whatsoever on the behalf of any purchaser or reader of the material provided. The owner of held dog training guide assumes any, and all risks associated with the methodology described inside the dog-training guidebook.

DEDICATION

I dedicate this book to my parents, Andrea Sutcliffe and Alex De La Garza, who let me travel with them when I was young and encouraged me to keep doing it. Also to my late grandparents, Bill and Nesta Johnson, who loved to travel the world and inspired me with their map of the places they had been.

I would also like to thank Camille for making this all possible! Without her backing and experience, I may not have made the move to Costa Rica.

I was greatly inspired by Gay Hendricks, author of *The Big Leap*. His book helped me overcome my fears and taught me how to keep from hitting my upper limit. **-Stephanie**

To my husband, Bob, who taught me how to move about freely in this world, to The Caretaker Gazette for helping our travel dreams come true, and to Andrea Sutcliffe for blazing the path to my first book. **-Camille**

Contents

Preface

About Stephanie by Camille

Stephanie made her appearance on my radar screen in 2005 before she arrived at Casa Iguana. Not surprisingly, our relationship began with an email. She had a few questions and was just generally chatty and I happily answered her.

We exchanged more than a few emails before Stephanie stepped off the panga onto Little Corn Island off the Caribbean coast of Nicaragua. She walked the sandy path to the other side of the island and arrived at our gate, larger than life, accompanied by her travel buddy and the staff with their luggage in wheelbarrows.

Bob and I were managing the lodge at the time and took to Stephanie right away. If you've ever worked in the hospitality business you can attest that you will click with precious few guests. When you do, you will always remember each other, whether or not the friendship continues beyond their brief stay.

Fortunately, Stephanie and I remained email buddies. She had a job which required she occupy herself until called upon to solve a problem, and I have an email addiction. There have been days in which we received and replied to six or more emails. Through the years we have shared both the mundane and the profound—everything from what's for dinner to secrets about our dreams.

When at last Bob and I found ourselves in Stephanie's house in San Antonio we were mightily impressed at the simple beauty of her home. We sat on the couch, told stories and laughed our way through a sublime evening. The next day, Stephanie took me out for a drive in her beloved vintage Camaro, a gold chariot if I'd ever seen one. We stopped at one of her favorite fossil hunting spots, and for the first time I saw the raw Texas beauty I'd always heard about.

Needless to say, after years of correspondence I feel I know Stephanie well. I've always been struck by her independence, strength and tenderness. Just when I'm thinking, "I wouldn't want to cross her!" she would write about saving a baby bird or bringing a tiny lizard in from the cold.

Stephanie is a fascinating study in contrasts. She has fearless business acumen and a deep passion for nature, is an excellent judge of character with a wide open heart, and has proven able to endure discomfort as well as appreciate the finer things in life. Despite a sixteen year age gap and other subtle differences, Stephanie and I have formed an enduring bond. Our friendship has been, for lack of a better word, a blessing. Many a time she has given me her ear, been my champion and my common sense.

What Stephanie did was very brave. I doubt I would have abandoned my life in the U.S. had I not been holding Bob's hand, but she did it alone. I often wondered if I could venture out into the world by myself and now Stephanie has proven that it can be done. So, while I was once an inspiration to her, she has now become my inspiration.

As I write this, I sit across the dining room table from Stephanie with a view of the Appalachians, both working on our book and pining for the tropical worlds we recently left behind. We share an appreciation for the nuances of a life without A/C and central air; a life lived with all the windows wide open. A life of heat, sounds and smells that are missing from our lives back home. We share a perspective that we now offer to our readers.

About Camille by Stephanie

Camille is my hero. She is part of the reason that I moved to Central America. I clicked with her when we first met, over many emails before my first trip to Nicaragua. It all started with me getting out a world map and looking for islands I'd never heard of somewhere in Central America. I saw a couple off the coast of Nicaragua called Big Corn and Little Corn. I liked the sound of Little Corn, since it was smaller and more remote. I started looking into it and found Camille working at Casa Iguana, where I would be staying.

Over the next couple of months, I emailed her to be prepared for my visit. I asked her if there was anything I could bring from the U.S. and she said yes! Kitchen towels and chocolate chips were the two things I remember most. I totally understand the chocolate chip craving, now that I have experienced what it's like to not get the sweeter things in life down there.

The day finally came on May 0, 2005, when my friend and I arrived on Little Corn and were met by Camille and Bob after a nice jaunt through the jungle. Boys put our luggage in wheelbarrows and led the way through the sand. She was a tall, attractive woman and I was impressed by her ability to speak Spanish to a couple who were staying there. I felt like I'd known her a long time even though it was the first time we had physically met.

She was always busy, as she and her husband managed the lodge. She was patient and willing to take time out of her day to enlighten us about the island. I recall seeing her standing in our little yard as she picked up a large sea bean from the ground. She seemed intrigued by it and asked if I had put it there. I said no and she said, "Well it's lucky to find a sea bean in your yard!" I didn't know what a sea bean was but found out they were large, sturdy seeds from trees or vines that wash ashore all over the world. I started to see them everywhere now that I knew what they were, and so began my sea bean collection.

She was excited to get the chocolate chips and made everyone fresh hot cookies that night after dinner. Looking back, I know they tasted way better to her than they did to everyone else since it'd been so long since she had any.

We stayed in touch after I left Nicaragua and I was fortunate enough to hear about the places they had lived during their lives. It was inspiring to me that people could give up everything in order to follow their passion. I wanted to be like her: a free spirit, doing what I actually *like* to do, not what I *had* to do. So with each and every communication we had, a seed was planted and grew slowly from an idea into reality.

Camille is one of the most down to earth people I have ever met. She's honest, sincere, helpful, friendly, perceptive, loving and nurturing. We both feel a bond with nature and the earth, preferring to grow things in the soil instead of going to the store to buy them. We can find pleasure in seeing a tiny seedling sprouting in the forest or a beautiful insect sitting on a leaf. It's nice to have the same values and perceptions, yet also being able to enlighten each other with new ideas.

Camille has wanderlust, and although she and her husband have "settled down" and bought a house in the U.S., the need to travel will always be with her. Even after buying a house, they moved to Africa for over a year and brought back unforgettable memories. She will always be my hero, forever my friend and an inspiration for many years to come.

MAPS

Ghana

Nicaragua

Tronadora

San Jose   San Antonio

Cocles

Panama

Costa Rica

Maps by Bob Armantrout

Introduction

Braud /brôd/ **noun** Fearless female; an adventurous, daring or independent woman.

We've heard enough people say, "Gosh, I wish I could do that!" that we decided to share our experiences.

Our book is based on emails written between March, 2012 and December, 2013 that chronicle Camille's move to Africa and Stephanie's move to Central America. We tried to show in an informal and largely uncensored manner what it felt like to abandon our old way of life and step into a new one.

We hope to inspire you to follow your heart without being hampered by fear or possessions. Your leap of faith may not involve moving to a different country. It may take the form of a new career, a healthier lifestyle, a different house or leaving an unrewarding relationship. With this book, we plant a seed.

Here are some reasons you should consider living abroad:

1. Experiencing a new culture is eye opening and makes you realize your way of doing things isn't always right or better.
2. Being outside almost all day opens your world up to new stimuli, and you feel connected to the earth and your fellow man in a way you may never have been before.
3. Living with only what you NEED isn't as bad as you think.
4. All of your senses become awakened (which could mean in the middle of the night), whether good or bad.
5. You will appreciate the smallest things that you used to take for granted.
6. You will be challenged almost every day, and each day will be different.
7. You will make new friends from different countries, which can in turn facilitate new traveling opportunities.

1

8. Your life will never be the same again.
9. You sometimes get the feeling there might be something more to life but you can't quite see it from inside your own culture.
10. You're curious and want to test your own boundaries by living life without a safety net.
11. You suspect mainstream media isn't telling you the whole story.
12. It will prepare you for life in the years of dwindling oil reserves to come.
13. You will get in shape, lose weight, gain muscle and probably get a tan.

That said, leaping off the corporate diving board isn't for everyone. Here are some reasons why living abroad may not be right for you:

1. You cringe at having to learn a new language and believe everyone will speak English.
2. You are afraid of any and every type of insect, large or small.
3. You believe your way is the only way.
4. You have no patience.
5. You've discussed terms like "Type A" and "Anal Retentive" with your analyst.
6. You can't imagine life without Starbucks.
7. You simply must have air conditioning and 500 thread count sheets to be comfortable.
8. Fast food chains are your main source of nutrition.
9. You can't fathom life without a car.
10. You are not willing to risk being forever changed. As they say, you can't go home again so don't leave if you don't want your life to change.

In Stephanie's case, she knew in 1998 that she wanted to live in Central America after visiting Belize. She looked into moving there, but it wasn't financially feasible and she wasn't mentally ready for it. It took many more years of traveling, inspiration and preparation, knowing someday she would finally make the move. It finally started materializing in 2011 and the preparation started. She knew that she had to start selling almost all of her things. The only items she would be buying from then on would be consumables. Many eBay hours later, the house started looking less like a home and more like a staging area.

The final phase of her mental preparation involved overcoming the fear of having nothing, of being "homeless," of learning a new language and then traveling and living alone in different countries. This was probably one of the biggest steps she had ever taken and having the encouragement of friends and family went a long way. Mostly, the desire to do something new and exciting, maybe even a little dangerous, was inspiration enough.

Once she put her house on the market and only had the bare minimum of possessions left, she knew there would be no turning back. She would quit her 20 year career and take the leap. She promised herself to live a year abroad before giving up, since it's too easy to quit early on. She had read plenty of stories about people who couldn't hack it for one reason or another, but she didn't want to be like them. When there's nothing tying you down, it is harder to give up and come back. She wanted a challenge and an experience that would not easily be forgotten.

Camille, on the other hand, had escaped the American Dream years ago with her husband, Bob, and was now deeply involved with their local community in rural North Carolina. They felt so settled that they purchased their first home since selling their house in 1997 to move to Belize. And then, out of the blue came a reason to leave their comforts behind and live abroad again.

In April 2012, Bob came across a job listing for a research project in Ghana, West Africa, and the travel bug bit hard. He was in between jobs at the local community college, was a perfect fit for

3

the position and Camille was keen to experience Africa. The fact that Bob had spent some of his childhood years in Ghana was enough to tip the scales in favor of the move. By the end of June they had relocated to Kumasi, the second largest city in Ghana.

This time they decided to leave their house unoccupied rather than rent or sell it. They spent the next two months preparing for their move: handing off responsibilities, getting their visas, putting their clothes in storage, eating down the contents of the deep freeze and making arrangements for the care of their house and gardens.

We have both run across many people who are intrigued by what we do. We have had the courage to travel to places that aren't in the Top 10 Destination articles. We've lived in conditions that many might find intolerable. Yet we are certain that living this way brings a certain "je ne sais quoi" that we would never experience otherwise. The thrills of submersing ourselves in other cultures outweigh any discomfort.

We are aware of our privileged status as U.S. citizens, spoiled by conveniences, isolated in our closed up homes, entertained and ruled by electronics. Our travels gave us the opportunity to come alive, to feel connected to the culture, the people and the earth.

As we sit together in this beautiful house in Virginia working on our book, we can't help but notice the lack of smells around us, the harsh feel of forced heat drying out our skin and lips and the constant chill in our hands and feet. No calls of birds, dogs, chickens, people or horns. No smell of food cooking, fires burning, flowers blooming...the smell of AIR! It is deathly quiet and sterile which we find stressful. We have everything we could possibly need in this house, yet we feel we're missing something. We both comment on our longing for the tropics again.

A word about the formatting of the book

We decided to keep the bulk of the book in the format of our actual emails. We edited out private, incriminating or irrelevant ramblings that didn't bring anything to the table.

Names have been changed to protect the innocent and the guilty. All amounts proceeded by the "$" indicate U.S. Dollar values. We inserted selected blog posts and added information, preceded by icons.

Icons:

 Information: More insight about the current situation

 Tip: Helpful advice

 Looking back: Our thoughts in hindsight

We hope you enjoy reading about our travels as much as we enjoyed living them!

PART I
THE EMAIL CHRONICLES

ADVICE FROM A TREE®

Stand Tall and Proud,

Sink Your Roots into the Earth,

Be Content with Your Natural Beauty,

Go Out on a Limb,

Drink Plenty of Water,

Remember Your Roots,

Enjoy the View!

- Ilan Shamir

1
AFRICA BOUND

Steph has a photography exhibit for two months at a local market in an attempt to make some money and potentially shift into a different career path. She is also planning a solo trip to Guyana for an Amazon adventure.

Subject: Hi!
On Mar 9, 2012 Steph wrote:

How ya been?

I got my pictures hung last week and have an order for three of them. I have my opening on the 22nd. I'm not sure that's really going to generate any sales, but we'll see. I'll have my step-dad be paparazzi during the event so I'll send ya some pictures when it's all said and done.

Anyway, it was semi hot lately and now it's 45 degrees and rainy! How's the weather there? The trees and flowers are all starting to bloom. Can't wait for actual spring! I bought some furniture for my covered patio so I can sit out there and enjoy the yard.

Well, e me when you can...have a good weekend!

Camille:
Congratulations on getting your art out there. I hope you sell some of your beautiful work. Wow - the backwaters of Guyana by yourself! Guyana makes me think of Jonestown. Is this the same country? The Koolaid vat is probably a tourist attraction.

Neither Bob nor I ever got any shots - not for Belize, China, Guam or Nicaragua. We drank Jack Assed Bitters elixir for its anti-malarial properties in Belize.

Our weather can't decide to be hot or cold, swinging from below freezing up into the 70's. The peepers are peeping, the Bradford pears are flowering and I already mowed once at work on March 1st.

Steph:
Yes, Guyana is the same country you're thinking of. I'll be sure to avoid any purple Kool Aid while there. It's what everyone thinks of when they hear the name...at least folks who are old enough to remember the story. That seemed to have given the country a bad rep. The other problem with tourism there is that nobody takes anything but cash (at least it's USD they'll take)...lugging around Guyana dollars would make me look like a millionaire since their largest bill is like a $20 USD equivalent. I'll have to carry over $2K with me. I'm not used to doing that. I'm sure I'll be fine though. The other choice is to WIRE money to their banks, which doesn't make me feel good either.

I'd love to take jackass bitters instead of the malaria pills. I'm afraid they will make me sick. I'm not sure if the bitters reach down that far though. I did a little research on malaria, and most of it was mentioned in Central America. I'd prefer to not chance it by taking nothing, since mozzies seem to love me to death. Malaria is the top killer down there too. I do plan on asking a lot of questions about medicinal plants from the locals and documenting it. Guyana is still fairly unexplored and the biologists, herpetologists, any-ologists are having a blast down there finding stuff.

 *Steph was shown a quinine tree in Guyana. Some of the bark was removed for her to taste and it was very bitter. They use this in a tea to help cure malaria. It doesn't have any of the nasty effects that the pill version does.*

Subject: Transit
On Apr 23, 2012 Steph wrote:

Hey, the Transit of Venus is happening the day after your birthday...last time in our lives we'll see it!

Camille:
And three days before yours! How exciting!

Speaking of exciting, there's a pretty good chance Bob and I may move to Kumasi in Ghana for a year. If he gets the job, we'll likely move in June!

Steph:
Holy crap! What will you do with the house?

Camille:
We're gonna leave all our stuff inside it and have our neighbors come by once a week and check the mouse traps, maybe do some laundry, hang out and keep the critters at bay.

Daughter Molly's boyfriend will come mow every other week in exchange for the use of Bob's car. Someone will start my car once in a while and drive it around the block or to town and back.

All linens and clothes will go into Rubbermaid containers. It's all quite exciting. Bob lived in nearby Accra as a child and speaks a little of the local language. We should know for sure in a week or so,but I can't imagine he won't receive an offer.

Steph:
So what is he going to be doing over there for work?

Camille:
He would be the project manager for the waste-to-biodiesel project. Very cool stuff! Plus, the position pays enough so I won't have to work if I don't want to.

Subject: Empty house
On Apr 23, 2012 Steph wrote:

Hell, I may just babysit the house for ya! I'm dying to get outta here and grow my own food.

Camille:
Would you really want to live here for a year? Well anyway, Jason has already agreed to maintain and harvest the garden for farmers market. Bob just finished planting six beds of potatoes! We didn't want to put all our personal stuff into storage so we decided not to rent the house.

Steph:
I've thought about it before. I just so want to get outta here and get my head straight....figure out what to do with my life. I'm ditching cable finally! I got an Apple TV and figure I'd prefer to save the $55/mo.

Subject: Job
On Apr 27, 2012 Steph wrote:

Any word on the job yet?

Camille:
No—we should know something by the end of next week. Bob will call on Wednesday if he doesn't hear from them by Tuesday. If we get it, I'll have three weeks to hand off my two jobs, get the house ready and pack for our annual trip to PA! Yikes! What's going on in your life?

Steph:
Wow, that's a lot to get done...but it sounds exciting. Are you looking forward to it?

Not much here. I got an email thread going with a guy who advertised on the helpx site looking for a "gal Friday" to volunteer in Costa Rica for a new marine science center they're setting up. I told him I could bring more to the table than just that. So we're getting to know each other and I'm trying to find out more about the opp. I'm just dying to get outta here and do something worthwhile, ya know?

Well, let me know what you find out!

 Great places to find free accommodation in exchange for work are helpx.net, wwoof.net and caretaker.org

Subject: Sunflower photos
On May 8, 2012 Camille wrote:

I'm so excited, I can't swallow! With so much to do before we go, I find myself plowing up my lists at 3am so I'm tired during the day. Handing off two jobs is a challenge, as is preparing for our annual two week vacation. Making plans and getting everyone to agree seems impossible at the moment, and we leave in 10 days.

We're looking at a wedding, cousins, friends, aunts and road trips with my brother and my Mom. And then there's the move to Ghana and all before the end of June!

Meanwhile, our daughter Amy is coming in from Asheville tonight, I've got wall to wall meetings and we're hosting potluck tomorrow evening. Thanks for bringing your willing ear into my life!

Steph:
Well you are welcome! You'll get it all done like you always do. Don't kill yourself trying, though. I'll leave you be for a while and you have a good trip up north and drop me a line when and if you can at some point.

13

Camille:
Hey there!

We're chillaxin' in DC and I'm getting caught up on personal correspondence

I loved your photos.

Steph:
Glad you liked the pics...those sunflowers were so amazing. I've never seen anything like it in my life. I must go get another look and take it all in.

There was so much positive energy coming off those flowers! I just wanted to stand next to them and stay there. It was a good day for shooting. Just after hard rains, early in the morning...sky was blue (no Photoshopping needed!). I love the last one too—its little yellow arms waiting to stretch out and wake up. What perfect little packages they are.

Subject: Happy birthday
On Jun 4, 2012 Steph wrote:

Gud mawnin friend! And happy birthday! What are you doing? Is your trip finished? Packing for the new one? Tell all! Will be thinking of you!

Camille:
Here's my obligatory birthday photo. Molly and Shane are coming over for spaghetti dinner and Bob will man the stove. He gave me a great birthday card this morning with three horses 'laughing'—the inside quote is "getting older is no laughing matter."

Camille's obligatory 58th birthday photo

Our family visit was both wonderful and taxing. It took a day or so to unwind and stop dwelling on our undone to do lists. I had a great time with my sister-in-law riding bikes and banging around together running errands. Bob and I had fun visiting our friend's farm and feeding their lambs and our last day at Ned's was really fun and relaxed.

But now I'm home and pretty much done with "work" and life is crazy good. The weather has been fantastic—we're able to keep our windows open all day and night. I'm spending time visiting neighbors, going for walks, doing yard work, cooking and not too much trip planning.

How have you been and what are you doing special for your birthday?

Steph:
I'll be in Sedona for mine...leave on Wednesday, going with Dahnelle, so it should be fun.

What day do you leave for Ghana? What will you actually be doing? Any kind of work? I'm so excited for you!

Camille:
Have fun in Sedona!

We leave for Ghana June 24th! I plan on having plenty of time to write as I will not be working a job per se. I will happily help Bob with anything he needs work-wise and do the bulk of the housework and cooking and tend the garden and laundry and water transfer and shopping at market. It will be a lovely time.

I like to stay busy, but here I was just plain overwhelmed and I let it happen to myself, so now am whispering in my own ear not to let it happen again.

Subject: Sedona
On Jun 12, 2012 Steph wrote:

Back from AZ...it was nice, but waaaay too dry for my taste. We had a great time. Sure is beautiful out there. Wish I had a few more days, though, to get everything done. Took a couple of nice hikes, had a good day at the spa and the town of Jerome was really cool.

Now to start getting excited about Guyana!

Hope all is well and you're not in too much of a frenzy getting ready to move.

Camille:
I'm doing fine! We'll be airborne before we know it. Your photos of Sedona were great as always, but I hear you about the dryness. I like green, good thing because Kumasi is pretty green.

Subject: Made it ok?
On June 29, 2012 Steph wrote:

What are your first impressions? I can't wait to hear about it.

Camille:

Thanks for thinking of me. Bob just got us online and I love it here! It has not been too hot, either. So much like Belize and yet different than anywhere I've ever been. We're working with a great group. Will have more time to write soon, I hope. So far, going to market, getting set up, cooking and cleaning is taking all my time and we are trying to figure out where to put our clothes because we don't have a closet or dresser.

Steph:

Of course I think of you, silly! All of the time! Well I'm glad you got there okay...I can't wait for updates and to hear how all is working out. I'm sure after a while you won't feel like a stranger in a strange land. Tell me about the kind of things you find in the markets and how you end up cooking them. I hope you're able to blog more once you settle in.

Subject: Settling in
On July 2, 2012 Camille wrote:

How is your day? It's almost chilly here! Managed to pull off a post, but haven't gotten our clothes off the floor yet.

Bob moving our bags from the courtyard to the house

17

Plastic Farm Animals

blog

Settling In

By Camille

Well, we made it to our new home in Adiebeba, a small neighborhood in Kumasi, Ghana. Despite some challenges and minor discomforts, we are just as excited to be here as we thought we'd be. When we walk to market, the sights, sounds and smells are surreal and intoxicating.

I'm writing this while standing at the tiled counter in the spacious downstairs kitchen at 6:28am GMT, Greenwich Mean Time, which also happens to be Ghana Time. It's 2:28am Eastern Standard Time. Our neighbors are already outside on the dirt street, dressed in bright colors, laughing and chatting in the lilting local language. A taxi has already come and taken our three housemates to work. Like Bob, they are associated with the fecal sludge-to-fuel project.

Bird calls fill the air, many of them foreign to our ears. This is a bird-watcher's paradise. We're seeing woodland kingfishers, pied crows, flycatchers, sparrows, doves and perhaps turacos. All our windows are open, letting in a delightful breeze. The sky is overcast as we head into the end of the rainy season. I don't smell any smoke yet, but it will come.

Most everyone burns their garbage. We like to joke that we love the smell of burning plastic in the morning. We are amassing our own pile of cardboard to burn but are affluent enough to send our plastic to the landfill because, unlike most of our neighbors, we can afford to pay for trash pick-up. We are rich by local standards. Our courtyard is fenced-in concrete and razor wire.

It's a Monday and a local holiday, which explains why the city water is not happening. On the weekends, when water usage is higher, the water delivery system is unable to meet demand. Bob said he got up at 4am *and was able to flush the toilet, but this morning the tap is dry.*

Fortunately, the house is equipped with a giant water storage tank which sits on the roof and fills with city water when it's running. All the taps in the house pull from the storage tank except for two of the three bathrooms. Unfortunately, we don't have a way to know how much water is in the tank. We're hoping it filled up overnight.

The Ghanaians always look clean and sharp despite the mud, smoke and exhaust. They are stoic or perhaps a little shy, and even if you smile at them they don't smile back until you say "good morning." One does not pass anything to another with their left hand. Water is a luxury, so due to sanitary constraints it is the custom to wipe with your left and eat with your right.

We stand out with our white skin and often hear the call "Obruni!" Another difference - we carry our stuff in backpacks and shoulder bags while the locals carry their parcels on their heads. It is not unusual to see vendors with large trays of bananas or peanuts meticulously stacked for weight distribution. Some even carry big square glass display cases, striding confidently between cars at the intersections. I have yet to see a slouching Ghanaian.

We don't drink the tap water. To replenish our supply we call a taxi for a trip to the Palace Hyper Mart with our empty bottles. It was a big day when we got set up downstairs with our very own bottled water dispenser.

Despite my defrosting it yesterday, the refrigerator upstairs remains at an alarming 65 degrees Fahrenheit. We are storing perishables in the small refrigerator downstairs. This morning I got up at 5:30 to take the leftovers upstairs for our housemates to take to work for lunch.

We take turns cooking dinner for five on two portable burners. Last night Louis told me he was wary of the local bread because he saw unpackaged bread stacked like bricks in the back of a truck being transported, presumably to a place where people would put it into plastic bags.

We have no closet in our bedroom, but I have found another room to hang clothes in; we are keeping our folded clothes in the pantry. In the absence of mirrors, I took a photo of myself in a new outfit before going out onto the street the other day just to make sure I looked presentable. We are looking into having a few pieces of furniture made, including a wardrobe with a mirror.

We chip away at our list, picking up little things like mayonnaise, duct tape and canned beans from the Melcom, which is only a 10 minute walk away. When we buy too much to carry home, we hire a taxi for 3 cedis, about $1.50.

Our housemates Lauren, Louis and Chad have been here long enough to figure out easy ways to get the things we need. We went to the circus Saturday, something I could never have accomplished on my own. They've discovered an amazing taxi driver named Prince who will be able to help us buy a washing machine, range and refrigerator. Perhaps he may even know where we can get a can opener and a functional broom.

2
LEAPING INTO LATIN AMERICA

Subject: Legally working
On Jul 6, 2012 Steph wrote:

Wow! You're in another world! Were you able to bring the Berkey with you or was it too big? Bummer on the water situation. I'll be curious to know how Bob's work goes and if he can change the world with a new way of providing fuel.

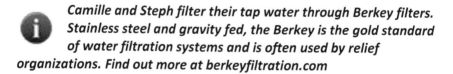

Camille and Steph filter their tap water through Berkey filters. Stainless steel and gravity fed, the Berkey is the gold standard of water filtration systems and is often used by relief organizations. Find out more at berkeyfiltration.com

So it gets cold there at night? I assume you only have whatever air blows through the windows?

This is my week back at work after being in training all last week, which was a nice stay-cation since I got out early every day. But now I have to study to pass this Security+ test in order to get my friggin' raise.

Hopefully I pass the first time or else I have to pay for the subsequent

21

test(s). Ugh. Hate taking tests.

Sounds like you're having some challenges cooking. Find any weird stuff at the market? I assume it is fairly easy to find veggies and such?

I hope the shelves arrived and you're getting things where you need them. I'm also curious what you brought with you besides clothes.

I also had another question and you are the only one I know who MIGHT know this. When you were doing the Nicaragua gig, was that basically a volunteer position and you were just getting room/board? I mean, did they pay you? If they DID pay you, how did that work? Was it just all under the table and you SAID you volunteered...since you can't actually work unless you have a permit. How was it in Belize?

Anyway, the original question comes from buying a one way ticket down there...how did you guys do it (I realize it was before the 9/11 thing for the most part)? Did anyone ever question your return ticket? What do you tell customs/immigration what you're really doing there? I mean, being honest, you say you're volunteering, but how long do they actually put up with that excuse before they think you're really working for money? Even though you might NOT be.

Okay, enough questions for today; hit me back when you get a chance.

Camille:
We didn't have room for the Berkey and since the house is already buying drinking water in five gallon containers, we decided not to try and filter the city water.

Yes, we did get paid, and no, we didn't pay taxes on it because we were living outside the country. Why, are you thinking of being their next manager?

We did have work visas, which we had to renew every three months in Nicaragua. In Belize we were volunteering and didn't have a green card or work visa so had to visit immigration every month and tell them again that we were sightseers and not working. After a year, we had to leave the country for eight days in order to come back in as tourists.

I believe we bought round trip tickets to both Belize and Nicaragua. At the time they were cheap to Belize - $250 round trip, and round trip is often cheaper than one way.

We bought a one way ticket to Africa this time. We may have to pay income tax because we own property in the U.S.

We recommend checking tax law before you go. The US only makes you pay taxes on income over a certain amount and while you do have to claim it, it's deductible as long as you are paying it to the country that you made it in. As it turned out, the Armantrouts did not have to pay income tax because it was income earned overseas and they lived outside the US for more than a year.

Subject: Decision made!
On Jul 10, 2012 Steph wrote:

I freed a baby gecko from a spider web in my bathroom this morning. I'm pretty sure he hadn't been bitten, so that was the good part. But he was stuck, and when I got him out the spider came runnin'! It wasn't easy to get all of the webs off...They were even around his mouth, but I managed to get them off and he tried to scamper away when I was helping him, so I knew all of his limbs worked. I made sure he could stick his tongue out then let him go by the faucet outside that had dripped some water on the grass and off he went! Phew...he didn't have much time left. I evicted the spider from my bathroom finally and put him out front so that there would be no re-confrontation. That gecko was about half the length of my pinkie finger! I'm glad I didn't squish it!

Well, I've decided to go ahead and move to Latin America finally. Just go and volunteer at some places and see where it leads me. Would you say that everything you did like that got you where you wanted? I feel that's what it'll do for me. So I plan to leave no later than next March. I haven't really decided which country yet...Panama will be in there though, plus I have a friend of the family who lives in the city so that would be nice to see him and helpful also. Got a lot of volunteer opportunities in Costa Rica and some in Belize, but I'm up in the air about Belize...I've never gotten the good feeling about actually living there. As much as I love it...I feel it's dangerous for me. Probably read too much of their news. So can you give me any advice, having been down this road before?

Camille:
Ha ha - you little rescuer, you!

Wow - I'm so jazzed to see that you are going to leap off into follow-your-heart land! What a brave Stephanie. I assure you, you will not regret it. Yes, our volunteering gigs were totally worth it. That year in Belize was one of the best years of my life! It gave us a new perspective, got us off the corporate treadmill, helped us get paying jobs overseas and was the gateway to more travel.

We're going to Lake Bosumtwi for some R&R today. Will return Saturday. Can't wait—no housework for TWO WHOLE DAYS!

Steph:
So did you guys have any problems with electronics in the tropics...any suggestions for keeping them alive?

Camille:
What we did in Belize is buy desiccant and a Rubbermaid bin for computer storage when not in use. We're not doing anything like that here and also didn't in Nicaragua. Taking out an extra warranty is also a good idea.

I bought a beautiful dress for 37 cedis ($18.50) yesterday that looked as if it was made for me.

Steph:
Cool! I can't wait to see it. What have you been finding at the market to eat?

I have tons of desiccant...did you ever have to dry it out in the oven or somehow? I don't know how effective that stuff is after being in humidity for that long. Guess whatever happens, happens right?

Subject: Can opener
On July 18, 2012 Camille wrote:

Bob and I went to Adum, where I found a can opener yesterday! We had a vegan lunch and took out a P.O. box.

Re: desiccant, yes, we did have to dry it out in the oven once in a while. Bob took care of this so I don't remember.

Have started drinking again and realize it's not good for me. Mentally or physically, so will stop. It crept up on me. A little drink here, a little one there and pretty soon I'm drinking every night.

We have just about every kind of vegetable and fruit you can imagine, plus locally made tofu, loads of beans and rice and pasta and canned tomatoes.

Last night I made pasta sauce with soy protein nuggets, a bulgur and chickpea salad with onion, chopped cucumber, fresh orange and lime juice and grated carrots, angel hair pasta, boiled chayote and yams and fried eggplant cubes and served wine...for the five of us.

Woke up to pee at least five times (effing wine). The Muslims woke me with their broadcast 4:30am call to prayer. Went back to sleep until 6.

Steph:
Sorry to hear about the drinking thing...but I know what you mean. I

can't drink much these days either, and it is weird how when you do start, it seems like you want it every day. If I drink too much, my muscles get super achy (I assume it's from dehydration) and it's really uncomfortable...like I can't even sleep.

Your meal sound yummy. Looks like I'll have to get on the vegetarian kick a lot more than normal when I move, too. Cooking for five people, huh? Sounds like a lot of work. But I know you like doing it for the most part and you're great at it.

Do you get the 4:30 wakeup call every day? I assume so. Whatta bummer!

Subject: Wow
On Jul 20, 2012 Steph wrote:

Did you see the thing in Panama in Caretaker's last night? I'm totally applying. It sounds so great and also meets my vision of what I think I'd like to do. I'm psyched about it! Check out the site if you have time and give me your thoughts.

The Caretaker Gazette is a great little publication, available both online and in print whose sole mission is matching people with opportunities all over the world. Bob and Camille discovered Casa Iguana through the Caretaker Gazette, which is where they met Stephanie. You can find them at caretaker.org.

Camille:
Yeah! It looks great to me too. Only thing I didn't see was if room AND board is included. Will they feed you or do you have to feed yourself?

Steph:
I'd have to feed myself but I expected that any place I went. I could grow stuff there (if it didn't get eaten by whatever).

Camille:
Ha ha! Reminds me of when we had an enormous sow rooting up the

26

garden at Casa Iguana. Bob had to chase it with the shotgun.

Speaking of iguanas, I've been seeing what I believe are red headed rock agamas in their breeding season. They have blue and orange and brown broad bands of color. Their back is shimmering aqua blue, their head and a section of their tail orange and the rest brown

Steph:
Oooo! I love leezards soooo much. How are things going over there? Feel like you're getting settled in yet? What have been your main challenges so far? How does Bob like his job?

Well I applied yesterday for the Panama position. We'll see! Keep your legs crossed for me!

I passed my Security+ test on Friday so that's out of the way thankfully! That also means $1K bonus...which I'd better get soon! I've also sent out a case of Berkey Lights to Amazon, so maybe I'll make some more sales...trying to rev up the old savings account before quitting life as I know it!

Subject: Panama
On Jul 25, 2012 Camille wrote:

How exciting! I'm so proud of you for following your heart! You belong in Panama with the lizards and close to the water.

As for challenges, Bob is under the gun but still not working too terribly hard. He loves it here, too. After the big dog and pony show at the end of August, life will smooth out, but for now the interns are going into the lab nearly every day.

We've got a good routine going, and after we get Bob's check deposited we can buy a washing machine and maybe another refrigerator and a real stove. But I've got it all down and frankly (don't tell anyone) I actually enjoy doing the laundry by hand. Dinner can sometimes be a struggle though. We started out taking turns but now I cook five nights a week.

We have all the creature comforts and plenty of good food and the weather has been great—cool at night and warm during the day. Rarely hot.

We're going to Cape Coast for four days tomorrow and not bringing computers. So expect radio silence. I'll bring one backpack and my journal and camera.

Well, better get to bed because we're getting up a little earlier than usual for the six hour drive. Our housemates are taking a tro tro and getting up at 3am! Bob hired Eric to drive us all the way. We didn't want to squeeze into one of those crazy Cape Coast tros with all the goats and shit. When we were out with Eric the other day, he pointed to a tro and said you could tell by the way it was loaded it was going to Cape Coast. The word on the windshield was "SERIOUS".

We saw another one like it farther on down the road with sheep tied to the top! So now we have a running joke about Cape Coast tro tros in this house. Can't wait to hear how the kids like their ride.

Tro tros are the cheapest way to travel in Kumasi, the fares ranging from 60 pesewas (thirty cents in 2012 and 2013) and up depending on the distance. These ubiquitous passenger vans typically seat 14, but often hold more than that as every fare squeezed in is one more dime for the driver and mate. It's the mate's job to fill the tro and often he will perch on a window rather than take a seat to make room for one more passenger.

Steph:
You know, it's funny you say that about the laundry. When I did it by hand in CR on vacation, I actually kinda liked it too. I don't know if the guy even has a washing machine in Panama. If not, that's ok. I'm just happy there would be hot water and a very nice looking stove/oven. All

I have are positive thoughts about this opportunity, which hopefully will come true. I had a dream last night that I got fired from my job unexpectedly! I was stuck as to what to do...leave the country now or wait. It was weird.

I'm glad the weather isn't unbearable...I thought it would be for some reason. Is it really humid? Do you have problems with bugs/flying/biting things? I can't wait to see the pics of your Cape trip...gosh, I wish I could be a fly on the wall down there with you! Sounds like you've taken the culture shock and move pretty well. Good for you. I'm so happy.

Subject: Ghana TV
On Jul 24, 2012 Steph wrote:

Wow...how are people taking this there? "State run television in Ghana is announcing that President John Atta Mills has died at age 68."

Camille:
No obvious signs of mourning yet. Will have to speak with our driver, Eric, and see what kind of impact this will have on the upcoming December presidential election. Will keep you posted. The president was in ill health, so his death was not unexpected.

Subject: Happy anniversary
On Aug 2, 2012 Steph wrote:

You two have been together about as long and me and my Camaro! I think I'm taking him to get sold this weekend...unlike you with Bob!

 *Steph sold her 1969 Camaro, her pride and joy of 19 years, which was a huge part of letting go. It was one of her dearest belongings.*

Camille:
Thanks! How sad... I hope you make a bazillion dollars!

Steph:
I wish too. Only worth $20K though. Selling at the wrong time (as usual).

Camille:
Have you heard from the Panama folks yet? You could always take this temporary position I saw listed and get down there and look for a long-term position.

We had a great time at the coast. I hate to admit it's another 500 photo month. I'm getting it down to 200 but it will still be 10 pages. Let the fun begin!

 Each month Camille and Bob publish an online photo album at troutsfarm.com.

Steph:
No, I haven't heard back yet. I saw that other Panama listing yesterday as well. I'm going to have to play everything by ear since I'm not leaving until next year.

3
LOUD MOURNING AT NIGHT

Subject: Life without Lauren
On Aug 10, 2012 Camille wrote:

Lauren left this morning, leaving me in a house full of solid male energy. She is taking the bus to Accra. I hope she doesn't run into too much traffic. I sent her off with tissues, ramen and biscuits (HobNobs, what the British call biscuits—not homemade biscuits).

They are burying John Atta Mills, our Ghanaian dead president, in Accra today after three days of lying in state. I read that Hillary Clinton was coming down to pay her respects.

Time to get on my feet and do some shopping. I dropped a five gallon water bottle on my right foot this morning while changing out bottles in our water dispenser. No doubt a bit of trepidation about stepping forward into a life without Lauren on some level.

Steph:
Oh yeah...gee, the death of the president seems like it was weeks ago! How did everyone take it and is it like here where the VP takes over?

Guyana is around the corner, so I've started updating my new blog Solo

Guyana (guyanatraveler.wordpress.com) as time grows closer. If interested you can follow it by clicking on follow (as I'm sure you well know) and will email you updates. Apparently the first week I won't have Internet but I'll still write up the posts and put them out there when I finally do. I'm stoked that this is my very first blog I've done so I hope it comes across ok.

Camille:
I just got caught up on your blog and love that you will be writing about your Guyana adventures. I have no idea how you will pack everything on your list (and more) into a backpack! You've definitely thought of everything as far as I can see.

As regards the dead president, the community has been in mourning clothes for three days (black and red) and is somber and united. Funerals are a big thing here, they last for days. The family is required to outfit themselves in new custom-made funeral attire. No wearing that suit from the previous funeral.

Hundreds of people are invited, they block off the streets and dance and eat all day. Ironically, a family that can't afford medical care will somehow manage to pull off a huge funeral after their child or parent dies. In return, guests bestow the family with gifts, allowing them to repay their debts and perhaps put a little money in the bank.

Often the body of the deceased is stored in the morgue for weeks or even months, giving relatives from all over the world time to travel home for the funeral. This explains why the hospital is a lot smaller than the adjacent morgue.

As you might imagine, the president's funeral is an especially big deal. The churches have broadcast prayers nonstop from midnight to 3am three nights in a row, ruining our sleep. Just can't figure out how anyone can think this is good on any level. Why can't they do it from 6pm (sundown) until 9pm?

Steph:

Wow...and I thought barking dogs at 4am were bad...I can't imagine what you must be going through. Strange how other cultures think things like that are ok to do for some reason. I assume ear plugs don't even help.

I didn't do much this weekend other than be domestic. At 102+ degrees outside, I can't find a good reason to go out other than first thing in the morning. Can't wait to escape this heat! No sign of letting up either.

 *Noises at night in different countries are quite different than the U.S. Steph recalls being alone in her casita in Costa Rica and hearing what she thought was a house being broken into across the street. She heard footsteps over glass and then thought she heard them coming into her yard. She called the police and tried to explain in broken Spanish what was going on. She was quite terrified until she found out it was some drunk throwing bottles from his car onto the trash pile which was on the street corner.*

Dogs, people, cars, motorcycles, bugs and other strange noises abound and it takes a while to get used to. Eventually it becomes so common you can fall asleep without a problem, but it was quite unsettling at first.

Subject: You won't believe this
On Aug 16, 2012 Camille wrote:

They are gearing up for a party across the street. The music is concert loud. Will likely insert earplugs tonight. Meanwhile the Muslims are dying down. Ramadan ends Saturday evening. Now we have all night Christian loudspeaker preachers popping up in the neighborhood. I liked what this guy wrote to the local TV station, which begins with "Though the very soul of middle class discretion and respectability, I am pretty sure that even some of my normally staid, hard working and stiff upper-lipped neighbors must have been discomfited by the 'I-stand-in-the-blood-of-Jesus' all night megaphone din that kept our neighborhood awake, a few nights ago."

Steph:
Wonder if they ever will ban the music. Funny how in different countries you have to deal with late night/early morning noises that we in the U.S. get our panties in a bunch over. Dogs barking at 2 a.m.? Unacceptable! Yet down south, it's a fact of life and I doubt anyone bitches about it. The dogs are there for security. Now the cows and chickens...that's another issue.

Camille:
Ha ha! The bitches are barking and no one is bitching!

I rarely hear our male goat bleat, but this morning I heard him. He sounds way different than the female. She's like "Blaaaahhhh, Blaaaaah" and he's like "Boo awww."

What's going on in your life? When are you leaving for Guyana? Please forgive me for forgetting the date. My brain is going.

Steph:
Ha ha, I like your phonetics there, very cute. I'm still laughing. Silly woman!

I leave next Friday to Guyana! WHEEEEEEE! I can't wait...although I think it's still raining down there. Hopefully it's not an all day thing. I see leeches in my future.

Subject: Feeling safe
On Aug 13, 2012 Steph wrote:

So how do the locals feel about y'all in the neighborhood? What's the crime like? Do you ever feel unsafe? Do most speak English? So many questions!

Camille:

Walking around as an Obruni can be both alienating and exhilarating. The children embrace me with exuberance and shyness if you can imagine this. Leaping about with their hands waving and then hiding behind their pals and/or mom when I return the greeting.

I rarely feel unsafe but I don't go out after dark alone. English is the national language and most people speak at least a little bit of it.

I do believe we could easily be robbed but probably not on the street in broad daylight. If I get in a conversation with anyone on the street, they invariably announce that they are going to come over to my house. "I will come to your house tonight." We've made it a house rule that we don't invite anyone inside the gate, although our trusted taxi drivers are allowed in to help carry stuff into the yard and into the house if need be.

For sure everyone assumes I'm rich and when I pull out my wad of bills to pay at the little neighborhood stores the point is proven.

My friends so far are all shop keepers who hope to pry some of these cedis (the local currency) out of my wallet. "Do you want plantain today? No, why not? You bought plantain from someone else, didn't you?" and "What do you buy at Melcom? I want to see if it is something I can sell you."

One exception is Mary's shop. She never pressures me and she is only a couple of houses down.

My friend Sharyl's niece is coming to visit for a couple of nights on Tuesday. I never met her but I asked the house if we could offer her a room and they agreed. Young boys and a pretty blonde in her twenties. So we bought a bed and I'm doing a little extra cleaning this weekend. How is your weekend? So much to do to get ready I'll bet!

35

Steph:
Well, sounds like you're in a pretty chill environment. Safer than Belize City! My friend Dahnelle is going to Africa for about a month and a half for work...can't remember where, but it ain't nothin' to write home about!

I had a dream last night that the guy in Panama with that Caretaker job wrote and asked if I wanted the job. I was so happy, almost crying about it telling my mom. Then I woke up! I'm sure he's found someone by now.

Yes, I packed yesterday. But I also trimmed the bushes out front and as I was sweeping the sidewalk a big muscle in my back freaked out and apparently got worse as I slept because it hurts today. I may need to get an emergency massage. So I thought I was doing pretty well on the packing when I weighed in at 16 pounds, but once I "truly" packed it came out to 22. Took out some things...21.1. Uuughhh. I'm sure my Go Berkey isn't helping matters. I need to look for a smaller backpack for misc. things like electronics.

Subject: Go-At
On Aug 19, 2012 Camille wrote:

So sorry you tweaked your back and can't get your pre-pack to fit like you wanted to. I really don't know any other person who plans as well as you do.

I would totally ping the folks in Panama. It never hurts to follow up. They might have found someone and maybe not. Perhaps they're waiting to see who writes them back just to be sure they really want the position.

I'll leave you with this photo of Bob and Go-At from this afternoon. One minute Bob was scratching Go-At on his head and the next he had scooped him up and had him in his arms. I was so jealous! Will have to try this now, copycat that I am.

Bob and Go-At, the Nigerian dwarf buck

Steph:

Yes, I emailed the guy in Panama but haven't heard back...and I say "in" Panama...he's out sailing the great blue somewhere. But yeah, you're right...I thought the same thing too. I doubt he'd "hire" me being that I don't know much about maintenance.

That was a cute pic of Bob with the goat. They're becoming like family, huh? They probably know that you guys won't eat them! Aaah, they just know nice people when they see 'em. :-)

Is there a rainy season there?

Camille:

It's true—I heard they can smell the difference between meatitarians and vegetarians. I'd say you likely have significant experience in fixing things after living by yourself in your own home for so many years.

There is a rainy season here and we are in it. The rainy season begins in April and ends in November, but the heaviest rain happens between June and September. After that comes the dry season and with it the heat and dust from what I've been told.

4
GUYANA!

Subject: Whatta time
On Sep 1, 2012 Steph wrote:

Hi friend! I am alive and well in Yupakari village waiting for darkness to fall so we can go out on the river for a boat ride. We are going to find creatures of the night! I saw my first caiman this morning. You can catch up on everything online at Solo Guyana. I've been blogging my face off since I got here. Been without electricity for six days. The jungle was amazing.

How are you doing?

Camille:
How nice to hear from you! I am doing great and am very happy to see your 12 new posts. I loved the photo of you and the tree boa and can't wait to get caught up in your adventure.

Heard a great story two weeks ago about an enormous boa eating a goat out of the neighbor's yard. This naturally made the man fear for his young children, and he has been clearing around the property since then to discourage snake travel into his back yard.

Our electricity is on. The water is on. And the neighbors are burning plastic on an overcast day.

Steph:
Good to hear from you as well. Thanks for reading my blog, been having fun writing it. It's 8:30am now and I'm sitting on the deck looking at the mountains. A hummingbird just flew up to say hello. Vultures are circling above me for some reason and the black-collared lizards are keeping me company. It's quite pleasant right now, but in the afternoon it can be unbearable. Luckily we finally got some rain to break the heat. But today the mountains are hazy again, so who knows what will happen.

It's a tough life out here for people, so it really puts my life into perspective. There's not much to do around here during the day so I've been forced to relax for once. Swing in the hammock and check out any wildlife that happens to come by. Been eaten alive by bugs but mostly still recovering from the betress. Bastards.

Betress ended up being chiggers that Steph got while blazing trails through the forest in Maipaima.

A man from the Netherlands and I are the only guests here, which makes it nice. He's a good fellow and we've done some tours together. Next week the place will have about seven people, so I came at the right time.

Glad to hear you have a little break this weekend. Crazy about the boa! Living in harmony with nature can be a challenge, as I am learning!

Camille:
I love, love, loved the posts you wrote about your adventure and read all of them. We've been losing power daily for the past four days, so it was a challenge to get online time.

What a terrible and challenging, yet rewarding life experience! You are very brave to sign up to extreme-roughing it.

I love that you wrote:

"I'm not sure if it's the sheer exhaustion I have been going through or the empathy I am feeling for the people here. I have cried more in the past ten days than I have all year. Maybe I'm amazed at the tenacity of their will or their ability to cope. They know no different. This little boy works harder than I do, yet I'm spending $200 a day to 'vacation' here. Believe me, this does not feel like a vacation. This has been a real eye opener for me, and although I will probably never come back, I'm glad that I did travel here."

Coincidentally, two of the three quotes Bob picked out for this month's Photo Album were very appropriate to your experiences:

"Travel is fatal to prejudice, bigotry and narrow-mindedness and many of our people need it sorely on those accounts. Broad, wholesome, charitable views of men and things cannot be acquired by vegetating in one little corner of the earth all one's lifetime." – Mark Twain, *Innocents Abroad*

"I thought how travel was composed of moments like this: discoveries and reverences separated by great inconvenience. These encounters, taken together, added up to one's experiences of a place—the inconvenience had to be forgotten and displaced by the epiphany." – Paul Theroux, *My Secret History*

Steph:
I'm in Houston now, having spent the last five hours in luxury on the plane in first class, writing my final blogs. Some guy gave up his seat to be with his family in coach, so I snagged it fast. Such luck! Thanks for your thoughts...I am glad you have enjoyed my writing and hope it all came across well. It was fun to do and I look forward to doing more when I make the move to Central America. Heck, maybe I'll write some articles for a magazine or paper or maybe someone will show enough

interest and have me write a book!

Subject: Photos of Guyana
On Sep 13, 2012 Camille wrote:

Morning! I just watched the slideshow of your photos. Beautiful as usual. So many great images! You have an eye for wildlife. I loved the crocs, caimans, turtles, smiling lizard and the other guys, the blue/green lizard and the iguana. Of course, I particularly liked your ox cart photos. It was wonderful to put the images to the words I read. Oh, and I loved the quote by Henry David Thoreau.

How has your experience influenced your perspective now that you are back in the States?

Steph:
Thanks for looking at them. It was so hard to get pics of the animals on the river when you're either moving or swaying in a boat or both (usually). I didn't catch the ones I wanted. Luckily I did a lot of videos.

I think whenever I come back from a rough trip (which is typically all of them), I always cherish the things that I have here a little bit more. However, with the big change ahead for me by moving down south, it's made it a lot clearer what I should be expecting. I know I won't have A/C, it will be buggy, uncomfortable, I'll lose a lot of weight...but I think I will be happy...happier than I am here.

I vowed to myself to not be afraid anymore and it's amazing what the mind can do. Once I set my mind to that, the only thing that scared me during the whole trip was the lightning. And that, I think, was warranted. So with that, I will be a trooper and take what comes my way and not give up even when I might want to. I promised myself to write a list of WHY I'm there to remind myself in the dark hours and to stay at least a year...but hopefully a lot longer. I honestly don't want to come back. At least that's what I believe as of now.

I saw a listing for Puerto Rico...do you know anything about that place? I've heard good/bad about it. It was a paying position though with lots of amenities on Snake Island. Woo hoo!

How are you feeling in Ghana now that you've been there a while? Do you look forward to staying or do you want to come back?

BLOG

Blam, Pow, Zap!!
By Steph

Last night a huge storm swept in. I had finally gotten to sleep (which is becoming a rare commodity around here), when I heard the wind kick up. It had been eerily still which is usually a sign of rain to come. I have been very lucky lately as far as the weather goes. When it has rained here, it is not that big of a deal. Little did I know that it could have been deadly. Here, I have been worried about the creatures with teeth, the blood sucking parasites and what lurks beneath the waters. Never did I think that I could be killed by lightning.

The wind was howling and the rain started up and beat ferociously against the thatched roof. I am upstairs in this house and a few backpackers came in last night but were sleeping outside. A couple of my wooden shutters slammed closed, making me jump. The lightning was loud and seemed very close. I counted the seconds between the lightning and the thunder. It went from three seconds to two and then that's when it happened. A loud crack, a super bright light, then a sizzling and a POW about five feet away from me in the corner of my room where the electrical outlet was. I screamed and jumped, fully awake now but glad to be alive. My heart was beating fast and I didn't know what to do. I wasn't sure if I should get up and go downstairs or remain horizontal and not stand up. I moved my metal flashlight away from me and took off my pants that had metal zippers on it, not knowing if either of those would work against me.

I remained in bed, too frightened to stand up and hoped the storm would pass soon. Finally the lightning tapered off but the rain continued to fall. Once things had subsided, I thanked my lucky stars and slept in til 7:00.

Camille:
Your fear of getting melted into your grave by a lightning strike was certainly warranted!

I've heard good things about Puerto Rico. A friend of ours lived in Vieques for decades before returning to the States in his 60's. Bob had a work friend in Virginia 15 years ago whose wife came from Puerto Rico and she loved her homeland. Other than that, no direct experience but my gut feel tells me that I would definitely live there. I like that it's close to the States, so cheap airfare if you have to travel back and forth. Plus, islands rock! The ocean breezes and the insulating effect of the surrounding water moderate the temperature so it doesn't get super-hot.

We are still living the dream here in Kumasi and happy to be here despite the difficulties of everyday life. Little triumphs can make our day. For instance, yesterday when taxi driver Prince and I went to buy drinking water, he said he saw an open gas (propane) station, so we high-tailed it back to the house and traded the water bottles for our propane tank and scored!

Three hours of taxi time (60 cedis or roughly $30) and I had filled our small spare tank (7 cedis), purchased a new large tank full of propane (110 cedis) and also purchased a charcoal stove (13 cedis) and a giant bag of charcoal (11) cedis. So, about $100 split four ways.

I was so jazzed! We have all been worried about running out of propane for cooking and have been having nearly daily power and water outages, so cooking dinner is always a gamble. We have three electric burners and three propane burners. The electric burners are low wattage and shut off before you can boil a pot of water. They are either on or off so I have quite a challenge not to burn whatever it is I'm frying, and rice is out of the question. So I end up using the propane to finish boiling noodles, cook rice, fry plantain, bread and fritters. That's when the power is on. When it's off, I cook everything over propane.

For nearly three months we kept hearing that there was a propane shortage, and when it comes in people queue up with their tanks and wait for 45 minutes. Every night I wondered if this would be our last meal on propane. The guys would heft the tank and say it felt pretty full, but how do you know? Our tiny tank is quite heavy empty.

Thank god for our great taxi drivers, who get around and notice what's going on. Prince knew where to get a new back up tank and the vendor had already filled it with propane. Refills will be 20 cedis and I'll call Prince when we switch tanks so he can keep his eye out for an open gas station. Then he'll call me and come pick me up with the empty tank and off we will race!

Despite (or perhaps because of) these challenges (and the potential victories) I am still happy to be here. Despite the dust, noise, uncertainties, occasional rudeness, shit on the streets, religious and political fanatics trolling our street with loudspeakers at 7am. Have I told you about the flying toilets?

That's what I found out they call human shit in a plastic bag. At first I wondered why all the street vendors use black rather than clear plastic bags. Turns out, due to sanitation challenges they come in handy for people who are in town and need to go to the bathroom. In Ghana it's acceptable to shit into one of those black plastic bags, tie it up and fling it somewhere, usually into the weeds. Thus the name flying toilets.

Anyhow, despite all these things, I am loving the experience. So many wonderful little vignettes. Tiny children suckling their mothers, kind eyes passing in the street, the apple that my new friend at the plumbing store presented to me this morning, beaming. Life without A/C is so much more to my liking than the isolated, sanitized world in the U.S.

That said, I do miss my community of wonderful friends and the way we wander around on foot to each other's homes and hug each other on contact. We have a great thing going in NC and a good thing going here.

Amazingly, it has not been buggy or even very hot here in the three months we've been here. The heat will change, the bugs likely will not.

Your experience in Guyana was really rough. It's hard to imagine you will find Panama (or Puerto Rico) as uncomfortable and challenging.

By the way, every time I see a lizard, I think of you and that's a lot! Here's the old agama that lives in our yard, hanging out on the front wall by the road.

The Agama lizard that hangs out on our courtyard wall

Steph:

Oh man...I haven't laughed that hard in a long time. Flying toilets, eh? Now THAT'S culture shock. I don't think that image will be leaving my mind anytime soon!

Thanks for the info on PR...good to hear. The island is semi-arid and says it has thin soils. Plants that need a tropical environment to grow probably won't work there. Odd huh? Although the weather sounds great, not getting over 90 typically and cool at night. I think it'd be neat to move there, but it's up to the guy at the inn, obviously. I told him I had ideas about money making ops for the Inn, so hopefully that will keep me in the back of his mind. He did hit my blog so I'm not sure if that's a good or bad thing.

Sounds like you have quite a few challenges of your own over there. What a pain about the cooking and water situation. I became aware of scabies as of yesterday...something I hadn't really given any thought to. I looked up what these black dots I saw on peoples' skin might have been and I only came across scabies. The black could be the feces of the mites coming up through the skin...and I'm not sure if that's what I saw, but I had no idea what scabies was. Then I got paranoid because I have some bites that still itch and I don't think it's scabies but may get checked out just to be safe. But that also made me think that when I live in these places, critters like that could become commonplace. What about over there? Any mites/parasites that are of concern to you? How do you think the quality of the bottled water is?

Any word on if you will extend the year out there yet? That was a good pic of the lizard, thanks for thinking of me and sharing it. Hope he doesn't cut himself!

Oh, how I hate coming into work. I can't wait to be "free."

5
WHAT'S FOR DINNER?

Subject: Menu
On Oct 2, 2012 Camille wrote:

I wish you had a recipe for me today! I keep making the same old stuff and need to plan the week. I think I'll make chili today and maybe some slaw to go with it. I hate to keep making the same thing, but if I don't plan tomorrow too, I'll have to shop both today and tomorrow. Sigh.

Meanwhile, looks like at least someone in our neighborhood will have dog for dinner. Check out my blog.

No, we don't have mites. We have ants and mosquitoes. The bottled water is fine. Sometimes we taste a hint of sea salt, though. We carry water bottles because we don't trust the water you can buy in plastic sachets on the street.

Heard anything yet about PR? I think it's pretty likely we'll finish out 2013 in Kumasi, but no final word yet.

Steph:
Hi! No, nothing from PR. He may be trying to get the person for this month together first, so I'm still hopeful! I gotta get outta this shitty job.

Loved your blog, by the way. Horrible reality of what people do to animals. I think if more people knew the process and conditions they'd turn vegetarian. We go to the meat aisle and see it packaged nicely and refuse to think about how the animal was raised and butchered just so we can eat dinner. I can completely understand your point of view and applaud you for not taking part.

Plastic Farm Animals
blog

Let Sleeping Dogs Die
By Camille

Sometimes reality hits you in the face whether you're ready for it or not.

I was walking to the Chinese store for tofu, coming up on the house where the rust colored dogs hang out, when I noticed two men doing something in the grass between the ditch and the compound wall. One of the men was picking up an animal. He held both front feet in his left hand and the hind feet in his right. The second man was holding a big woven plastic bag just like the one we bought a load of charcoal in.

I immediately identified the animal as a dog and because it was the same color as the dogs that habitually sleep outside that same wall, a scenario developed in my brain. A cherished pet had been struck by a car and was being rescued. Or it was dead and the body was being removed by city employees to wherever road kill dogs go?

Out of the corner of my eye, I saw the men look my way, so I turned, and getting a better look there seemed to be some life in the unfortunate animal. Maybe there was hope for the dog after all. My face reflected my internal narrative with a mixture of sorrow and hope. As I met his gaze, the man swung the dog into the bag and reached down for something else.

49

I think my look of concern made him smile. Picking up a second dog, this one a black one, he asked in English in a slightly teasing voice, "You like this?" He held up the dog and its head swung back to reveal a gaping gash where the throat once was. Obviously, the dog's throat had been cut. Cut the way I've seen deer hunters bleed out an animal before butchering. Probably hacked with a machete or "chopped" as they say here.

Confused, I answered "No," and kept walking, stepping aside to miss a small puddle of drying blood. It was unclear whether he was asking if I liked dogs in general or as pets or did I like dog meat. It was pretty clear these two dogs were headed to someone's kitchen and it was best that I continue on my way.

To be fair, I've often joked that I'd eat road kill if I were hungry enough and feel better about it than eating factory farmed meat. I've never been squeamish about meat. The neighbors raise chickens for food and the goats in our yard are being raised for breeding with the intention of eating the kids. After we leave Kumasi, Go-At, Aponche and Nwansane will likely turn into meat.

My attitude had always been: animal protein is animal protein, no matter how you slice it, and I've chosen not to partake. However, our vegan diet has taken a hit since moving to Africa.

Last Saturday Bob and I discovered a new shop in the neighborhood that stocks good cheese, delicious beans, bread, spices, dried fruit and our favorite mayonnaise. Our new expat friend generously invited us to join him while he ran his shopping errands and we happily hopped in and returned home with 101 cedis ($50) worth of food, including three packages of cheese.

Grilled cheese sandwiches are now the latest culinary craze around here. I tasted the Swiss and one of the cheddars and was reminded how much I once loved cheese. I have yet to eat a grilled cheese sandwich but I have to admit that today Bob's sandwiches smelled mighty inviting, even after the trauma of seeing what I saw a couple of hours earlier.

I realize there's a lot of wiggle room between grilled cheese and dog meat. But my nonchalant attitude towards animal products has been shaken by the haunting image of a black dog with a hacked throat. When I arrived home, the goats gathered around like pets and I felt a pang of sorrow knowing that they may one day end up on someone's dinner plate.

Subject: Female companionship
On Oct 12, 2012 Camille wrote:

I made chili again for dinner last night. It made us all sweat. No wait, we were sweating already. It's really not chili weather down here but the guys love my chili. We ate it with flat bread and cold salads, cucumber, green bean and cole slaw.

I had a little incident today. On the way home from my morning trip to market for tofu, I met one of the neighbors outside her gate down the street. We said our hellos and I pointed out our house (I'm too friendly) and she says, "I'll come see you." A lot of people say this and I don't know how to take it or respond. Well, in future I won't be pointing out my house and if someone says they'll come to visit I should probably ask, "What for?"

Well, she showed up at our house a couple of hours later. She just walked up and let herself in the gate. Bob saw it happen and was not pleased. Although he was on a phone call, he called out to her that she should always call out "ago, ago" (knock knock) because we might have dogs. So I went out and walked her to the gate and felt terrible.

I wish I could just make friends as if I were in the States. But we really can't have people just letting themselves inside our compound, nor would they feel good about us letting us inside their walls. Plus, whenever we get close to someone here, we risk them asking us for money. Bob has already lent a sizable amount to our good taxi driver Prince to get his car repaired.

It is becoming increasingly clear to me that I crave female companionship. Never thought I'd hear myself say this. Thank god I have you and my other email girlfriends. The male energy in this house just isn't doing it, so when I go out I am super friendly with the ladies. Sigh...

Steph:
Hi! Yes, I know the culture shock will get to me as well, wherever I end up and that's nothing you can ever prepare for. So did you even visit with her or did she just leave? Seems pretty awkward, but if people don't like others in THEIR personal space why would they do that to you? Odd that she wouldn't announce herself first too...but I don't know how they work down there either.

I don't hang out with women on my "off time," nor do I really speak to any even on the phone except occasionally. I guess maybe I'll go through the same thing as you at some point. I'm glad you can at least talk to me over email and your other g/f's as well. I'm always here for you! :-) Apparently the girl goats aren't doing it for ya!

I'm so ready to get out of here...just still mentally preparing what I want to take with me and I guess a lot of that depends on where I end up. Then selling my stuff is an ongoing process.

Camille:
Can't believe it's Saturday already again! What are you up to this weekend?

Haruka said both men and women alike these days are sensing the lack of female energy in the world and so are craving it. Interesting concept and I can totally see this. As in yin and yang, war and peace...

Steph:

I'm just waiting for Julio to come over. We're going to Boerne for a wine/chocolate festival, but we're going to have lunch there first, since I don't really want chocolate for lunch, ha ha! I thought I was going to sleep in but that didn't happen. The neighbor's dog barks way too early in the morning, so that happened at 7, just enough to wake everyone up and THEN they bring it inside. Guess I should be getting used to that, though, for when I move. NOT looking forward to hardly ever getting to sleep in but I guess I'll just go to bed early down there.

Other than that, just glad it's Saturday...been having a hard time tolerating work ever since I got back from the trip. I can't leave that place soon enough!!

It's overcast but they say it should get to the mid 80's. We might stop in at Boerne Lake if they're not charging to get in and lay out a blanket for a while. I'm sure we'll finish up with a bbq or something and a scary movie...a typical "date" night for us! Not much else to report so far. I'm sorry you don't have any girlfriends nearby...wish I was there with you! We could play with the lizards and goats. :-)

 Julio was Steph's longtime boyfriend in Texas before she moved. They remained friends after she left.

Subject: Work
On October 20, 2012 Camille wrote:

Hi! How's your week coming along so far?

My good friend Pamela emailed me the Hunger Games on audio and I am loving housework with someone to read to me!

Steph:

So far my week is starting out with the typical users that call into the help desk that I can't stand talking to. This one in particular is from Boston and his accent and rude behavior is just outSTANDING! I can't wait to get away from this b.s.

Camille:
Morning! Ha ha—we call them Mass-holes. Those assholes from Massachusetts. Really arrogant in general. And yes, that's a generalization and stereotyping. Too bad so many individuals willingly prove the point for us.

Hope you found a way to laugh with that Boston-ite. I regard these types as a challenge and am pleased when I manage to break through their upper crust.

Steph:
HA HA HA! Oh man, that was awesome. I LOVE IT! I was literally laughing out loud for ONCE at 7:40am in the office.

Subject: Hurricane Sandy
On Oct 30, 2012 Steph wrote:

How you doing over there? Hope there was no damage from Hurricane Sandy at your NC house?

Camille:
I'm doing great but sweating like a mule and heading to the shower before going back into the kitchen. When I take out the compost and see those brightly colored agama lizards scurry I always think of you.

I spoke with my mom and emailed my brothers, cousins and sister-in-laws to find that my family is weathering Hurricane Sandy on the East Coast. The rains were anti-climactic. My friend Pamela prepared for a tsunami on Maui, which produced little more than three-foot waves.

The longer I'm here, the harder it is for me to reconcile the dichotomy between hunger and eating animals. While in the States, raising animals for meat consumes a fair amount of resources and creates tons of waste, here in Ghana the animals roam and scavenge, fertilizing as they go.

54

The next door neighbors now have three puppies. We're all wondering if and when they will begin butchering them. I can't imagine what those little dogs eat that comes for free.

Well, in the shower for me. I'm sweltering in a puddle of sweat. The hot season is coming. No A/C for us. I suppose I could have turned on a fan. Duh!

Subject: Halloween
On Oct 31, 2012 Steph wrote:

So my house will go up for sale in the beginning of December for my goal of being out around March, if not sooner. I'll start sending out feelers around mid-December to people and see where I end up. I'm still leaning on Panama just due to their six month visa. I don't want to have to jump around TOO much, you know? I'd like to settle a little first then move on. Plus I'd like to see Panama finally.

Does anyone there observe Halloween? Are you guys having a party/dressing up?

Camille:
No trick or treat here. It's just another hot day.

Animals are awesome but can be just as spoiled and bratty as humans. I'm thinking of the goats. The more we feed them the more they fight over the food and cry at the door for more. I guess they're more human than we give them credit for.

The guys have started throwing handfuls of raw rice to both the chickens and the goats, and you should hear them! Bob, watching from the window, tells me the chicks are attacking one another. I've seen chickens eat a dead chicken. Don't know how it died.

Seems the more I see of the world, the harder it is to be idealistic and yet the more compassion I feel. Seems like a dirty trick to feel so much

55

love for creatures that are willing to tear themselves apart. I'm talking about people here as well. Guess that's why old folks are so interesting. They have all these feelings and knowledge battling it out inside their heads. I'm just beginning to understand a lot of things and yet the more I know, the more baffled I am.

6
SHOPPING FOR PATIENCE

Subject: Shopping center
On Nov 7, 2012 Steph wrote:

Jeez, whenever I see anything about Ghana I perk up wondering what's going on:

News article online: *Dozens of shoppers have been rescued after a department store collapsed in the Ghanaian capital Accra. Around 40 people have been pulled out alive by rescue workers but at least four people who were inside the multi-story Melcom store have died.*

I know you're not in Accra, but with all the shopping you do it always scares me so I just gotta ask....you okay?

Camille:
I heard about this today, too. Eric's wife, a nurse here in Kumasi said eight were killed and there were a lot of injuries.

We have a Melcom just up the street and I was shopping there several times a week until they pissed me off and now I go elsewhere. Places like Ababio, where we were returning from this morning when a big orange truck slammed into the back of Eric's taxi.

I was in the back seat but seem to have suffered the least. It was a long day waiting for the police, filing the police report at the station, hanging out in the hospital for a clean bill of health. They took our blood pressure and asked us for 100 cedis each even though it clearly states on the medical form provided that the fee is 2 cedis and change. Crafty bastards.

Love the name on the truck that hit us: "God's Way." Guess we got in God's Way!

Plastic Farm Animals
blog

In God's Way
By Camille

All things come to those who wait. In this case we were waiting in traffic when an explosion pitched us forward. No warning. No screeching of brakes. Only a sudden impact from a truck coming up behind us, plowing into Eric's taxi and knocking us silly.

We had been sitting in heavy traffic pointed in the direction of the Palace Hypermart when the brakes failed on the truck behind us. One minute we were chatting idly and the next we were rubbing our necks.

A little dazed, it took a moment to understand what had happened. Ironically, my first thought was of the drinking water bottles behind me in the trunk. Bob's first thought was for his wife in the back seat, and then the water bottles. It's silly that we'd both think of the water, but trauma works on the mind in strange ways.

We twisted in our seats to see the windshield of a large truck looming over the rear window of Eric's Nissan Twister. Then we began feeling ourselves for injuries, afraid to move, yet feeling the need to get out of the car. My collar bone was slightly sore, as was my neck. I realized I had a headache. Bob and Eric were both touching their heads and necks. We had hit the taxi in front of us and were sandwiched between the two vehicles.

I tried the door and it seemed stuck, but pushed a little harder and gingerly got out. I made my way unsteadily towards the curb through a gathering crowd of concerned pedestrians. Bob stood in the street, leaning on the roof of the car with his head in his hands. I felt faint, a little dizzy and I definitely dazed, not quite sure what to do next. My right knee was skinned where it had pushed into the back of Eric's seat.

Eric surveyed the scene and took off to fetch the law, a hand on his jaw. None of us were bleeding but we all had headaches. The concern of the bystanders was comforting. The driver sat in the cab and talked with the crowd. "God's Way" was painted on the windshield in bright yellow letters.

Thirty minutes later, Eric returned with a policeman in a black and white uniform and carrying a newspaper. Without acknowledging us, he took some notes, writing them down on his paper. Then he sat down in the shade with his newspaper to wait for the tow truck.

Eric arranged transport to the police station and the hospital, in that order, and asked us to sit in the back of a parked taxi. We hesitated. Bob said his appetite for sitting in stationary taxis was very small. But he agreed and the men moved the five gallon jugs of wate,r and Maui Recycling Service reusable grocery bags full of food into the car. I watched in apprehension as Bob picked up the water bottles, recalling stories of cracked vertebrae breaking under the stress of unusual movement, rendering the victim a paraplegic.

We tried to relax in the taxi while we waited for the police officer to release us. I passed the time by looking at Bob's pupils, asking him to close his eyes and then open them, trying to remember how to spot the signs of concussion. The ditch beside us reeked. Our skin glistened with sweat in the 90 degree heat, leaving a bit of a slick on the vinyl upholstery. We finished our water and I caught myself eyeing the sachet vendors but listened to Bob's advice not to trust street water.

Eventually we found ourselves at the police station, where the three of us filed into a darkened room. I tripped over a pair of sandals and turned to see a uniformed police woman napping barefoot on a wooden bench. The officer asked Eric for his driver's license, used the information to fill out a medical form and put the license in his pocket. His cell phone began playing "Happy Birthday to You" and he took the call while we waited. By now I was very thirsty and pretty sure my headache would subside if I could take a long drink of water.

Eric asked for his license back but got a shake of the head in answer so off to the hospital we went. We presented our forms to the doctor. He asked us what effects we were feeling from the accident and a woman took our blood pressure and then he asked us to pay 100 cedis each.

After some bargaining, the men struck a deal—200 cedis for the three of us even though the form says the fee shall be 2 cedis 10 pesawas. By this time we were past caring and only longed to get home, drink cool water, shower off the shock of the day and get some down-time.

Finally we arrived at the green gate and dragged out our groceries and water bottles. It was 3:30pm and may have been the longest five hours of my life.

Steph:
Oh jeez...what a bummer. Is everyone ok? It seems so packed there, how could he have hit the car? What a pain...I'm sure Eric isn't very happy either. I assume the taxi is still drivable?

So what'd they do at the market to piss you off? Are they always trying to gouge you for more money because you're white? How does it feel to be the minority?

Subject: Melcom
On Nov 9, 2012 Camille wrote:

Turned out the truck had no brakes! Bob and I are fine, as is Eric. Don't know yet how his car is doing and how much of a bribe it cost him to get his license back. We hope the truck owner agreed to pay for repairs.

Oh. Melcom. Well here's that story. On September 10th I bought my usual load after checking my back pack with the grun guy at the front door. I was spending at least 100 cedis a week there. I had my usual challenges of having to step aside for the surly attendants whom I encountered in the aisles, ducking workers unloading goods. (One day they were restocking and a 10 foot display shelf fell on top of me. They felt bad. Like any place 'round here, there are a few nice employees and everyone else seems ready to spit in my face.)

The cashier upstairs was changing the drawer and asked me to go downstairs to check out. So I went downstairs and stood patiently behind a family with a huge basket and checked out, but the cashier didn't put stamp on my receipt so the guy at the door wouldn't let me pass until I went through a second line. By now I'm pissed and telling him, "You just watched me pay! Do I look like a robber to you?"

To no avail. I knew it wasn't the help's fault, but still...

I asked to see the manager so I could file an official complaint. The manager tried her best to explain why it had nothing to do with mistrust, only concern for our safety. I asked for some letterhead. She brought a blank piece of printer paper. I wrote out my complaint, added my mailing address and phone number, asked that they contact me and signed my name.

I told the manager there were many other ways to ensure correctly charging the customer for goods bought and said, "I think this is just about giving people jobs." She agreed, laughing. I left feeling a little better but never heard from the upper management. The manager probably crumpled up my painstakingly long note and tossed it.

I promised not to shop there anymore and have only been back once. Plenty of other places to shop.

As for bring a minority, I'm happy for the opportunity to see what that feels like, but being white in Ghana is nothing like being black in the U.S. In many ways being an Obruni gives me an edge, yet that edge comes with a price. I feel honored and pestered at the same time.

Steph:
Yes, I can see where patience/tolerance will be part of my new lifestyle as well...It'll be hard going against the grain of what I'm used to here in the U.S. But oh well...gotta take the good with the bad I suppose!

Well, yesterday was great. Julio came over after I got my hair cut and we took the bikes downtown, ate lunch outside, rode, laid on the grass, ate a cupcake, had a rum punch and rode s'more, then came home and bbq'd some chicken.

So today I guess I'll be domestic. Clean the gecko poop off the garage walls, blow out some of the junk and see what I can sell or throw away.

I got a $500 international Berkey order yesterday morning through my website for once and then sold a Berkey Light on Amazon on Friday. Good stuff! Looks like it might be a good month!

Subject: Harmattan and patience
On Nov 13, 2012 Camille wrote:

Happy Tuesday! That's great that you and Julio are still keeping company. What is he going to do when you fly the coop? Congratulations on the Berkey order.

Patience: before we moved to Belize to manage Mountain Equestrian Trails (MET), the owner told us, "If you come to Belize with patience, you'll lose it. If you come without patience, you'll learn it."

Nice quiet morning here so far. Woke at 6am to the smell of burning plastic or tires. Wasn't sure exactly. Will probably wash windows. We have never lived anywhere this dusty before, and the Harmattan has not begun yet. Harmattan is when the winds shift to blow dust and grit down from the Sahara. Bad times, from what I hear.

The other night, while walking home from Sunday night pizza, people were calling out to us. Adua cried out, "Afia!" laughing. I waved and laughed back and said to my housemates in mock complaint, "We're local celebrities!"

Sometimes they'll call after me for half a block, but I keep on walking. I don't think they're being malicious, but because I'm an Obruni they probably want money. But in the case of one older woman in Adiebeba village, she wants me to come into her house and meet her grandchildren so they can see a white faced person and not be afraid.

Steph:
Funny to think that a child would be scared of a white face. I totally recall when I was a baby and we were traveling up to Virginia from Texas to move. We stopped in New Orleans and outside of a shop they had a full sized "mammy" manikin standing there. I remember FREAKING OUT because she had a black face and I thought she was real. My parents got a kick out of it watching me scream...I don't think I was crying...I just didn't understand what it was! They have a picture of me next to her and I seemed to be smiling/wiggling to get away or something. I remember it like it was yesterday. I'm sure it'd be the same for the little girl there and you. It'd be funny to see her reaction.

Subject: All is well
On Nov 15, 2012 Camille wrote:

Mmmm, smells like burning hair or feathers outside. I am sweating so much my clothes are sticking to me. Have to be careful when pulling on spandexy tops these days because they get stuck and rip. Almost ruined one of my favorite tops this morning.

Steph:
You poor thing...how hot is it there? Will it get worse? What do you drink besides water? Can you make any fruit juices?

So what's the deal with your stay there? Have you decided or has it been decided for you how much longer? Didn't you move in June? I can't remember now.

Camille:
It's been in the mid 90's. I drink water and tea. I have a hot cocoa in the morning and sometimes I'll drink half a hard cider, but I don't drink the juice. Water gets boring but juice really isn't calling my name. Justin makes horchata with rice, vanilla and cinnamon, and I'll drink a few ounces of that. When we go out I order an Alvaro, which is non-alcoholic, fizzy and very tasty. Sometimes we get ginger beer, which I really like.

We can get beer here. There's a Guinness plant down the road, but the "stout" they brew for the local market is nothing like the real thing. Bob's been working with them on using some of their waste product to make biodiesel and has confirmed that the recipes are different. He says the stout tastes like ditch water with engine oil in it. I had one a few weeks ago and it wasn't THAT bad. The best beer available is Castle Milk Stout, from South Africa.

We got here in June and have decided we will stay through the end of 2013 if the project is extended.

I enjoyed watching the goats go ape shit for raw rice earlier, fighting for every grain. Oh, and I saw a man walking down the street yesterday with a big cathode ray TV on his shoulder.

7

BITTERSWEET HOLIDAYS

Subject: Tarantula Thanksgiving
On Nov 23, 2012 Steph wrote:

Had a T-Riff T-day! Caught wild tarantulas! They were all living in the parking lot in front of my aunt's house. I've never held one before, but these were really nice. Their little feet really stuck to me! I have to look up how that works. We stuck big blades of a weed in the hole and they'd pull on it. I wondered how they had such a strong grip. When they'd come close to the top I noticed it was only one foot that was creating that big pull. It was wild! They were neat.

What'd you end up doing? Tofurky time!!

Camille:
That's lovely! You are in your element with such a huge spider in a way I could never be. I suppose I would let one crawl on me but not without trepidation.

Bob used to poke a stick into the tarantula hole outside the MET cantina for after dinner entertainment and to draw the guests away from the table so the staff could clear the dishes.

Most of the time he was able to pull out the spider to the amazement of our guests. I was usually in the kitchen helping button it up, so never noticed they hung on with only one foreleg. Amazing how creatures all adapt different strategies.

Well, I have to walk over to the Chinese shop to pick up some tofu I paid for yesterday and feel this does not count against me for "shopping" on Black Friday since I'm not in the U.S. Not to mention buying water yesterday.

All three shops I went to on Wednesday were out of bottled water, so I left my empties at the third place and waited until the truck came up from Accra to deliver. We were also out of tap water for 36 hours. But between sachets and roof top water storage there was little inconvenience to us.

Justin said the KNUST (Kwame Nkrumah University of Science and Technology) students he's working with had been without tap water for three weeks! This morning we have drinking water, tap water and electricity. I feel very wealthy—lots to be thankful for here!

Steph:
Yes, it was very exciting and I loved being with the spiders. I guess, once again, fear holds us back from many things but once you take the time to got over it, the world opens up to you.

That was funny about your Black Friday shopping...naturally I didn't either, as I have too much stuff to get rid of anyway to even think about wanting anything tangible at this point.

Well I have a possible volunteer job on the horizon...I just hope I'm accepted. It's for a jaguar rescue/rehab (along with other animals) in southern CR on the Caribbean side. The long term volunteers don't work at the center but instead in the jungle (at this very nice looking lodge that I would have to pay $10/day to stay) releasing the animals back into the wild.

So I talked with one girl at the center and she encouraged me to submit my application, which I have done. I'm super excited, as this is EXACTLY what I want to do. So keep your legs crossed for me! My cousin actually went to that jaguar place recently and said it was the highlight of the trip, so that was good to hear. It has also gotten good reviews by volunteers who've worked there. EXCITED!

Subject: Poem
On Nov 29, 2012 Camille wrote:

Congrats and good luck! I'm trying to get tickets to see Vieux Farka Toure, the Jimi Hendrix of the Sahara and I wrote a poem last night. Second poem since high school, I think. Both written here in Kumasi. Developing countries are inspiring!

When in Ghana

I live in Ghana now
I drink cocoa in the morning
I wear a thick gold ring
I sit on a wooden chair
At a wooden table
I eat plantain and turn little red tomatoes into sauce
I wear a skirt and walk along dusty dirt roads
riddled with ravines
I step over plastic water sachets and piles of shit

I wake with the roosters
My underwear is crispy after hanging on the line
in the hot equatorial sun
My skin is brown, my feet calloused
I've worn socks four times
in as many months
I live in Ghana now

I don't drink water from the tap
even when it runs clear
I wash dishes with cold water
I take cold showers and scrub my feet with a brush
When the electricity is on, I charge things up
I bring a flashlight with me when I go upstairs to cook dinner
When the taps are dry, we use a bucket to wash and flush
When the water and lights are both on I run loads of laundry
in our fancy washing machine

At 3pm the children spill out onto the streets to play
like I used to after school
I'm a white haired obruni now
I carry vegetables on my back, waving at the kids
I admire the agama lizards and plantain eaters

I say hello and ask people "how are you?"
I try to be nice and fair and good
I live in Ghana now

Steph:
I liked your poem! I'm listening to Vieux now...he does sound a lot like Hendrix...very cool! I hope you have a great time going to see him.

I heard back from the CR place and apparently I won't be living in the jungle. I'd start out at the center instead, which I'm fine with, but now the housing situation is up in the air. They're in talks with the owners of the jungle lodge about the reintroduction of the animals there...so I don't really know what that means other than it sounds sketchy. I'm still hopeful this will work out though.

Still working on getting the house ready for pictures and the market...I should be done by this weekend. My car allegedly sold for $16,500 but I won't see that money for at least another month which doesn't make me happy at all...nor do I believe the hype until the check has been cleared, so I'm semi stressing over that too.

Camille:
Don't count your chickens before they hatch. Another thing I heard a lot as a kid. You are wise.

I am so psyched you may be moving to Costa Rica! I really love Central America. Africa is fine, but it is not Belize.

Plastic Farm Animals
blog

African Music
By Camille

I am rarely as moved by music as I was by Vieux's band of three guitarists and three drummers. His sound is an infusion of African and electric blues, at times very traditional, sometimes bluesy (think Stevie Ray Vaughn), even psychedelic. Vieux Farka Toure has rightfully been hailed as "The Jimi Hendrix of the Sahara." All of this beautifully moving sound is made more poignant by the current strife in Mali.

David Bromberg sang, "You've got to suffer if you want to sing the blues" and Vieux is a great example of the intense beauty which can come from suffering. Over the past week there have been numerous stories about Malian musicians being threatened with having their tongues cut out.

A couple of months before even considering a move to Africa, Bob put on some music one evening in North Carolina that nearly brought me to tears. "What is this?!" I asked. It was African. Later I came to view this experience as a sign that we should move to Ghana.

Last night, engulfed in African music I again had tears in my eyes. My heart felt like an enormous, molten thing, a volcano exploding quietly within my breast. At times my face ached with emotion and I found myself unable to swallow. My hands were little comfort. They flew up to my face and fluttered back down to my lap.

Subject: Jaguars and housing
On Dec 3, 2012 Steph wrote:

Well, I think the jaguar place has accepted me as a volunteer but the cheaper place to live in the jungle ($10/day) is now up in the air. She wants me to hang out at the center for the first few weeks which also means a more hefty price of accommodation at $15/day, which I'm not thrilled about. They're figuring out something with La Cieba in the jungle, so hopefully she'll have more concrete news for me in the next month. I may try to look for a house to rent that might be cheaper...only problem is that this is in a touristy part of CR and right near the beach so it may be hard to find...but we'll see what I can do.

The house goes up for sale on Thursday! Getting a little nervous, excited, slightly jittery!

Camille:

I am so proud of you! Only one in 1,000 would take the plunge. Heck, if not for Bob, I'd still be in the U.S., no doubt, and you and I would not have met. Plus you are so super organized. Yes, very proud. I brag about you to my friends and even strangers who say, "I could never..."

Steph:

I was just going to write you...I checked your blog and saw that you went to that show. I'm going to listen to some mp3 clips on Amazon and see if it affects me the same way. If so I'll download some. I liked what I heard in that YouTube clip for sure. Not often that music can make you have that kind of emotional response...I love stuff like that. Some of Steve Vai's songs do that to me also...bring tears to my eyes and there weren't even words in the song!

Well thank you for being proud of me...It was YOU who inspired me to do my own thing so don't think you didn't have a part in my decision. LOVE YOU!

P.S. I'm on lesson 49 of my Spanish podcast!

Plastic Farm Animals
blog

Nwansane's Swan Song

By Camille

Chad's goat, Nwansane, died in his arms last night. She had suffered from bloat and scours (gas and diarrhea) all day and he had tried to help her by making her walk around, massaging her stomach and feeding her oil.

After dinner, I heard a goat crying out in pain or fear so I grabbed a

71

flashlight and went outside, where I found Chad sitting on the top of the third set of stairs with Nwansane on his lap. As I stood there she went into convulsions and after a few seconds she was still. Chad held his hand in front of her nose and thought he felt her breathing. I reached under her jaw where a horse's pulse would be and felt nothing.

I felt so helpless! The best I could do was suggest he lay her down in the fenced in garden area away from the other goats. He stood up carefully, as if not to disturb her, and slowly walked down the steps. Her head was flopping, her eyes open and lifeless. I untied and opened the garden gate and they passed through.

On my way back into the house, the other goats, Go-At and Aponche, came to greet me. I bent down to caress their soft coats, hoping they would provide Chad the same comfort.

Subject: Sniff sniff
On Nov 26, 2012 Steph wrote:

I was so sad to read about the goat. She was so cute. Poor little thing, I'm bummed.

BTW, where is Columbia U located? Is it NY? That's who Bob works for right?

Well, I got an offer (low) on the house the other day and only came back to them with $1K off and I'm not movin' from that spot AT ALL. It's not like I'm in a rush...matter of fact I need to kinda wait at least another month before I feel comfortable about it. That way I can get all my shit done like taxes and not have to stress about sticking around here. So as of last night she hadn't heard back, which is fine with me. I obviously pointed out that I spent $6K on the patio, $700 on the fence, $500 on the water heater two months ago. I just don't understand how six years ago this exact same house without all of those things was appraised for $180K or whatever, but now it's worth less.

Dad sent me money the other day so that was sweet. Beefing up my savings account...that should help pay my first year's rent down in CR at least, ha ha. If I survive that long!

Camille:
Yes, the death of that goat really hit home, reaffirming our decision not to "own" animals again. You must feel the same way after your beautiful iguana, Kiwi, died. Just not worth the pain.

So will you do Xmas on your own? What's Julio up to? We'll probably eat alone. No big deal. We aren't as big into Christmas as we were as kids.

I do hope you get the price you're looking for on your house.

Steph:
So what causes the bloat? Is it what they eat or drink? Scary. What if they all die (I hate to say that)...would he get more? Ugh...yeah the death of animals SUCKS, which is one aspect of volunteering that I'm not looking forward to. I'll be crying a lot.

Yes, I will be alone for Xmas as far as I know.

I'm just happy I get a four day weekend finally. Can't wait to sleep! It froze here again last night. Ugh!

Subject: Merry Christmas
On Dec 24, 2012 Steph wrote:

Just a quick note to wish you a Merry Christmas and Happy New Year!

Peace, Love and Good Happiness stuff....

Camille:
Thanks! Same to you. If we're lucky, the power will come back on today. We have water, though, and do not want for anything. Lots of food and solitude. Just the way we like it! Are you at home?

Steph:
Merry Xmas...yes, I'm at home...SICK. Think Julio got me that way or it could be allergies, which is odd because I haven't had allergies in a VERY long time. Drinking hot tea with ginger and honey and cranked up the hot water heater so I can try to steam this stuff outta me. Yucko!

Subject: Last day of the year horoscope
On Jan 1, 2013 Steph wrote:

Make new resolutions that you stand a good chance of sticking to: "A journey of a thousand miles begins with a single step." Give thanks to the Universe for the many blessings that you have.

YEAH! Wheeeee, here I go!

Happy new year!

Camille:
Nice! Did you make some resolutions?

Here are mine:
Paddle my own canoe
Learn all 57 African countries
Learn how to stop short of losing my temper (see #1)
Have the courage to be imperfect
Have the compassion to be kind to myself first and then to others

Steph:
No resolutions for me...those just tend to come as they need to, but I DO like yours! However, taking a shower the other morning I wondered why I was so nervous and semi worried about my move and then I put it aside and realized for once: this is going to be GREAT! I'm going to be in a place that I love, the ocean as my front yard, the jungle as my back yard...working with animals! Why would I be worried about THAT!? For the first time I felt relief, like this is what I've been waiting for my whole LIFE! Now I can't wait for it to get here! Aaahhhh...It's ALL in your head.

Amazing what we can talk ourselves into (or out of).

I called Julio yesterday, who was doing nothing as well, so I invited him over. We had leftover Chinese ribs and salad for lunch, made cookies for munchies and then I made chicken tortilla soup for dinner and watched Workaholics. So it was fun...better than sitting around doing nothing!

Now I'm back at work (after my alarm didn't go off AGAIN, but I was only 20 minutes late in getting up this time). Just waiting for the day I can call it quits. Oh, got paid for the Camaro too and the check didn't bounce. Another chapter of my life closed.

Camille:
How lovely! Bob and I are having the same kind of idyllic days, not much to do, all day to do it, total privacy. We've been sharing chores (garden and goats) and he's been walking to market with me every time I go. I love to walk and talk. If he can do one thing to make me happy, that is it. Join me. Help me. Be with me, especially walking, commenting on the scenery, baring our souls.

The Harmattan dust is upon us, increasing the need to clean five-fold. The rest of my time will be spent writing, reading, laughing, emailing and talking on the phone with family and friends. Bob hooked me up with a Skype-to-phone account so I can make unlimited calls to the States. Life is good.

Now back to you. You are definitely on the right track. Following your heart. Letting go of stuff. Closure on the sale of your beautiful car. And it IS scary stuff. Especially on your own. On some level you must be sad to leave Julio behind and all your friends, of course.

Steph:
Wow...I'm glad to hear you're scaling back on your work and will have more YOU time...good for you. I think it'd drive me crazy to have to clean so much...I can barely do that in my own house on a monthly basis! However, I have to keep it pretty clean now, never knowing when

someone will be by to see it. I've come to the conclusion that others see it a lot cleaner than I do so I'm not knocking myself out over it. Who cares if there are some spots on the mirror, you know? I'm not going to obsess over little things. From what I recall when I went looking for houses, most people didn't even TRY to keep it clean...and I've gotten feedback saying the house shows well so that's good. Now, for someone to buy it!

Almost time for lunch...delish chicken tortilla soup on this cold wintery day. It actually sleeted earlier. I can't wait to hit the jungle and be well and warm again!

8
SELLING THE HOUSE

Subject: The weather
On Feb 4, 2013 Steph wrote:

Enjoying your pictures as usual. I wasn't thrilled to hear about the dead cobra, but also didn't see the picture of it anywhere!? What's the story there?

So what is the latest on staying in Africa? Do you have any exit plans yet?

Camille:
We're here through 2013 and who knows after that. Bob is positioning himself to stay employed on projects like this and there are endless opportunities in Africa. We'd love to go to Peru, but for the sake of a paycheck may stay in Ghana or go to Kenya. This will all change dozens of time during this coming year.

The easy answer to what is our exit strategy is no one knows!

In other news, our daughter Amy has arrived for a five month stay. We are real excited she will get to experience the culture of her father's childhood and she's going to help me cook! Which is a good thing because while we were in Accra to fetch Amy, I started having pain in my foot which I now think is related to a mess of long simmering varicose veins. Guess my days of standing barefoot for hours on the terrazzo floors are numbered.

The cobra was on the rice walk page and we didn't kill it, just wanted to get a look after the rice farmer told us he'd run into one tangled in his bird net and killed it an hour before we crossed paths with him.

Subject: Cobra
On Feb 5, 2013 Steph wrote:

Wow! 5 months! That's a long time…well good for her! Nothing like getting that experience while you're young! I'm sure ya'll will have fun together.

Ewwww hate to hear about foot problems. Mom always warned me about wearing high heels and that eventually it'll all catch up to me.

Poor cobra…too bad he killed it. And a spitter at that! I'm glad Bob didn't skin it. Poor thing.

All I know is I'm sick of cold weather. I'm sure when I get to the jungle I'll be sick of hot weather too, ha ha…oh well. Cold sucks, that's all I know. And with everyone and their dog getting the flu around here this year, who the hell knows what's being spread around.

Camille:
Even on the hottest day, I still know I'd rather be uncomfortably hot than painfully cold. My bones ache when it is cold. Even in the house. Can't sleep without knee socks because my shins hurt. Dry, scaly skin from forced air heat. I can do without all that.

I hope you have a great day, my friend and that your body decides to behave itself. It is still cool so I will do a little stretching and then put on my backpack to shop for tofu and cilantro. Amy and I are making pad thai and mapo tofu for the evening meal and Kat is coming over at 3pm to learn how I make my tofu-based dill dip.

I am also very jazzed about making a vegan freezer ice cream substitute to help us through these hottest days of the year. I may make this while Kat is here just for fun. I'll blend up tofu, a cocoa syrup that I can make over the stove, vanilla and soy milk and put it in the freezer. We can test it before she leaves!

Steph:
Let me know how your ice cream comes out...sounds interesting. How is Amy getting along there?

Camille:
Amy has fit in as if she were born to this place! I'm impressed with how adaptable and resourceful she has been. Her druthers, of course would be a life in the forest somewhere rather than a squalid, teeming city of a million, but she's been a trooper and has totally throw in with us. She's cut my kitchen chores in half!

The ice cream was as hard as a rock. So thawing and stirring before serving is what I will do with my next attempt.

So what is on your plate today? I plan on meeting my girlfriends for an afternoon chat at Kumasi's poshest hotel. So far today, I cleaned up a shredded disposable diaper on the lawn outside our compound, blogged, swept, did laundry and mopped.

Subject: House offer
On Feb 7, 2013 Steph wrote:

I got an offer on the house last night and this one may actually go through but too soon to tell. Offered $170K, wants all the outdoor furniture, so I countered with $179K and explained that's what I paid for the house ($179.9), put in a $6K patio, put in a new water heater, etc. It's a single woman and it appears she really likes the place so we'll see.

Camille:
Congratulations on the offer on the house and I do so hope it goes through. I like the idea of a woman living in the beautiful space you made.

Steph:
I have a feeling already that I'm gonna be sick of CR food pretty soon after I get there. I guess luckily I'm in a town where different food is available, but I'm going to be cooking most of my stuff and living on the cheap, so gallo pinto and casados when I eat out will get monotonous real quick. Oh well...at least I'll HAVE food I suppose. It's just funny how you get used to variety here and when you can't have it you REALLY crave it.

Well, have a good weekend...I'm going to have five days off next week into the following so that'll be nice. Will try to get rid of some furniture during that time.

Camille:
Did you get a counter offer on the house yet?

Why do you have so much time off next week? We are going to the lake for two nights and probably won't be doing email. Next week it's Mole National Park with no Internet as well. For a whole week. I hope we see elephants!

My dad contacted Columbia University and asked them to send Bob home. Sigh...Bob and I both wrote apologies.

Steph:
The house sold today!

I decided I might as well use up my vacation time so I'm just taking a chunk of time off at once since it's combined with a holiday. I may put in for another day tomorrow since I found out the house sold.

I'm happy to hear you'll be getting away. I hope you see elephants too, that'd be so cool. What's up with your dad? Why'd he do that?

I just listed a bunch of stuff on eBay and sent off things to friends to keep for me. Gotta get rollin'!

Camille:
My father is concerned for our safety because of the recent events in Mali. He never liked the idea of me moving to Africa in the first place and even though Mali is 800 miles north with terrible roads between here and there, the conflict has him spooked.

Congratulations on selling your house and for holding out for the right offer. Still weird that they are not going to look at the house first, but heck, we've done similar things. When we bought in Virginia we flew from Colorado for a look but were 99 percent sure from a few faxed photos that we would make an offer. A month later we were moved in! Seven acre horse property was all we needed to know.

Steph:
I found out those people probably did see the house after all. The guy was out of town when he sent over the paperwork. I'm just surprised they still offered full price but I'm not complaining. The inspection is going on now so I'm at Panera waiting it out. Got my personal cell phone activated today for the next month and just waiting to quit my job.

Subject: Photos
On Mar 11, 2013 Steph wrote:

Two things before I forget: goats, neem.

I remembered I needed to buy powdered goat milk to take down to CR for the baby monkeys. It makes me wonder why they aren't raising goats there. How would you rate, in difficulty and expense, raising goats and do you guys milk yours or are there special kinds they use for milking? I'm pretty sure I've seen goats in CR.

81

That neem tree, I wonder if it was the same one I took a pic of in Guyana that was so beautiful? And if it was, I'm mad I didn't ask more about its properties. I took a similar picture of the leaves against the sky and they look mighty familiar.

I'm down to two weeks left. Whoa. I think I sold my Prelude, though, which is a huge relief. Now the furniture doesn't seem that important. I mean it IS but you know, car was more of a headache. She's going to come by to test drive it Friday or Saturday and I can keep it until the last minute.

Made my reservations to leave on the 27th and get this: I did a bunch of legs on the trip for going to VA from CR in June, then to Houston for a few days, then back to CR for about $1300 and all but one leg of the trip (SA to CR) are in FIRST CLASS! Holy god, don't know how that happened but I am seriously happy about it!

Camille:
Interesting about the goat milk. I have not seen anyone milking goats in Africa but milk is not something Africans can easily digest. These goats are all meat goats and I'm not sure if there is a difference, but I suspect there is because milk cows and meat cows are different so why not goats?

Come to think of it, dairy isn't prevalent in Latin American cuisine, either. I assume our little sweeties are meat goats.

I can't believe you are leaving in two weeks already.

Nice piece of luck getting first class tickets. Wish we'd had that on our 13 hour flight last June.

We're throwing a little party this Saturday—our first potluck bbq and we just got invited to a party on Sunday at the home of an expat family newly arrived from Ireland. Wouldn't miss the opportunity to party with the Irish on St. Pat's day!

Subject: Final countdown
On Mar 14, 1013 Steph wrote:

I've been so busy trying to sell off all of my stuff on Craigslist, to neighbors, friends, etc. I'm really getting down to the wire here. Tomorrow is my last day of work...hallelujah! I've been waiting so long for this day to come (like 15 years!). Hard to believe it's really happening. I'm getting anxious and excited, but I know this is the right thing to do. I'm closing on the house in a week and a half. That's two days before I leave so I guess I'll crash at a friend's house since I won't have any furniture. Weird, eh?

I purchased my travel insurance, and it was $467 for 6 months, which isn't bad at all. Even gives me a few weeks' worth of U.S. coverage when/if I go back there. The pickin's are pretty slim for CR though...only a couple of docs in San Jose on their list, but really this is for major events that hopefully won't happen.

On top of all this, a guy I used to work with at the bank who is my age suddenly passed away in his sleep last week and his service was today. Serious bummer...we had all gone out fairly recently for dinner and drinks too, so this was a real shocker. They say it was heart failure. It sort of makes me stand back and realize that decisions like the one I'm making should not be put off for some later date that may never come. You just never think about dying at this age, you know?

Camille:
Your life is beginning to sound like a movie! That's such a classic story line—a work mate drops dead and you decide to leave your job and try on a different life. Only you decided months ago. Seriously though, that is real sad and sobering. Even if it does prove to you that you are doing the right thing. I'm amazed at how much hard work you are doing to make it all happen. Congratulations on your last day of work!

Meanwhile, my social life has suddenly blossomed. After meeting Kat at a party, I was invited to the Golden Tulip for coffee with a group of expat women from all over the world. There were more than a dozen of us. Gina (she's Italian) brought flowers and there we all sat in the poshest hotel in Kumasi, sipping our drinks as if we weren't in Ghana at all. Then someone realized it was International Women's Day. Now my life is beginning to sound like a movie!

Steph:
My departure is around the corner and quickly approaching...I'm stressing. Getting every single item out of the house is beyond impossible, but it has to be done. I haven't even started packing yet. That's another issue. Two bags, one girl. Gooooooood luck! Really, I should only be taking one bag, but I'm sure I'll pare down eventually and get down to it. Jeez...I'm seriously overwhelmed.

I put a three month deposit on a little house I found in Puerto Viejo, not too far from Jaguar. I'll have to get a bike, although I think walking only takes about 20 minutes. The house looks cute enough, big veranda, large lush yard. It's close to the pulperia (grocery store) and the beach is a one or two minute walk away. Not bad huh? I do have to pay for water and electric. Internet will have to be done by a USB stick that takes a SIM card, which I'll get down there. I also unlocked my Blackberry and bought an LG phone that came unlocked for a spare just in case.

So my other bit of news is not a good one...the buyers have postponed closing so I won't be here to sign the papers. Yeah, don't even get me started on how I feel about this. I had to assign a friend of mine to have power of attorney and he agreed to go to closing for me and do it. Unbelievable, after all of this rushing to get out of the house on time for THEM when I really could've used a couple of extra weeks, this is what I get. Well, no need to bitch about it I suppose...things happen for a reason right?

I found a guy to buy my Prelude for $2500 and can give it to him the day before I leave so that worked out. The lady who originally wanted it backed out. I hate to say it, but I feel like I'll miss that car more than the Camaro. I guess after 19 years of having the Camaro I'd sort of fallen out of love with it. However, I can't think about it too much or I'll start to lose it. I can't believe how little I got for it and the fact they repainted it broke my heart. I didn't want to see it and I'm so mad they did it. Well, this is all about giving up things that are replaceable right? I mean, not that I could ever get MY car back, but it's just a car at the end of the day I had a good run with it and got what I wanted out of it. Best boyfriend I ever had!

Camille:
The logistics are staggering and something I don't have to deal with too much, thanks to Bob. I wonder if I'd have been able to pull off what you are pulling off.

That's sad about your cars. Cars mean a whole lot more to us Americans than just transportation. They represent freedom and autonomy. But I do feel you'll get over it. We gave away the horse that we had owned for ten years and we got over it eventually. It helped that he went to such a good friend.

Guess what? Gina has a stone pizza oven and bakes the most amazing pizza. She told me she cooked and sold her food when I met her at the Tulip, so I ordered up some pizza and lasagna. I got a taxi to go pick it up and it was raining hard. We got lost because I'd been to her house only once, in the daylight, and it was raining so hard I could barely see.

At one point I rolled down the window, but it was broken and wouldn't go back up. Our driver was pissed and I felt like shit. Finally Gina got her driver to bring her car to where we were sitting in the taxi and we followed her home.

When we walked past the blazing pizza oven into her house, it was like another world. For one thing they had hardwood floors. Not terrazzo.

85

There were flowers everywhere and beautiful wooden furniture. The table was elegantly set for a dinner party. Gina invited us in warmly and tried to get us to sit and have a glass of wine.

Turns out her husband owns a wood working plant which makes parquet floors. A different world, I tell you!

9
LIFE IN PUERTO VIEJO

Subject: Made it!
On Mar 29, 2013 Steph wrote:

Well, I'm HERE! Landed fine, stayed in the city overnight and took off to Puerto Viejo yesterday. I'm "borrowing" Internet from a signal I'm picking up since I couldn't get that USB stick for my laptop (not in stock). It's painfully slow here. There's a little café down the street, but they charge quite a bit for Internet and she's not always there, so I'll limp along with free until I can get my own.

So I finally ventured out into my yard today to see what was there after it stopped raining (which went on ALL night and morning). I found the lime tree with a lot of limes on it, some very hard though...not sure what that means considering they look ripe. There is a little perch where I can put fruit and such for birds so I did...a little leftover banana I had for breakfast. Then I saw a big ol' morpho flutter by and land on a leaf...right after I snapped the picture it flew away.

I will look for a spot to plant the jalapenos and see if they even grow. Not that I eat that many...I just like planting things. My mom told me recently that when I was little, she'd find plants sprouting out of her houseplant pots. Apparently she finally caught me planting orange seeds and whatever else I could get my tiny hands on and the riddle was solved. So it's in my blood apparently to be a farmer of some sort.

My first night was interesting. A lot of noises, wind, rain, strange cat howls and loud motorcycles. But it all calmed down eventually and I was really surprised there were no barking dogs and no roosters waking me up. WOW! What a treat. It will become even quieter after all of the tourists leave on Sunday (Holy week here).

I found one problem, though, with my doors to my room and bathroom. If you close them, they lock. So if I accidentally do that and don't have my keys...? Ugh. It's a pain to remember to carry them around, but I must. Ahhh, the challenges so far.

Jeez, I almost keeled over when I saw the price on the register today. Luckily the grocery store (not a supermarket) is very close to me. The downside is that the prices are high. Puerto Viejo town is far...would have to use a bike to get there. Back in Texas, I'd spend about $45 a WEEK on groceries. I got a bag and a half for $50, most being necessities and simple stuff. Yikes. I didn't even dare look at wine prices. Not needed. Looks like I'll be losing weight here. Ha ha!

I'm not here long enough to grow my own stuff unless I rent for another three months, although I will plant those seeds from the jalapeno for sure and whatever other seeds I can get my hands on. I need a machete to cut the coconuts open...but all of a sudden I'm seeing blood in my future. I think I need a lesson first. Evi said there was a tree in my yard with some kind of fruit that has 30 times the amount of vitamin C in oranges. She also said there are guys that come around selling stuff and there's a farmer's market in PV each weekend. I'm down with that.

The bathroom is larger than I expected. The suicide shower does NOT work for some reason, which doesn't make me happy. There are only three settings (of course pictures, which make no sense, but I have used these before). I hate cold showers. I will insist it gets fixed.

Suicide showers are on-demand shower head fixtures that are hooked up to the electrical system. Typically not a good combination in a shower, hence the name. People have gotten electrocuted from stepping on something metal or adjusting the head while standing under the running water.

I have seriously had to use my Spanish here. Thank god I listened to those podcasts at work. It's coming back to me. Luckily at the place I ate dinner tonight a girl spoke English. She was from Luxembourg and has been here for three years now. She looks young. She says she's a gypsy and looked like one, with short spikey hair that looks like she cut it herself and a few scraggly pieces of long braids hanging around her face.

So I sit here in my bed, 8pm, listening to the rain and feeling very damp. The papers I had written on are limp and I wonder what kind of havoc this is going to play with my electronics. Luckily there are very few bugs. Actually none are even being attracted by the light above me. There are two small geckos on the wall, keeping things in check but I have to assume they are hungry. I'm grateful to not have to sleep under a net.

The beach was nice...black sand, only a few people but big waves. Nobody got in beyond their waist. The riptides are hellish here. I was amazed to see a bunch of Red Cross tents set up all along the roads on the way down (due to the holiday weekend). These people are prepared for anything it seems. Of course there will be accidents and drinking this weekend.

Well, all for now. I slept almost 11 hours last night and did it feel great! Hope to do the same tonight.

Camille:
Love the story about you planting orange seeds in your mother's potted plants!

I'm so glad you made it and thrilled to hear all of your news. As for shopping, wow! We are lucky that food is pretty cheap here in Kumasi. Tofu is only 50 cents for half a pound. I can pick up more vegetables than I can carry on my back for $20. I hope you find those cheap local markets soon.

That must be torture to be on the beach but not want to go into the water for fear of riptides. At least you have rescue crews there. If something were to happen to one of us, I wonder how easy it would be to find help.

I'm jealous though. Always wanted to go to Costa Rica. We loved Belize....

But back to the concept of safety. Back in the States I hear that nice motherly types are showing up at gun rallies with loaded assault rifles!? WTF? No wonder people all over the world think every American carries a concealed weapon. In a lot of ways, Kumasi is way safer than the U.S.

Wait a minute—reality check. Did I tell you about our German friend who was robbed twice? The first at gunpoint and the second time, well, the robber did not get away with Andrea's car and probably lost his life after the beating he took from the night guard.

So, not all that safe here either. But at least I can get away with speaking mostly English.

Steph:
Hey, cookie! How are you? No, you never told me about your friend. Yikes. I often wonder if women aren't as much as a target as men. I'm hoping not to have any problems. I tend to send out a vibe of not being vulnerable, regardless of my stature.

I went into Puerto Viejo (PV) today (3km from here) to check out the farmer's market for cheaper fruit. The walk didn't sound too bad. I mean, I've spent plenty of time walking in the jungle before so this should be a piece of cake. Plus, it was still early and fairly cool and not many people out.

I stayed on the shady side of the road and it was nice. I'd look up at the trees, hoping to see a sloth or a troop of monkeys. I didn't see those, but what I DID see were those HUGE banana spiders with their giant webs up in the electrical lines. There were probably 50 to 75 of them along this one stretch and I was walking almost right beneath them. Not that they'd fall on me, but they were a little scary. Some had babies in the web...they were all just chillin'.

I looked to my right and saw the beautiful Caribbean and it was blue this time. This is the first day the sun has been out since I arrived. The water was calmer over here than it is at my beach. I got to PV and saw a huge pig roasting. Then I popped into a bakery which was crowded but the breads looked and smelled great. After asking directions TWICE to the farmer's market I found it. I got some dried sausage, cucumber, tomatoes, potatoes, onion, mango, green beans and a bag of oranges. The fruits/veggies set me back about $7 and the sausage was $4.50.

Naturally it was heavy. It was getting hot and I didn't feel like walking back home. I had the tourist office call me a cab and got a ride for $4...best spent $4 yet! Oh, the bakery line was too crowded, so I passed on the bread unfortunately.

I dropped by the Center today to deliver the goat's milk for the monkeys. They had tons, which made me feel better. I saw the volunteers cleaning extensively, one girl had a monkey on her head while she worked. There was a parrot talking to himself and screaming like a child. A couple of deer roamed around. A toucan with some missing toes harassed everyone and everything. They wish he would just free himself (he has the option of doing that) but he won't. And apparently that's kind of how it works there. They take the monkeys out to the forest each day and if they want to come back "home" they do. Sometimes they spend the night (but rarely) and some find troops that have adopted them. So it seems pretty cool. No forcible releases...they go when they feel it's time.

I felt bad for the baby sloths because they stay with mom for a very long time and these didn't have a mom. They're so sweet...I can't wait to nurture them. What a great job...being mommy to loveable creatures.

So I will start a week from Monday and maybe sooner since some volunteers are leaving. Can't wait! Sure as heck beats resetting passwords under fluorescent lights. Oh, and I can walk to and from work via the beach. What could be better than that? My house is closing on Tuesday and I wanted to be around for that.

I'm busy, still figuring out how to live without a microwave. I made my first dinner in mi casa...took a while. Had to take apart a whole chicken, which I wasn't expecting. I'm cooking on a two burner gas countertop stove, which is a challenge. Surprised I didn't burn the place down.

What took 30 minutes back home takes an hour here. Challenges....now to figure out what to eat for breakfast each morning when I go to work. I'll have the same six hour stretch between breakfast and lunch there. I dig those fluffy pita pockets though. I am spending way too much time in the kitchen between washing and drying dishes each time I use them and cooking. Thank god I have a lot of time. Messes me up to get dark around 6 though. Feels like it should be 9 by now and it's not even close.

Camille:
What a cool place to work! It sounds like Daktari or Born Free or something. Dr. Doolittle.

Funny, I never pictured you sitting underneath fluorescent lights resetting passwords, because your emails over the years were all about your animal rescues, the work you did in your yard and so on. All the stuff you did outside of work. What a treat it will be to do work that you are excited about and love!

You hit the mother lode of cheap food I guess. Isn't that great you can grab a cab for so cheap? I always keep 3 cedis in my purse in case I buy too much produce. Then I just stop walking and look like I need a ride and cabs come screeching to a halt.

Hah—I have not had a microwave for so many years I can't remember when. Oh, and the gas burners—they really can be scary. Ours has a habit of flaming on. Someone melted the plastic knob into a glob before we moved in, so if I want to use that burner I have to use a knob from one of the other burners. You absolutely cannot turn your back on this thing. Oh, and one day someone was making toast in the toaster oven, went into the dining room and the thing flamed on while they were out of the room! It's a little tricky, I tell ya!

Subject: Patience
On March 30, 2013 Steph wrote:

Hi! Well my house didn't go to closing yesterday. You can't imagine how pissed I am. The buyers claim that their renters trashed the house and they have to pay $20K to fix it! Then something about their job transfer, the list goes on and on. My realtor says it's not legit excuses and they will pay me $2K and the $1,200 but I'm not going to settle for that. Serious drag here. I can't relist it until this gets resolved. I still have to pay my mortgage in a house I'm not even living in. UGH!!

The effing rain is driving me nuts, not to mention sleeping on moist sheets isn't my idea of a good night. It gets dark at 5:30pm so I was in bed by 8, felt like 11...I wake up around 11 thinking it's morning.

I start work tomorrow since I know they need help. More later.

Camille:
What?!

Before we moved to Belize we considered keeping the house and renting it out. Well, the mortgage was so high we would never have been able to cover it with rental revenue. We simply couldn't ask that much for that place. Plus we would have had to hire a property management firm to oversee the situation. That would have cost $150 a month, plus the difference between what we could ask and what we had to pay the bank.

So we sold it and took the $40,000 loss. We'd only lived there a year. Bob said if we are going to lose an arm, better to cut it off at the shoulder than work on it one inch at a time.

Well, I hope you find some comfort in your new job and that the sale of your house irons itself out.

10
THE PRICE OF PARADISE

Subject: First day
On Apr 4, 2013 Steph wrote:

Well, it was my first day and as I was having fun with some baby monkeys, one promptly decided to pee on me. I was able to avoid the full effect of it by holding his tail out beside me, but still. Something I'll have to get used to, I guess!

It was a loooong, hot and physically demanding day. Started out cleaning the huge monkey enclosures which was disgusting, honestly (after breakfast, too). After that, which took about an hour and a half, I took food out to the other animals and was able to take a break before the tourists came in. They are here daily except Sunday. We need to have everything ready and presentable by the time the tours start. No exceptions! While the tourists are here, we get to spend time with the animals (if you're lucky enough) or you have to do the laundry, gardening or help in the kitchen. Thankfully I got to sloth sit, which sounds easy but when you have four or five babies who all want to crawl in separate directions, it's not.

Lunch is around 1pm and then we clean again and feed, then wrap it up

95

around 3ish. So each day is different as far as assignments, so that the work is split up evenly between everyone. Some work is easy, some isn't. Bad thing is by the time I got home, showered and prepped dinner the sun was almost down. This may not work for me.

Camille:
Ahhh, monkey pee on your first day. I hope you don't get used to THAT! Go-At likes to pee on his beard and eyebrows so he can rub his manly smell on Aponche and everything else that reminds him of romance. So I put a bar of soap outside in a mesh bag and hung it on the faucet so I can wash him off my hands before coming inside.

Well, the other day a bar of soap I had set down went missing and I didn't think too much of it until I saw Go-At licking the mesh bag. Guess he's gotten a taste for soap. Maybe it'll help him smell better. They say goats will eat anything.

Ha ha! Sloth sitting. You traded password setting for sloth chasing! You're right, I can't even envision chasing a sloth. I picture you moving in slow motion like the million dollar man. Or woman.

What can I say but hang in there. Especially since you're surrounded by sloths and monkeys. Heh heh...

Subject: Towels on the line
Apr 7, 2013 Steph wrote:

Hey woman...I still don't have Internet thru my laptop, hence my quiet lurking. I was wondering what the secret was to making towels soft when drying in the sun? If anyone knows, it's you! They're stiff as a board.

Doing okay here, work is hard and very physically demanding. I may ask to switch to four days a week...It's killing me, but I have to wait a bit first probably.

How are you doing over there? I'm about to buy some cacao pods! Yum, love those. Did a video but takes two plus hours to upload, so not doing it at this restaurant...will have to wait.

Camille:
I take the towel and ruffle it up between my hands and work my way all around the surface of the towel to soften it. One or two uses will achieve the same result. I downgraded to a smaller towel for just this reason. My underwear is crispy too. I do the same thing with them, sometimes as I am folding them. Crispy underwear takes some getting used to.

Hard work can be fun but too much is too much, so no amount of getting used to it is gonna help. It will just break you down.

Trust your instincts, but like you said, you may need to wait a little. If the work doesn't kill you! What do you get in compensation for all your work?

Steph:
The towel did get a little better after I used it...thanks for the tips. I get nothing in compensation so I'd better not be given a hard time about asking for four days a week! Jeez...experience and loving sloths and monkeys is what I get.

Camille:
O.K. then—they are taking advantage of you and I would not hesitate to tell them the truth—that this is simply too much for you. Who knows, perhaps after you adjust you can give more but you don't have to say that. Take care of yourself first. What happens if you wear yourself out and get sick? Who will take care of you then?

Steph:
True, that...I'll ask my friend Poo here...about to do a post on her birthday party last night.

Subject: Poo
On Apr 7, 2013 Camille wrote:

What fun seeing her dancing in the street with Doc Martens on! Poo doesn't have any hair!

Steph:
She shaves it off. Prefers it that way. She just loses a lot of weight here. Most all non-locals are really skinny. Hope not to get that way myself!

Camille:
Heh, heh—I lost a bunch of weight on Little Corn running my ass off. Skinny Minnie I was.

Much love; Bob and I were bragging about what you just did to our friends this evening. You are WAY cool!

Steph:
Ha ha, thanks. At least I don't feel guilty eating sweets at night anymore!

Crashed Out Creatures

By Steph

I got moved to the smaller sloth area, which was good and bad. It was so hot and the sun was shining right on their new structures. I stretched a blanket across it to shade the kids. I had a sloth around my waist in a blanket (sloths like to be warm, but seriously...it was brutal). Luckily Palma and Fernando were staying on the structure for once, eating, and so was Tyson, who would occasionally bite the babies arrrgghhhh...such aggression (hence how he got his name). Fernando has taken a liking to the rope we have strung across the area, cruising fast toward the caiman enclosure. And let me tell you, getting a sloth off of ANYTHING is a serious job, especially when you can't touch them. We can touch their claws, but they have a super grip. So my bright idea of just sliding him slowly back down the rope didn't work at all.

I forgot to mention something about the sloth. Since I wasn't allowed to touch Fernando, I had to pick him up with a blanket when I needed to get him off the ground. So I would put the blanket in front of him and he'd just climb onto it and then I could wrap him up and take him back to point A. After an hour or so, when I would do that, he'd avoid it like the plague! Amazing. He knew that the blanket meant getting off the ground, back to a place he didn't want to go. That didn't take long at all. So then I'd have to pick him up from the top, but then his little claws would cling onto the grass and it was hard to get him. Smart little dude.

Subject: Wedding
On Apr 18, 2013 Camille wrote:

Love your sloth post!

Our first Ghanaian wedding, billed as the Solemnization of Holy Matrimony, was anything but solemn: a long ear-splitting affair complete with karaoke, graphics, humor, dignitaries, Bible readings, microphone feedback, backup singers, a long sermon, cacophonic music, fabulous hats and a sermon delivered with rabid fervor.... It was the absolute worst wedding we've ever been to. Long, loud and, well, just painful. We left after three and a half hours with another hour and a half to go. Some of the music was fun, though, and I found myself dancing. The rest of it was hard to listen to because the musicians were not all on the same page. It often sounded like they were playing two or three different songs and their microphones were turned up so high they kept squealing with feedback.

Oh, and the preacher (bless his heart) or maybe it was the MC, took the opportunity to single us out as the only five white skinned people, even asking us to stand up so the other 400 people could get a good look. But you know what? I've been here long enough already that it didn't bother me. I'm the star in everyone's little story here just like in China. It's like being on TV whenever I leave the compound.

I hope no one peed on you today. Or took a bite out or pooped on your shoe.

Steph:
Wow, that wedding DOES sound bad...gave me a headache just reading about it! Well at least it's over. Weddings are never good unless they're yours I guess?

Subject: Fed up
On Apr 18, 2013 Steph wrote:

I will say the wildlife here is pretty cool. Just updated the blog page with some pics of a green basilisk that's in my yard at the moment.

I will go to three days a week after the 26th, thankfully. I decided to go ahead and ask for it before I ended up killing myself. It's nice to sloth sit when I can get it, but she pretty much makes you pay and then gives you a relaxing job, which is how it should be. But my body...omg...ouch. I'm getting a massage tomorrow which won't last me but a day or two I'm sure. They are expensive here but found one for $40 an hour so hopefully it's good. I refuse to pay more and the going rate seems to be $65. No thanks.

So I've decided not to come back to this area in July but look for a place In the Central Valley instead (possibly Arenal by the active volcano). I want some comfort and nicer weather. I'll pay a little more, but I think it'll make me happier. I can find something to do in the area for volunteer work I guess. I'd like to stay in the animal department but all this cleaning up after them isn't what I'm digging. There are lots of rivers, forests, coffee plantations, gardens, etc. in these towns, so I'm sure I'll find something. And even if I don't, that's fine too...not like I'm making any money. Although, if I give tours I could get tips. My Amazon biz is kind of ramping up with spring now, so that's bringing in something. I'll work on that more too so I can add other items. I just want to RELAX for once! And I want a CUSHION to sit on. I've resorted to bunching up a towel to sit on this plastic chair. I hate it. My feet are always swollen from sitting like this. Never get to go "inside" to hang out...getting eaten by bugs of all kinds daily. I just want a break, you know? Yes...you know.

Camille:
Good decision and always a difficult one to make. Seems life is made up of deciding whether to stay or leave, continue in the same way or change something.

I hope you find something that pays for your time. Volunteering is the perfect way to get there because you get the exposure and make connections.

Another Kumasi Monday. After Amy gets up we'll shop for produce. It'll be good to shop before the heat settles in like a hot iron, pressing down on everything.

We had an excellent night at Nik's pizza last night. Cook's night out. Sophie, a beautiful young lady we met on the bus to Cape Coast joined us. The synergy was palpable as we dove into deep conversation about cultural practices here in Ghana and how they affect health. She is studying jaundice in babies and making connections between the problem and the causes.

Sophie told us she has been in Kumasi for eight months and has not met any other expats outside of her work at the hospital!

 *Camille realized that she and Sophie shared the same conundrum (the running joke around here is if you want to meet other expats all you have to do is hang around the bus station) and decided to do something about it. So she created a Facebook group called Kumasi Expats which became a successful platform for expats to connect and share resources.*

This morning I listened to Michael Pollan's interview on NPR regarding his new book, "Cooked," and realize how our health in the U.S. is also affected by our culture. Interesting ideas to ponder while I sweep and mop.

Steph:
It finally stopped raining here and was sort of cold last night...first time I didn't have to use the fan. Hopefully it'll be the same tonight; it cleared up so we'll see. Was able to do laundry finally. Jeez...took advantage while I could and did lots. It was 90 degrees today and with all of that rain over the past few days, humid.

Also, I haven't been feeling good lately either. Stomach issues. I think I'm getting why all the people here are super skinny. I'm filtering my water, but I do go out and eat sometimes and I know restaurants probably don't. Plus, there's no hot water to wash dishes with (not sure it matters) so I may just be contaminating myself constantly. Either that or it's working around the animals (and feces) all day. I just don't feel like eating and my stomach is constantly churning. I'm waiting to see what happens with what I ate today. I've been tired and lethargic, too, so I don't know what that's all about. Have a headache, but it could be from looking at the computer too long. Simply didn't want to do anything today.

 *Apparently the filter Steph was using had become* .. *jointed from a plastic piece making it worthless, so more than likely it was due to drinking the water.*

I finally made tortillas yesterday! That was a pain. They're okay, better than store bought for sure. Not a popular item down here apparently. I made two batches, thinking I had learned from the first but I didn't. Now I know to make them bigger and to knead them longer I think. I didn't have any measuring cups so I just eyed it. They tasted fine, just small.

I had wanted to make picadillo with the ground beef I found yesterday, too, but wasn't up for more kitchen time so I did it this morning and THAT took forever. I only have a small six inch or so nonstick pan to do it in, hence the time spent. It actually came out decent and I had that for breakfast in my 'tilla. Plenty of leftovers so I froze some. Forced myself to eat a PB&J for lunch; just seriously not hungry at all. Might not even have dinner...don't really want to work tomorrow but I still have time to figure out if I'm going in or not.

My god, these people are putting on an addition to this house across from me, and the hammering and sawing and drilling are driving me crazy! SILENCIO POR FAVOR! It's always something, isn't it?

Camille:
Paradise always comes with a price. In Nicaragua the snorkeling was extraordinary but we pined for privacy. Here, depending on the day I either love it or have had enough. It's worse for Bob because he can't

take the heat like I can. The power goes on and off pretty much every day, as does the water. Seems to get worse and worse. We have decided to go home in December. For now at least. Until the next big job presents itself as a temptation to remain expatriated.

Steph:
Phew...I'm sort of glad to hear you're going home. You've been out there long enough it seems and you've worked your ass off! I'm worried about your foot/leg, that a clot might show up and get lodged somewhere. I wish you'd have it looked at soon.

I've always had a problem with swelling up. If I walk too much my fingers swell and I'm sure my feet too, just don't notice it. I don't know what that means, do you? I remember being in Mexico at a bar on a swing drinking and when we went to leave, I couldn't even get my shoes on my feet swelled up so much!

I'm still not feeling hungry. I didn't go into work. I'm just drained like never before. I bought some watermelon and pineapple and mangoes off the truck today so I made a watermelon drink trying to get some fluids and vitamins in me. I'm just SO not hungry. I'd love to treat myself to a nice dinner out tonight but hate to waste it (well, I'd bring the rest home). I guess I'd just hate to not enjoy it, so we'll see.

Have fun at the party and I hope you feel better soon.

11
THE WORMS CRAWL IN, THE WORMS CRAWL OUT

OUT ON a
BLOG ⎯⎯⎯⎯⎯⎯⎯⎯ LIMB

Daiquiri's Anyone?
By Steph

I haven't had any appetite for the past few days and I felt like I should force feed myself something tonight. All I could come up with that was appealing was half a peanut butter sandwich. Off to the dark kitchen (it's always a thrill to turn on the light). Grab the bread, peanut butter and tea out of the fridge, go back out to get my glass, rinse it out in the sink. Put everything on the counter and for some reason I look over at the blender only to find...HOLY CRAP! Now let me tell you, this is no ordinary blender...it's one of those huge glass ones so the spider may LOOK small, but I swear to you, I actually screamed when I saw it.

Now I like spiders, ok? But something about one on my blender, on my counter, right next to the sink I just visited REALLY left me with no appetite. Like I even had one to begin with. I look at the fixin's for my sandwich...I look at the spider. I contemplate even making this stupid thing or just turning out the light and abandoning all hope. I look up at the light and see a gecko taking all of this in. I know he's not coming down. Hell, he's probably just as terrified as I am. I'm not about to get a better look at this spider by turning the blender around. I just know he'll jump or run right toward me if I do. Note to self, wash blender in morning.

I did make my sandwich, though, and managed to eat it, but now I have to go back in the kitchen and put the dish in the sink. Or maybe I should just let the ants eat the crumbs. Cause if I go back in the kitchen and that spider is gone......uuuugggghhhhhhhhh.

Subject: Spider
On Apr 26, 2013 Camille wrote:

Yikes! Finding a huge spider in your blender would surely kill your appetite! Hmmm, I need me one of those. But seriously, I do hope you get your appetite back. I'm going back to bed and do my best to get some more sleep. I have no energy today which makes everything look scary and dire.

Steph:
How are you feeling? Any better? I did go out to eat last night and I was craving pizza so went out for lunch after I went to Playa Negra's hardware store to find...FOAM! And yes, they had it for my stupid hard bed, and only $25 for 3" thick stuff, too! I can't wait to get it. Now to wrangle someone into taking me there to pick it up. It's really not far. Some volunteers at JRC have a car so I may ask them tomorrow and buy them some drinks or something. The guy at the store did say they could deliver it but like an idiot I didn't ask for how much. But then he found out of course...they always have a way...that I'm not here with a guy: "Nobody wanted to come to the Caribbean with you?" So I don't really care to give him my address. Boy, they sure are forward here. So I will try to score that thing ASAP. Then I guess I can sell it before I leave.

I got some heartbreaking news when I went into work this morning. Little Fernando (the baby sloth) had passed away last night. This was very unexpected for a lot of us who had no idea he had been sick the past couple of days. I didn't get any details on what exactly happened, but they knew it wasn't going to be good. Luckily, I believe he was with Encar when it happened, so he wasn't alone. He was so sweet and always made everyone smile. The volunteers and tourists alike fell in love with him at first sight. He will be sorely missed. It was a difficult day.

I knew there would be bad days at the center. I guess I'm fortunate that it's taken this long for something to happen. I'm just glad that Fernando was saved when he lost his mom and that he was surrounded by people who loved and cared for him. I wonder how little Palma feels, since she spent every day with him. I didn't see her today, but had been taking care of her on the days it was raining. Poor kids.

I cried for quite a while and if I think about it I get misty all over again. Such a bummer. I really liked Fernando. Another baby sloth smaller than him came in the other day, but I haven't seen it since. Sucks to lose your mom like that. I hate it. These poor babies.

Steph with Pungulino the porcupine

A Fondness for Porcupines

by Steph

I decided the other day that I wanted to do some enrichment programs for some of the animals that are never let out of their cages. This means finding something to keep them occupied and entertained and changing those things so they don't get bored. I've always thought that I'd like to do that and it'd make me feel good to help animals in that way. I would have to research what they do in the wild and what other places have done in the past that have worked and also build the items that they would be utilizing.

I have a fondness for the porcupines. Nobody likes them in the same way as the sloths or monkeys and so they don't spend time with them. I've always been one to stand up for the rights of the spiky, toothy, not-so-cuddly creatures, and this sweet 'pine with the broken foot that didn't heal correctly was no exception. So yesterday I talked with the owner and she was all for it, as was Poo. I figured I'd start with the 'pines and spend some time in the cage with them (even with their bad smell!).

The little one, whose name I found out was Pungulino, came out and grabbed onto my finger really hard (wasn't sure if he was going to bite me or not) and then climbed onto my hand and arm. His little feet were cold, so I wondered if he just wanted the warmth. Anyway, I doubt many people would let a 'pine climb onto them without freaking out, but I did and we had a nice little bonding session. He climbed on my shoulder and sat there. Then he curled up into a little ball on my chest and fell asleep for a while. I really enjoyed the time I spent with him and had already looked up an easy enrichment game that I was going to bring in today to see how he liked it. I put him back by his house and said, "See ya tomorrow," and left the enclosure.

So needless to say, it was heartbreaking to see the owner taking him out of his enclosure this morning by the tail, dead. I immediately felt like I had done something yesterday, but I couldn't imagine what it could have been. I didn't feed him anything, I didn't take him outside. I wondered if maybe he had been sick and after finally getting some attention and love felt it was okay to let go. Kind of like people do when they're very ill. I feel horrible and responsible in some way. I know it's hard to understand being emotional over a porcupine but he was very sweet. I had so many plans for him to make him happier.

Camille:

So sorry to read about your sloth and porcupine. I also love the animals too much, which I realize is the big part of my problem with the goats and chickens at our place. They aren't our animals, so Bob and I don't get to decide how they are cared for, yet we end up cleaning up after them and, as regards Nwansane, watching her die in her owner's arms.

I can't help blaming myself for throwing kitchen scraps on the compost pile even though that was the approved goat-feeding protocol. We threw scraps and leftovers and the goats picked out and ate whatever they wanted. Even if it killed them.

We went to a great party this weekend at a beautiful place far outside of town and we're bringing pizza to Kat and Agye's tonight for dinner and trivial pursuit. Life seems normal when hanging out with people who speak English. Plus we are all "socialists" as we like to joke. Kat is making salad to go with the pizza.

Amy is at the lake, so there are only four of us in the house until summer intern Allison arrives May 15th. I've decided to transition out of my role as camp cook and the guys have already begun to shop and cook for themselves.

They butchered Nugget, the last rooster (at a friend's house), and cooked him on the charcoal grill last night. I never went upstairs. Didn't even want to smell it. But I agree with them that if they are going to eat meat, they should feel capable of killing and processing it.

Bob is over Ghana and was the happiest I've seen him lately after booking our flight home in December. We plan on spending five nights in Morocco. Maybe some camel riding!

Congratulations on your new bed. How much longer will you be at the reserve?

Steph:
Thanks for the kind words. I felt sick and left work early today...although I'm just overall still not feeling great. I was happy the other afternoon when hunger finally struck me after what felt like weeks. But it hasn't really come back again. My stomach feels bloated, I'm not hungry, and I'm tired and lightheaded. I at least try to make fruit drinks and keep somewhat hydrated. Noticed today my lips were dry and I was craving water. Not to mention it's 94 degrees today. At least there's a tiny breeze. I tried to sleep when I got home. Nope...wasn't gonna work. So I don't know.

I have a few tomatoes I need to process and got in the mood a few minutes ago, but now I don't have the desire or energy. I hate that kitchen. I hate this floor...I hate a lot of things about this house. I know how Bob feels...I'm counting down the days 'til I get back to the States and get some 'luxury'.

I'm glad you decided not to cook so much and that they're finally doing it themselves. Good for you! I noticed you had socks on with your sandals and cocked my head over it...'til I remembered about the swelling. How's it going?

Subject: Piece of cake
On May 8, 2013 Camille wrote:

Just got a text from my walking buddy, Manu, who makes cakes and she

111

says she can make me a chocolate cake with cherry cream today if I want. Do I want?! Perfect timing. Looking forward to diving into the second piece of cake I've had since arriving nearly a year ago.

Two amazing things: Manu's cake was springy and moist and I found local ice cream to go with it. Sophie and visiting friends Bep and Phil were here and we all ate too much stir fry and then too much cake and ice cream.

The second amazing thing is that all three are in the final stages of becoming doctors and Phil offered to take a look at my foot. From what he's saying (he hasn't looked yet) surgery is no big deal and the only way to fix the problem so I am pretty sure I will have it done by a surgeon at some point. No big deal. Heh heh.

When's the last time you had a team of future doctors in your kitchen chopping up vegetables for a stir fry?

Steph:
Wow, that's awesome he was able to look at your leg! Too bad he couldn't fix it on the spot as well. Drag. And no, never had a doctor anywhere in MY house!

The stupid burning of the brush finally drove me out of here, which is a good thing...I needed to get out anyway. So I was going to do the beach first and then the chocolate place but it was already noon and I was sorta hungry so had chocolate fondue for lunch! Ha ha...and a fresia batida (strawberry with milk and ice blended together) to go with it. It was good and around $6 with chocolate to take home (bought bananas at the store). Then I went back to Punta Uva again. I got in the semi shade under a palm frond and listened to music on my phone and got in the beautiful water a few times.

Stopped by the chocolate place again to pick up my leftover chocolate, buy a couple sticks of their hand rolled chocolate, a piece of cake and a brownie. Funny how I'm just not used to how "natural chocolate cake"

112

and brownies are supposed to taste. It tastes odd to me...it's not that over the top sugary sweet American style cake you know? But it's good all the same knowing it's REAL.

Then I went by my store to get green beans, red pepper flakes and a habanero so I can make my stir fry...although I can't guarantee that will happen tonight.

Funny you mention the cake. I had a dream last night I was delving into a homemade chocolate pie and the crust was to die for. I even resorted to buying "normal" chocolate icing (like the kind in the States) then looking for some kind of cake to put it on. They all suck here. Then I noticed my neighbor has an OVEN. I doubt I'll go through the trouble of making a cake, but I feel ya...and for me it's only been...well I did have a piece recently but it was horrible...two months plus.

Subject: Worms
On May 8, 2013 Steph wrote:

I've lost 15 pounds in five weeks. God, it seems like I've been here an eternity. Only five weeks? Talking to my neighbor...she says everyone has stomach problems here...even those who have been here a year now. She mentioned getting an anti-parasitic drug every six months at the pharmacia. Did you ever have to do that in Belize or Nicaragua or wherever else you lived? Did you ever KNOW if you had parasites for sure?

Camille:
The vet told us to deworm ourselves every three months because of the "environment." Our doctor friend in Ghana said they never deworm themselves, but if we were at all concerned we should take a stool sample to the doctor and they can tell right away if we have a problem. Amy investigated natural dewormers and found pawpaw (shit, now I can't remember the English word—oh yeah, papaya) seeds were good, as were ginger and garlic. Anyhow, we use ginger and garlic in pretty

much every meal (coincidentally, or not, they are the underpinnings of the local cuisine) and she came up with a fruit smoothie recipe using the seeds and flesh of the papaya (not skin.)

Chad left his goats out yesterday and only one returned. The buck went looking for poontang.

It is so much quieter without the roosters and it smells better already without that stinky goat. I miss him. That's part of the problem. I get too attached. I try not to think about them eating Nugget, roasting him on the charcoal grill upstairs. Wondering what they did with his bones.

Steph:
Jeez, someone might make a meal of that goat if it's not found, huh?

I do know about the papaya seed thing, but I had also read about someone who took them and it didn't work at all. I'll just grab those pills on my way outta here and see what happens. I was hungry this morning so that's good. Thanks for all the info. I eat garlic and ginger as well.

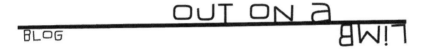

BLOG

Burger in Paradise
by Steph

I was finally feeling hungry the other day so I decided to go down to Playa Negra and visit The Point restaurant, which is an "American Sports Bar." Not what I'm into personally but they allegedly have great burgers and I hadn't had one since I left Texas. Plus I wanted to be on the beach, near a bar and people just to be safe...so this was perfect. I ordered a coke and sat down. Unfortunately I felt like I WAS in the U.S. due to the number of Americans there. I didn't acknowledge anyone...really wasn't crazy about getting into a conversation and of course you can't help but overhear what people are saying. I don't know what it is about

Americans and why they think it's okay to drop F bombs all the time, with other people around at a restaurant. God, it was annoying. I almost couldn't wait to leave. It's like they think since they're in a different country, it's okay to forget their manners. I can see why foreigners have a negative view of us. It was guys like this one.

The burger came out and looked great. I had a feeling there was no way I'd be able to eat it all though. Overall, it wasn't too bad. A little dry. At least the fries were homemade, albeit a little tough. Bacon was a nice touch. I don't get bacon around here. It will satisfy my craving for a while. The burger and fries (which came with it) cost about $10.50. Ugh.

As I sat there listening to the mind numbing babble coming out of this guy's mouth, I couldn't help but notice the magnificent almond trees in front of and over me. We feed those leaves to the two toed sloths. The almonds have an almost neon green pod, and they contrast beautifully on the black sand beach as they wash ashore.

Camille:

I liked your latest blog. Stupid Americans. We find ourselves pining for lights on and water always flowing from the tap and garbage pick-up, but when I get "home" and smell a fire I get all nostalgic for the developing world. I guess were never satisfied.

Why do they call it developing anyway? At least in the case of Africa, this world is knackered, beat down and nearly finished. I wouldn't call it developing unless you mean developing a case of worms or dysentery.

12
UNRAVELING

Subject: Unraveling
On May 9, 2013 Camille wrote:

Re: developing. This subject gives me no end of food for thought. What I see here in Africa is a post-colonial unraveling. Bob lived here 40 years ago when there were still timely British trains running on well-kept tracks with beautifully appointed dining cars. Crystal, china, linen, etc. And he flew on Ghana Airways.

Now the tracks are littered with vendors, and the trains a distant memory. Everything is shipped in by truck. Foreign companies have stepped in to run the airways. Ditto for the shops, hotels, etc.

The inevitable conclusion is that the Ghanaians are unable to step up to the plate, unable to fill the shoes formerly filled by their British lords, unable to join the developed world. Perhaps unwilling, but I don't get that sense. All the Ghanaians I meet are upset that the power, water, trash and roads don't work.

The problem lies at the top. Corruption is a way of life. Cops stop everyone and hold them until they hand over 2 to 20 cedis, depending on the condition of their car.

Once a Ghanaian makes it to the top, he stops working. Public officials build lavish homes. The kings or chiefs live in palaces and sit on stools. Or lately, plastic chairs. Their villagers cook, sit and sleep on the ground. The chiefs are elevated. They get to order others around. They don't have to DO anything. They are at the top, where everyone wants to be.

In a sense, the U.S. is the same. Poor white folk hang onto the status quo, smoking cigarettes in the single-wides they've mortgaged for four times their value, playing the lottery and hoping to make it big one day. To buck the system would dash their hopes of rising to the top. As long as they support the pyramid model, they have a chance, so they continue voting against their best interests—against national healthcare, welfare, public education. For corporate rights, low taxes for the rich and a strong military to protect our "freedoms." The freedom to take resources from other more disadvantaged countries. The freedom to enlist, and so receive a free education if you survive your tour of duty. It's all a gamble.

Religion ties neatly into my hypothesis. People believe in God hoping that this is their ticket to heaven, a better life. If you don't believe, you don't even have a chance. But if you do, well, that is all you need. You don't actually have to be NICE to your neighbors. In fact, religion gives you permission to hate them for their abortions, sodomy and other social abominations. As Bob points out, religion is a form of Cargo Cult culture in which if you do the right thing, you will get something for nothing. Praise the lord. Much to chew on. What do you think?

Steph:
Yes, definitely a lot to chew on there. I like your observations and how you can put it into words...quite fascinating actually. I'm glad I can be your springboard for these thoughts. You should write for a magazine or something.

Hey, what are your experiences with cutting bananas from trees? These suckers are taking FOREVER to grow, much less ripen. I read if you cut them down they do ripen faster. I have just cut one off so far to test that, but it still seems too young to even cut down just yet. You know more about the triangle banana at this point. How long do those things take to get mature and when do you cut them down? When they finally start turning round?

I guess you saw the CR listing in Caretaker's yesterday (today?). I'm coming back July 11th after my border run and he wants someone for the 9th. Plus it sounds like it's even farther off the beaten path than I already am. Not sure I'm up for that again so soon. Might want to try civilization before stressing myself out any more. Sounded kinda cool though. Too bad there wasn't more info.

Camille:
I always waited until the bananas were getting round to cut them and then let them turn yellow after cutting. In NC we put the green bananas in a brown paper bag with a slice of apple because that was supposed to speed things up.

How are you feeling these days? Sounds like you got your appetite back. We both got a serious stomach bug several weeks into our new adventure and solved it with three days of Cipro. Pains, nausea, diarrhea. Bob heard that it takes seven years, your body to learn how to fight the microbes in a new environment. So, as much as I dislike taking antibiotics, Cipro is my new best friend. I've taken it at least three times this past year.

Steph:
Oh, jeez...you may want to curb your enthusiasm for Cipro. That stuff is baaaaad news. Mom just sent me some stuff on it. I'll find it and forward to you. I looked into it as well when I got some to take to Guyana and wasn't thrilled with the stories I was reading about it, but took it anyway since I hadn't taken any in many years. I don't want to

take it again unless there is absolutely no alternative. I may have to go to the doctor soon. Was going to go today but nobody answered the phone. I'm very tired.

Subject: Mother's Day in C.A.
On May 13, 2013 Steph wrote:

Happy non-mother's day! My mom's in Wales at the moment. How's your mom doing? I haven't heard you mention her lately. You know Mother's Day is a pretty big deal down in C.A., but it rained today so nobody was at the beach. Unlike the U.S. I didn't smell any bbq or sense any kind of celebration here. Odd, huh? It rained so hard last night, I couldn't even sleep. You know how the sound of rain on a metal roof is. Sometimes it's nice to fall asleep to; other times you wonder where it will start leaking.

Riding my bike to work in the rain isn't a ton of fun either. Luckily my shorts are those quick dry kind, but my face always gets battered and wet. Rain jacket is a definite necessity here.

Camille:
Happy non-mother's day to you too! That's cool your mother is in Wales. My mom is doing just fine. Loving her life. We talk on the phone every Tuesday and I am typing her stories into Word for posterity.

Change is in the wind at Casa Kumasi, with a new person moving into the house on Thursday and possibly two more. Bob is actually fixing up the Boy's Quarters under the house for two inhabitants. Those rooms are nasty, a bit like Elmina Castle (the slave castle) smelling of pee and mildew and with iffy plumbing. They may have to use our bathrooms and certainly share our kitchens.

Amy is going home soon. :(The three of us are going to Accra for three days on June 9 to see her to the airport. Where are you going and when?

119

Steph:

Eeew, your basement doesn't sound too appealing. Those aren't things you would see in a listing for a rental is it? Wonder if they know what they're in for. Do you know these people?

I'll be off to Virginia June 18 until July 7, then to Houston, then back here.

Subject: Army ants
On May 18, Steph wrote:

I had to make a stiff drink before writing this one out. I have only ever read about this or seen documentaries describing what just happened.

Two words: army ants. After it stopped raining, I went out to grab my $6 cocoa powder for a recipe I was going to make. I came back and noticed about 20 very large black ants on the verandah in the corner. Hmm, okay. I got the broom and swept them off, knowing full well this is only part of the story. I look down and it's like watching water in a stream. There are (tens of?) thousands of these ants (oh, and of course they're NOT small) swarming all over the ground and going in different directions. Some toward my neighbor's yard, some toward the front of the house and some toward the back.

Oh, this can't be good. I carefully walk around to see where they're coming from and it appears it's from beneath the cinderblock under the house. And I mean POURING out of it. Then some start coming up at the other post. I sweep and spray around that post too. Then I start seeing geckos and lizards climb up on my porch. Another bad sign. I look down to see ants almost everywhere. It reminds me of the story I heard about in Guyana where someone was sleeping then felt they were getting attacked by ants. They went out of the cabin, turned on the light and found these ants marching through...devouring every living and dead thing in sight. They waited it out, because honestly, what else can you do? They said it was cleaner after they left than it was before they were there. These ants are also used in the bush for sutures to hold wounds together. They make the ant clamp on then cut it off at the neck...holds the skin in place and heals quite nicely. Obviously you have to do this quite a few times depending on the size of the gash.

Speaking of that, I attempted to get pictures of these guys and TRIED to watch where I was stepping but one bit my foot. Let me tell you, it does not feel good and it's still burning slightly. So I text my landlord because I'm confident she will know what's going on here...and my assumptions were correct. She said, "Yes. These are the cleaning ants. Don't sweep, don't touch. Just leave them go through. They leave as they come. Leave the house and come back in two hours. They will have gone. I had them yesterday at my house."

I got nervous when I saw them starting to climb up onto the roof and I could even see them up there through the clear plastic sheeting. They are still climbing up the post and along the gutter. I'm just hoping they sort of forget about the interior of the house and stick to the outside of it instead. ESPECIALLY since it's about to get dark in an hour.

So, life in the jungle...It's always SOMETHING!

Camille:
Ahh, yes—army ants. We had them in Belize but they weren't as big as the ones you had. We also had the suture ants. But both features in one ant, yikes! Glad you survived! Now I know why my mother was so worked up about them when she visited Costa Rica.

Ours DID come in the middle of the night. We woke up, of course, and noticed the cat was dancing from one foot to the next. When we realized what was happening—the place was crawling with ants—we grabbed our pillows and the cat and fled to one of the cabanas and settled in for the rest of the night.

In the morning they were all gone with the exception of a few who had gotten confused. Round and round they went on a bucket lid, somehow

121

unable to figure out how to get off the bucket. They ate all the bad things in the house—cockroach and scorpion parts were strewn here and there. We were pretty happy about that.

One evening Rolando saw the army ants coming towards the cantina and we had guests, so he and Bob took flour and made a big circle around the cantina and rooms that the ants would not cross. I was skeptical but it worked.

All is well here. Bob had a bunch of my favorite things shipped down with a visitor from the States this week—Belizean hot sauce, Dove chocolate, nutritional yeast and raw almonds. Yum! Guess he knows the way to my heart.

Steph:
Marie Sharp's habanero hot sauce. Yep, I miss that too. I had a huge bottle that wasn't even opened that I had to leave behind in Texas, killed me.

It rained like crazy again last night and the mozzies are now relentless. I can't wait to move.

Speaking of moving, the lady that's buying my house is supposedly moving in today to rent it until closing on the 10th. Goddamn, this better work out. At least I'll be getting paid I suppose.

Camille:
I walked nearly four hours today and I'm tired out. Walked 40 minutes to the Golden Tulip and back to hang out with Elisabeth, Kat's good friend who is Austrian and also married to a Ghanaian. Then I met a new Obruni, an Australian, who will be here for a year, and showed her some of my favorite Ahodwo shops. We walked for an hour and a half and then I walked home while she caught a tro.

Bob is getting the rest he deserves after working so hard to coordinate and facilitate two days of project meetings, which culminated in dinner for 22 of us on Tuesday evening. The weeks leading up to this have been hectic for him. Poor guy.

We have a new housemate. A kid without much common sense. Plays on his computer all day. Didn't know what to do when the power went out. Knows how to cook nothing much. Eats out and lives on ramen. He's only 22. Bob and I are showing restraint. We feel like we should be helping him more than we are, but know we haven't the patience.

Other than that, life is chill. A thunderstorm is rolling in. As per usual, I'm writing before heading to bed. Pleasant dreams!

Steph:
God, I wish the mozzies would stop biting. It's driving me nuts!

Oh, I saw my first snake since I've been here in my yard today! Cute green guy with beautiful big eyes.

Well your new roomie sounds just greaaaaaaat. Why is he there? Yeah, kids that age are pretty helpless. Hard to imagine we were that age once, huh!?

God, it's hot today and I'm in long pants so I won't get eaten up so much. I need a breeeeze!

Subject: Margarita Road
On May 26, 2013 Steph wrote:

I FINALLY decided to walk up Margarita Road, which is right across the street from me, to see what was going on there. It's the jungle side of the road. I saw this pretty German shepherd walking toward me, and she greeted me and started walking with me. It sort of seemed like she wasn't a stray...looked fed and all but had no collar. So we walked and walked and then it looked like it was going to rain so we turned around. She had been panting and I figured I'd get her some fresh water when WE got home. Oh boy...I kind of knew what might happen here. She drank out of a puddle and that made me feel bad.

I got her some fresh water and she gulped it down. Then like an IDIOT I got her a small piece of chicken. Yep...I'm pretty sure that's what sealed my fate. I walk her to the gate, she leaves, and before I can get back to my verandah, she's back. Got in through my dumb bushes. Ugh. I've walked her out twice now and she keeps coming back.

So I take her out again. She sees a dog across the street, barks and runs after it. I turn to walk back then hear a car laying on its horn and I just cringe. I was pretty sure she wasn't hit and that was confirmed when she came back into my yard. I was happy she was okay, but my GOD...I can't get RID OF HER! She's a good girl, no doubt. But I really don't want her here. I guess I should see where she's getting in through the bushes and try to block it off. I don't know if she has pups somewhere because she looks like she's nursing. You'd think she'd need to tend to that at some point. I'm trying to ignore her, but her big brown eyes keep watching me from the yard.

Camille:
Oh, geez, that's all you need is a dog. I'm glad she didn't get hit.

My latest passion involves walking too. I've been using Google Mapmaker to add street names to the map of our neighborhood. I tell you, it doesn't take much to tickle our fancies, does it?

Subject: Earthquake
On May 27, 2013 Steph wrote:

Well, THAT was certainly an interesting evening. I was in bed, dreaming, until I was jolted awake by what felt like my bed balancing on the top of a huge bowl of jello. It felt like some giant had reached into the refrigerator that was my bedroom and shook the bowl back and forth to see if it had set up yet.

Something started banging on my roof then something fell off of the ledge next to my bed and then I knew immediately what was going on. Ironically, I had JUST been reading a guy's blog that night about his time in PV and he described going through his first earthquake, too. Clock said 3:43am. The dogs started barking, the howler monkeys started yelling and the shaking stopped.

Once I had my wits about me, I knew I should probably go outside. Then I was worried about the huge trees and electrical poles and determined I was somehow safer in the doorway of my bedroom. I stood there a while and nothing else happened. Boy, I've never felt anything like that before. It was somewhat terrifying. It's almost indescribable how the bed just felt like it was floating on water...the legs of it knocking against the floor...I seriously felt like Linda Blair in the Exorcist for a fleeting moment. The howlers would NOT calm down for a long time.

So I go back into bed. I stay awake thinking about what just happened. Then I realized that I'm about a foot above sea level and the beach is one minute away. I got on the Internet to make sure there were no alerts out. I highly doubted there were any warning systems here unless the police go around with a loudspeaker, and by that time it could be too late. I figured I could hightail it up Margarita Road (probably run into the dog again) if I needed to get to higher ground.

So I type in (as I had just done the day before) "earthquake costa rica" and in big red bold letters on the first page, it read: "5.6 magnitude earthquake 12 km SSW of Guabito, Panama." I click on the link and see that it's very close to where I live. Obviously it took a while to get back to sleep. Soooo, that was a little freaky!

 ***They tore that house down to build a new one after Steph left.***

Camille:
Wow! Never a dull moment in your life, is there? What's next I can't

125

imagine!

Ha hah—you had a Linda Blair moment! I've felt tremors before but nothing quite like what happened to you. I'm glad the house didn't fall down.

This is hard to believe, but we have been in Kumasi for one whole year. I've learned a lot during this year. Here are a few of the things I've learned:

White towels are a bad idea.

When someone laughs, it doesn't always mean 'Ha ha" but rather "Tee hee, I've let you down, but won't do anything different next time."

If you say hello to people on the street, know that one out of five will respond by asking you for money.

When the next door neighbors light a truck tire on fire, they are fixin' to butcher another one of their dogs.

You can get used to the feel of an ant crawling up the nape of your neck and resist flicking it off while carrying a hot pot.

You may never get used to watching someone pick their nose in the middle of your conversation.

Always do a load of laundry when both the power and water are on.

13
BIRTHDAYS ABROAD

Subject: A tip!
On May 28, 2013 Steph wrote:

I got a $20 tip at work today! Couldn't believe it. NEVER been tipped before. Some girl from NY had come back again today to hang out with the sloths, which is what I was doing and we talked for a few hours...It was nice...then she reached into her bag and gave me money! That was super nice of her.

Sweet dreams!

Camille:
Congrats on the tip. I hope you don't spend it all in one place.

It was only 69 degrees this morning and at 8:15 has only climbed to 76. My hair is down. The fan is off and I'm not sweating. Perfect time to do some yoga!

We plan on hosting movie night down here this evening, and Sophie is coming over to help make spaghetti sauce.

Can you watch movies down there in the hinterlands? We pay dearly for

Internet, which Bob uses to download movies, then we project them onto the wall. It's great fun! We've been eating dinner and watching the Simpsons.

I do miss playing cards after dinner but we plan on doing that on Saturday, the day before Justin leaves us for good. I'm going to be sad to watch him go. He is such a pleaser and always pitching in.

I must say Allison is very much like Justin; she is very self-sufficient, shops for herself, cooks, works out and is always pleasant. Our other new arrival is pretty helpless, but Bob and I decided not to keep rescuing him after a couple of days in which we realized he does not listen to anything we tell him.

Subject: The skinny
On May 29, 2013 Steph wrote:

Just real quick because the gardener is on the way, here is a pic of me recently so let me know what you think!

Camille:
Well, you look thin but not too thin. Not haggard. Your ribs aren't sticking out yet and your arms still have some meat on them. You look athletic and beautiful (as always.)

Steph:
Well, thanks. It bothers me that I can SEE my ribs through my chest though...but not much I can do about that. Eat more ice cream sandwiches! I DO like those.

I treated myself to breakfast out after getting the RIGHT inner tube for my bike (which I also successfully put on and didn't take an hour and a half!). I had coffee, juice, fruit and pancakes and the friggin' bill was $8 (4 colones), I had 5 colones on me but she couldn't find change! So she ended up giving me back 2 colones instead! Ha ha...now that's more like it! At least they're honest here. I gave her almost a $2 tip anyway so I guess it kind of evened out.

I have a feeling I'm going to get hit with rocks by this guy's weed whacker soon. I'd better go....talk later.

Subject: Movie nite
On May 29, 2013 Camille wrote:

Sophie came at 4ish and she, Allison and I made salad and sauce. Bob and Justin made fish on the charcoal grill in aluminum foil packets. Chad made pasta. Allison makes a mean salad dressing.

We ate and watched the second half of "Lincoln," washed the dishes, made up a bed for Sophie and we went upstairs to eat chocolate and play six hands of Big Two, the card game Justin taught us.

After Bob and I went to bed, the younger folk played some more cards. It was so nice and family-like with everyone working together and then relaxing around the dining room table. It was just like we used to do at my Nana's after Sunday dinner when the neighbors would come over and we'd all play pick up sticks.

So, no complaints tonight. I hope to get a glimpse of your book soon. Very cool that you are writing one. I wonder if we took all your emails together could it be a book? Your stories of rescuing birds and lizards, dealing with co-workers, etc. And your photos - will your book have photos? It really should. Or else you should make a coffee table book. You could call it "lizard lips."

Steph:
Lizard lips...that's cute. Good idea, though. I love coffee table books! Yes, we could totally borrow from emails and blog entries to help write my book. I am just rambling in it now, not quite sure the point I want to make and not sure what to emphasize and what not to.

Oh, you had asked me if I watch movies. When I have the patience and remember to do it, I do. I had copied a bunch to my laptop but most of them didn't work. If I stream, it has to be early Sunday morning and I'm not exactly in the mood for a movie then. Maybe my connection will be better in Arenal too.

I did make more sangria. The lady that sells stuff on the side of the road was out there today. I noticed she had the water apples, which I needed. I had stopped buying from her because I didn't think she was very nice to me. I would always say hi, would buy things from her but she would just look at me as if I didn't say anything to her. Not even a smile. She seems like an angry person to me.

But today was different. She was chatty but she speaks fast so it's hard for me to understand her. I had my hair down for once and she asked if I colored it and seemed surprised when I said no. I bent down for her to see all the gray hair on top. She asked my age and told me hers (she's actually only 41 but looks older than I do). She talked about the fresh pineapples she had and said they were very sweet and yellow. The stalks were still attached to the bottoms of some and they looked really good, so I bought one for the sangria, although I already had some in the freezer. I also got one water apple and one avocado that's hard as a rock. It was under $4 for all of it. Not great, not bad. The pineapple WAS out of this world though, unlike any I've even had here before. They were shaped differently too...more of a conehead look than uniformly rounded. A different light yellow and sweet beyond belief. So the sangria was good even though it hadn't sat for long. I used merlot this time.

Wow, almost 9...I should crawl into bed and rest my hands. My hand has started killing me from typing on this laptop though...very annoying and won't go away...my left hand. I may end up getting a real keyboard and mouse in the U.S. to avoid this.

Camille:
We have a similar pineapple here, tapered, white fleshed and sweet. Interestingly, they are ripe when green. They call them Cape Coast Pineapples because they come from Cape Coast.

That is a real problem with your hands. Do you think it's arthritis? Sucks getting old. What do you have planned for your birthday next week?

Steph:
Re: my hands...It's from being on this stupid laptop too much. They get stuck in odd positions that my muscles aren't used to, so it stresses out little ligaments that take forever to heal. I'm sure it's what arthritis must feel like, especially in the morning. I can feel it in my left elbow and even pinpoint the muscle that is sore.

For my b-day I think I'll go to this Italian place for dinner that's supposed to be really good, albeit expensive. It's okay, right down the street within walking distance and apparently it's a must-do while here. They say it's probably the best in all of CR. We'll see. Then I really should do a snorkeling trip. I have a feeling I'll be underwhelmed, considering I use Belize as my baseline.

131

Well now you're going to laugh. For the two and a half months I've complained about not having a fan out on the verandah, I realized I can take the one in my room off the wall, which I finally did this morning, and now it's blowing on my back. Ugh...what an idiot. They even have a bracket to hang it from on the other side of the porch but I'll keep it on my back instead. Stupid, STUPID me.

Subject: Coati
On Jun 2, 2013 Steph wrote:

Baby coati...look at the nose on that girl! She's adorable and so small.

Camille:
Cute! Bob is whisking Amy and me off to the lake today to celebrate my birthday. We'll stay with Elodie and Kojo at the Green Ranch and go riding tomorrow. He said the plan is for me not to have to do any work on my birthday. He is so sweet. Just wants me to be happy. Tall order, I know.

We return Wednesday. I'm bringing my journal, sketch pad and Kindle but not my computer. Just started reading "Gulp"—an interesting and well written trip down the alimentary canal. What are you reading these days?

Steph:
God, I meant to ask which day it was...your b-day was on my work calendar and I didn't transfer it over to my personal email. I was thinking it was the 8th, but I'm sure I'm off. Well you won't get this anyway, I don't think, until you come back, so happy birthday. Glad you will get away from the house and enjoy yourself! That was nice of Bob to suggest it.

I've carted this book around with me for ages and just can't get into it. It's about some woman who relocated to Mexico by herself and I did want to read it but keep putting it off for some reason. I think I'm a little too ADD to read sometimes.

I'm completely stopped up from whatever blew in the other day and I can feel it working its way down into my throat. My eyes are puffy and nose is stopped up. I can't ever get a break.

Well again, happy birthday! They just seem to come faster each year huh?

Love you!

Subject: Birthdays
On Jun 6, 2013 Camille wrote:

Ha hah. You can't read because you're starring in your own story right now. Seriously, when we first moved to Nicaragua I tried to re-read one of my favorite books, "One Hundred Years of Solitude," and my brain refused to get into it. A couple of months later after we were all settled in and used to our new job, I picked it up again and devoured it like a box of fudge.

My birthday at the lake on the 4th was perfect! Well, as near to perfect as you can get in Ghana, anyway. The Taxi broke on the way into Elodie's, so there was some waiting around while the guys crawled underneath the car. But once we got there everything was great. Elodie has become family and we had Amy there, too. After spending a month at the Ranch, Amy and Elodie are as close as mother and daughter.

Camille's 59th birthday with Elodie and Amy at The Green Ranch on Lake Bosumtwi

And then there are the horses. I was thrilled to ride Quasar who was so grown up and sensible it surprised me. When I first met this beautiful mare while horse 'shopping' with Elodie, I found her immature and a bit spoiled. But Elodie saw her potential and took her home and started her under saddle.

Elodie really has a gift with animals and people alike. Quasar was a joy to ride and the meals were great and all that special time sitting on the deck. Truly a great getaway. It was so nice of Bob to whisk us away to paradise for a few days!

Steph:
Well, my neighbor was nice enough to have some friends of ours go to dinner with us for my birthday at a highly rated restaurant. There were five of us and we had a good time. Then we went to the bar where Poo was having her going away party, so basically one of the more exciting birthdays I've had in a while. Nice to be able to celebrate like that, even though I usually am out of the country for my birthday. This one was a little different...not a 'vacation', right?

Oh, and after all this time, my house finally closes in a couple of days. THAT was ridiculous.

Steph's 43rd birthday

Camille:
Well, that's a heck of a birthday present, your house selling. How nice you got to go out and feel special. Guess we're both having a good

birthday year.

Turned out I went to the zoo on your birthday. I'd been wanting to go and Sophie volunteered to go with me, and then Chad and Allison ended up coming with us too. It was much nicer than I expected and we all had a good time. Got some hysterical pictures, too!

Steph:
Well, I'm in the final days of being here, which feels strange. It's only been three months but feels like five. I've been going to the beach almost every day because I know I'm going to look back wondering why I didn't.

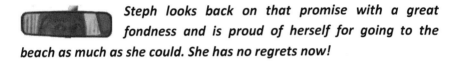 ***Steph looks back on that promise with a great fondness and is proud of herself for going to the beach as much as she could. She has no regrets now!***

Anyway, I'll go to VA for a while and then come back down here to live near Arenal Lake (and volcano). I've lined up a house there on a month to month (smart this time) to see what's going on. I'm looking forward to it. Should be nicer than this one (which shouldn't be difficult, honestly).

How are things going over there? Any new drama with housemates or locals? Ha ha!

Subject: Home call
On June 21, 2013 Camille wrote:

Oh my god, you would never guess the half of it! One of our housemates nearly died of heat stroke! Seriously, this was way over the top. When I called for an ambulance, they hung up on me. Then I went running around the neighborhood looking for a doctor while Bob and Allison packed ice cubes into his armpits. Finally they were able to get him up and into a taxi, took him to a hospital, where they ignored him completely. The good news is, he lived. But I never want to go through something like this again!

Are you back in the old US of A yet?

 ***When someone meets their maker in Ghana, they call their
death a "home call" as in God has called them home.***

Steph:
Unbelievable...that's an amazing story. Wow it's like something out of
a movie! Crazy what happens when you leave the States, isn't it? That
would never happen there. God, I hope he ends up being okay in the
long run. You'll have to let me know.

Well, being back in the States is weird. I got a little stressed in the
shuttle from one side of the airport to the other crammed with people
and children behaving badly. I'm gaining weight as I write though...Mom
is feeding me well and I'm indulging in junk food like never before.
You'd think I was gone for years.

Something amazing happened! You know, I joined that house sitting site
about a month ago. I was just complaining that nothing was coming up
and it was a waste of money. Well, I got an email from someone
yesterday asking if I'd be willing to sit their house in CR for FIVE
MONTHS!? It's in Turrialba near a volcano, situated in the mountains
and in a dairy farming community. So we Skyped and I'm pretty sure I'm
'in'! Wow, right? It looks like a really nice house with a huge yard, plus a
large outdoor covered area with a grill, bar and a couple of small fish
ponds. I totally can't wait. I wish you could come out there, but alas...

Camille:
How lovely to be back at your Mom's with your appetite back. I hope
she wasn't too shocked at your skinny self. Congrats on the house sit.
Don't tempt me. Seriously...

14
FOOD, FEAR AND FUN

 Steph lives in a rental for one month in Tronadora, Costa Rica, before going to the five month house sit in Turrialba.

Subject: Arenal house
On Jul 11, 2013 Steph wrote:

Rental house on Lake Arenal, Tronadora, Costa Rica

I had a good workout going into town today. Walked for about three hours. It didn't take long to GET to town, but it did take time to go up and down that hill each way. The town itself is pretty flat. I wanted to have pizza but the place wasn't open. I did find the bakery, though, and got a beautiful big cinnamon loaf for about $2.50 and a good ham and cheese roll for a dollar. I made my way around the tiny town to find some "forest" that ICE owns (the electric company here, pronounced 'E-say') and saw tons of saplings. I thought it might be that place that planted the trees. I asked if they needed volunteers and she said no, so I guess it's not the same. I saw there's a butterfly farm, too, but I'll save that for another day.

So I finally go to relax outside tonight and sure enough there was a troop of howler monkeys right in front of the house! Took lots of pictures, but only a few came out. Then I talked to my neighbor, who showed me the sloth that lives in his tree...a cute two toed who was sleeping in the mandarin tree.

Oh, so I'm in bed last night and right as I was falling asleep the bed shook. Not as bad as last time, but that's an unmistakable feeling. I wonder how many tremors happen - I just don't feel them while standing. It'll be interesting to see if it happens again tonight.

I'm kind of digging the weather, even though it rains without much warning. But it does pass quickly because of the high winds here. I haven't broken a sweat just sitting around yet. Even this afternoon was pleasant, although I did sweat a little due to all of the walking and wearing a backpack.

Tomorrow I'll walk the other way and see how far I can get and what I can see. This is horse country and a great way of getting around. I've seen a lot of guys on horses and a very cute guy walking in town ;-) ha ha...of course I said hello.

Camille:
Thanks for sharing the photos. How very cool that you have howlers so close to your house! I'm glad you like your new home.

Tremors—I was feeling something like that for two days in a row but it felt more like blasting than tremors. Hope the top doesn't blow off that old volcano while you are there!

I really liked this line from your post: "Clouds hung low and heavy, tripping over the tops of the mountains along the way."

Did you make your chicken dish? We're going out for pizza tonight and several other expats are going to join us.

Hope you are having a fabulous day.

Steph:
Yes, I made chicken & rice but with no lid...I had to use a muffin pan to partially cover it and that didn't work too well...had some crunchy bits in there. I did make a great peach cobbler last night though! I wanted to eat the whole damn thing after it came out of the oven.

Today I'll take a walk to a place I haven't been to before. There should be some nice views of the lake, and maybe if I'm lucky I will find a path down to it, although I doubt it. It looks steep so I may be out of luck. Ironically enough, there are leveled lots in back of my house (I climb through the barbed wire) and there are nice views of the lake without the electric lines in the way. I might just have a picnic up there one day! I will take my stuff today to lay under a tree just in case. It's a beautiful day!

Subject: Paddle boarding
On Jul 16, 2013 Steph wrote:

Well, I met a guy yesterday who gave me a ride back from the marina, and he asked if wanted to paddleboard with him today...he's taking lessons. It was weird, I thought he was an expat...blond hair and blue eyes but he's a Tico. So weird to think you can have someone who looks like that, but I guess it's the Spanish/European influence. My two great uncles were blond also. I'm trying to get the scoop on him from my landlord, who says she does know him. I've asked if he's okay to hang out with. He seems nice, but don't they all? She says she thinks so, he's done a lot of work for expats here, so he must be trustworthy. He's sitting a very nice house down the street from me.

So I guess I should text him and see what's up...will let you know!

Camille:
I'm glad you have an opportunity to enjoy male companionship, and it sounds like he can be trusted if he's done a lot of work for expats. I cannot picture a blond haired, blue-eyed Tico and was unable to locate any photos, but apparently it isn't that unusual given their mixed European and Indian ancestry. Our Ecuadorian summer intern has brown hair and blue eyes and cannot tell us what her ancestry looks like, as no one seems to know.

Steph:
So yesterday...we go to the lake for Joel's wakeboard lesson and thankfully I get to go on the boat for free! It was just us and the instructor, who is Dutch and has been here for about five years now. Nice guy, runs a good business there doing that and kite boarding. So we stayed for about an hour and a half, and I got some good pictures of both of them and some video...it was fun.

Then we went to his friends' house near the lake who are from Dallas. The woman had made some homemade cinnamon rolls that were great. She makes her own English muffins, which I got to try too. We went to Joel's house (he stays at a few different houses) and he made me a bead bracelet and picked some of his beautiful white ginger flowers for me, which smelled so good!

Then he bought us beers (I actually drank mine...I hate beer) and took me down to the lake, where there was a sandy area and we hung out there for a while. Then he took me to this lady's house for dinner which was awesome...typical casado...pork, rice, beans, plantains, flatbread...It was great.

She sent him home with a bunch of peppers and PASSION FRUITS, so I got some of those too. Oh, and some of the "tamales" they make here. He's a real nice guy...he takes care of a few houses in the area and does some gardening and construction and mechanical work on boats and such. Everyone seems to like him.

It was strange, it felt like the ultimate perfect "date" but it wasn't a date (I don't think?). It's not like he was trying to be romantic or anything, it just ended up being that way. It was uncomfortable for me because he was trying to hold my hand and do nice things, like massaging my feet then burying them in the warm black sand. But I just let go...enjoyed it and accepted what was happening. But honestly, it was soooo nice to be treated like that and going to pristine places with nobody around...it's sort of unexplainable, really.

So I've made the passion fruit juice this morning and mango salsa. I guess I'll invite him for dinner since I have the tamales and I need to make some chicken tonight. The housekeeper is here...ugh...for seven HOURS. Huh? I figured maybe two or three...they totally make a day out of everything here including gardening, housekeeping, etc. Nice lady, but I wasn't banking on that long, so I guess I'm kinda stuck here for a while. I'll make another peach cobbler for dessert tonight since I already killed the last one.

Subject: Bread and snakes
On Jul 21, 2013 Camille wrote:

What a fun day you had. How was dinner with your Tico? He is very cute and you are lovely as always.

Allison and I went to Ingrid's yesterday and she showed us how she bakes her bread. She sent us home with a loaf. Naturally, we ate plenty for breakfast—eight slices between Bob and I!

Steph:

Yum, that looks good! I'll break down and try making bread at the next house, but it's so easy to go to the bakery and get one too. But no amount of money can buy that smell of it baking in the house!

Yes, been having dinner or lunch with Joel everyday it seems! Tonight he'll come over for some stir fry and the chocolate cake I finally made. I found some cocoa powder in Tilaran so I bought two bags. I ended up using the one I bought in PV for the frosting just to tidy up. It came out fine, but a little grainy from the powdered sugar...I'll survive.

So yesterday he took me to Volcano Brewery and taught me how to skateboard...granted it was just my first lesson but he was a good teacher. I found out that I'm left footed, kinda like being left handed shooting pool. Not sure what it is with me and sports with the left hand thing but yeah...whatever. He kept wanting me to do it like he did, but it didn't feel natural...so he determined I was left footed. It was fun.

Then I had a paddleboard lesson from Dan, the guy whose house he sits/stays at. So much fun fun fun here! I hate to leave!

Camille:

Bob and I are going out to dinner with a bunch of expats we've not yet met. Should be an interesting evening. It's threatening rain and all my taxi drivers are busy so we'll just walk up the street and catch one. It isn't far. We could walk if it was going to be earlier in the day and not so overcast.

Bob and I are trying to eat better, so I make a big bowl of fruit for breakfast, a big salad for lunch and steamed vegetables and beans or tofu for dinner. I do sneak a little soy sauce into the mix here and there. This tahini/lemon dressing with a little soy sauce I've been making plus nutritional yeast is making everything palatable.

We can't think of a better place to do this than here where fresh produce is abundant and cheap.

Steph:

Joel brought over a cassabanana, which of course isn't called that here...I can't remember what he said. Guya something. It smells great but I read the only way to eat it is raw or make it into jam. He says it can be put in soups or eaten with fish. I sort of don't want to open it up. Between that and the guava it smells awesome in here! I was going to do a post on the ick factor on the guava but when I opened one up, it didn't have the worms in it. I'll find one eventually and do it. I got grossed out because I was going to make a drink from them and when I cut them open I saw worms in all of them. The gross part is that I ate one the night before and may not have looked closely enough or could've been lucky that it didn't have any.

The one I ate was from my neighbor, the other ones were taken off a tree roadside, so who knows. I found another tree and took some. I cut open the ripest one and nada. I have a few others here but they smell good. Maybe I'll look tomorrow. They looked like maggots...think they were from fruit flies and those were the larva...they also call them fruit maggots or something gross.

I think Joel is having a bad day. First, he crashed on his bike but he didn't appear that hurt when he showed up. When he got here he noticed a cow by my house that he said had been his and had been stolen, so that sent him on a goose chase as to find out who it belonged to. He was all pissed off about that and wants to get the police involved but apparently says the brand on the cow might be gone or not visible anymore due to the age. Then around noon I walked to the lake to meet him there. He was helping Mark with some lessons on the wakeboard with kids, and Mark got mad at him like he didn't want him teaching them, so Joel walked away in a huff.

THEN he said we'd go to Tilaran to get gas and a drink, but his jeep was driving all f'd up and it was freaking me out and it was starting to rain. I didn't feel safe in it so he took me to his mom's house, and we get in a 'normal' car so he can take me home, but instead he drops me off at

144

Mark's house even though I told him to drop me in town because it's shorter and I had a long walk home in the rain. Not to mention he was driving like a maniac and THAT was freaking me out. He tells me again that he's "testing" the car. Why do you have to test them when I'm in them all the time!? He said that about Mark's, too. Ridiculous. So he had some attitude with me when he dropped me off. So yeah...I'm just sorta glad to be home. Phew.

And he pissed off the dog too...he took me to his new house so he could change. We had the dog at the lake but he had put her in the jeep when we left. She got out of the jeep at his house and wouldn't get back in, so he tried to catch her and that spooked her and she wouldn't come back, so we left her there. I can't blame her. I was pissed at him for doing that. So who knows if she finds her way back here or to her 'real' house.

Anyway, a lot of drama for today, more than I've had all year! I'm sure you're exhausted from reading it, so that's all for now.

Subject: Worms and drama
On Jul 30, 2013 Camille wrote:

A bad day indeed—sounds like he went from bad to worse. Sorry you had to be around him. I'm glad you guys didn't crash or something. Hopefully he has recovered himself and apologized.

Oh, guava. We don't even eat guava anymore due to the ick factor. I do believe there really are worms in everything we eat unless it's been blasted by pesticides. So worms or chemicals, it's our choice. This morning I sifted through some of our flour and sure enough it has worms in it. Guess that's why old recipes all called for you to sift the flour first.

Even if I sifted it all and put it in the refrigerator, the worm eggs must already be in the flour to begin with. Eric laughs when I ask him about worms and he says, "If you eat in Ghana you are eating worms."

Seriously, ick!

Wishing you a no-to-low drama day! Let me know what you do with that cassava banana thingy.

Steph:
Yes, he did call and apologize, which I commend him for. He made me a fish dinner here last night which was good and bad...too much to get into, but his sense of basic sanitation is poor. I did have to spell it out to him since body language didn't seem to be getting through, that I wasn't interested in a physical relationship with him. We'll see what happens with that one.

I did a video today on the cassabanana. It tasted pretty good, I should munch on it so it doesn't go to waste!

 Steph was told that you can put the cassabanana in a closet to keep the moths away.

Camille:
I watched your video and it is obvious you put a lot of time into researching the cassabanana. Well done, and you are beautiful to boot. The blog about the guava is sobering and as I mentioned before, the reason we eschew guava.

It's chilly here. I noticed Albert, the guard across the street, was wearing a football jacket at 6am when I got up to start a load of laundry. The water came back on last night and was still on this morning, so I wasn't taking any chances.

Glad to hear Joel apologized and not surprised he's looking for a deeper level of intimacy. I'm finding here that if you open the door by greeting people, they will usually try for more. Not in a sexual way but by asking for money or a phone number or "where do you live, I'll come to your house." It has gotten old and my patience for it is gone. I realize I shouldn't go for walks with our young enthusiastic interns because my attitude is embarrassingly sour.

On a positive note, yesterday I went for tofu, bananas and avocado and while waiting for a gaggle of young boys to meander across a narrow system of boards that span a muddy bog, I noticed the boy in front was holding a home made truck. Made of tin cans and cast off wheels with a pull string made of audio tape. You can't make this stuff up, and I'm happy to report I see something amazing like this every time I go out, as long as I keep my eyes open.

A bit later, of course, we were greeted by another group of children. When we returned the greeting, they asked us for money.

BLOG — OUT ON a LIMB

Jeep Jitters
by Steph

Riding in the jeep with Joel was never fun for me. It was a 1974 Toyota. I was surrounded by all metal with absolutely no safety measures in place. The only glass was the windshield. There was a constant smell of burning oil wherever we went that fried a few million brain cells I'm sure. He was having some problem with either the brake or differential locking up one or both of the back wheels. It often felt like we were dragging and the steering was...well...not steering. It had so much play in it that it seemed we never really went straight. I'm not surprised...he drove that poor thing like it was indestructible. He had it in the shop for a while but got it out before everything could get fixed.

So one day, we're going to meet his cousin on the other side of Tronadora to take him to his friend's house. It had started drizzling a little bit and we were on steep, rocky, slippery roads. I keep hearing Kevin in the back of my mind saying "Joel has a jeep with bald tires!" after they had been stuck in the mud at the bottom of a hill one day.

147

He's not driving slowly either. Rain is pelting me from the side, making me cold and agitated. We get to the house and the guy wasn't home, so Joel proceeded to turn around.

The mountain side had a ditch; the side looking out onto the valley had a ditch, a barbed wire fence and a steep grassy ledge. As he's forwarding and reversing, we get stuck on the valley side and he can't get the jeep to go forward. He's backing up more and more and I'm staring at the barbed wire and a few cows thinking that I could be going through both soon. The rain is still coming down and I'm too scared to remember I'm cold. The wipers don't work so the dirty windshield is streaked and the image ahead is blurry. I'm getting a really bad feeling in my stomach that this could be the last of me. I'm holding on to the frame of the jeep tightly as the wheels spin, dig into the mud and we skid sideways toward the road. Luckily he was able to pull out of it and I breathed a sigh of relief. I live another day!

Steph:
So have you stopped picking up the trash out front yet? It's amazing how different cultures deal with issues, isn't it? As a collective effort and through education, fines and guilt, the U.S. managed to turn people around from littering for the most part. Who knows if it weren't for those millions of dollars of TV ads, signs, stickers, would it have worked?

And even about people in general...like you say about men like Joel...they don't want a girl FRIEND they want a friend with BENEFITS. And I suppose it's the same for guys in the U.S., but at least they've been "trained" on how to treat a woman and understand body language. I don't know, it's difficult unless you just want sex. Even then, he was trying to claim me as his own, so they take it a little far here it seems.

He's being pretty good though today, after explaining for the third time to him what the deal was. But now there's a weird tension, so I'm kind of glad I'm leaving soon.

Thanks for checking out the video and saying I look good. ;-) I need some practice though. But yeah, I like finding out about these fruits and trees so it's fun.

Well the poor dog got left at the lake today because she wouldn't get in the truck, but she was here when I finally got home. Then Joel picked me up in his jeep and she just stayed here (for once!). I went to go see the owner today but he wasn't home. She's in for a big shock when I leave and don't come back.

She's probably been fed better and gotten more exercise and attention with me than she ever has over there! Wonder why she even came over here in the first place. Weird.

Okay, making dinner and packing...

15
NO TURNING BACK NOW

Subject: Moving to San Antonio
On Aug 9, 2013 Camille wrote:

How are you settling into your new San Antonio home? I love reading your blogs and yes, I am still picking up trash off our little lawn outside the compound walls.

Steph:
The house is great and so are the people. The yard is wonderful to have and keeps me busy. I'm glad I didn't go into town today because it got cold and rainy. Although it's cleared now, it's still cold out! Well, 70...feels cold to me! I did another video today but I need to stop being so monotone. Comes from 20 years working the help desk I guess.

So I heard from the hot 20 year old last night. Actually, I initiated it by asking if he knew where I could buy a flat screen TV. I thought the TV here was one, but it's a tube...just looks like a flat screen. That means I can't connect my Apple TV to it and I don't want to burn out my laptop by watching things on it. Figure I'll just try to score a cheap used one and that way I can have it in the bedroom. Anyway, he was interested in getting together and he said maybe tomorrow so we'll see. I'm sure he has NO IDEA how old I am. It might make him sick to find out. But man...he sure is hot. Regardless, it's nice to have someone to hang with that speaks English and I can practice my Spanish with.

How's the biodiesel project coming?

Camille:
Whaa? What 20 year old? Oh, you! I'm amazed at your energy. But then, I guess I was just as good/bad when I was your age. Sure have slowed down. Plus, I'm married.

While it's "technically feasible" to make biodiesel from the oils in poo, it isn't anywhere close to rational. Fecal sludge is the stuff they pump from septic tanks and by the time they empty the tank most of the oil has already broken down. Not that there was much to begin with because it's 95 percent water. So success in terms of the participants writing up their findings, yes. And it got us to Africa and paid off our credit card debt. So yeah.

Allison left today. I'm going to miss her, she was so easy to live with, sensible, a good listener, happy to walk with me, capable and low maintenance!

Please tell me about your newest play pal!

Steph:
Well he's not a play pal yet. And may never be when he finds out how old I am. I thought I would see him yesterday but didn't hear from him, so no biggie. Anyway he was here at the bbq and he works with tour companies taking photos of the tourists having fun, and I guess he leads kayaking, rafting adventures as well. So it was a good way for me to talk to him and say I was interested in finding a volunteer job in that sort of field. But I'll tell ya, there is no shortage of good looking guys around. But you know small towns...I gotta watch it. ;-)

I helped a family make something like 800 tamales the past couple of days. Today they are selling them, so I bought some, then gave them about $25 more since it was a benefit for their family member who had had a heart attack. Guess they need help paying bills or something. Anyway it was fun and it was an immersion in Spanish that I needed. Then I got home to steam the tamales and the water doesn't work! Good thing I took my shower before I went over there.

Then this morning I weeded the little garden next to the ranchito and planted some jalapeno seeds there. Luckily it wasn't that difficult since the dirt is nice and moist here so it came up easily. I also planted some green bean seeds and some mamon chino to see what happens (in pots in a different location). You'd love this yard...wish you could see it in person.

So the young guy came by in the late afternoon. It didn't turn out well. He would stand WAY too close to me or sit RIGHT beside me. I showed him around the yard and found a way to distance myself physically from him by sitting behind the bar at the ranchito. So we come inside because it's getting dark and he again, sits right next to me, like no room to even move, and I'm getting weirded out.

Then he announces that he's going to "try something." Proceeds to get up, bends down and started kissing me! I had to push him off and say that I didn't feel comfortable doing that...I didn't really know him, etc. Might as well have been speaking Greek. He tries to continue and I keep telling him no, which still isn't getting through.

Well, you know...that kinda stuff just doesn't fly where I come from. So I tell him he needs to leave. It's getting to the point where I'm physically pushing him toward and out the door and I'm fixin' to punch him in the face in order to knock some sense into him.

We get outside and you won't believe what he said. He grabs my hand and goes, "Feel my boobs!" and places it on his chest. I wasn't up for an English lesson at that point and just told him to leave. Unbelievable. I wanted to laugh but I was too disgusted. Guys here just don't seem to get it. So that's the last of him (hopefully).

Well, I should get back to studying...I'll do it outside, although that leads to many distractions. Or maybe I'll wait until tonight, so much to do!

Steph got inspired in Arenal to start painting, which was long time dream of hers. She painted her favorite tree with watercolors she found in the house and decided to keep practicing.

Subject: No turning back now
On Aug 13, 2013 Camille wrote:

I can't wait to see your watercolors. Loved your blog about making a mountain of tamales. It's cool you could be a part of that.

Just said goodbye to Elisabeth, who stopped by while her son was playing tennis. We ended up telling stories about ourselves for nearly three hours! Like you say, friends are like gold.

Silly boy. Guys always assume women get aroused by the same things that would arouse them. Nudity, peck pinching, etc.

Have I mentioned you will never be able to go home again? Seriously, this year will have damaged your ability to "fit in" forever. Maybe.

Steph:
I totally get what you mean about being ruined on going back to the States. I really don't intend on it anytime soon, so that makes it worse too. I don't think I'd like it, but I suppose I'd get used to it again. I would just know what I was missing, which sucks. Anyway, time will tell!

I felt guilty about not exercising, so I took a walk to Santa Cruz up the VERY STEEP mountain (there was basically nothing there at all). So I feel I got a workout. The uphill took 45 minutes and the downhill took 30. Jeez, I'm gonna be sore tomorrow. Olivia is going into town on the 8:00 bus and I'd like to join, so hopefully I'll get up in time (I'm sure I will). I need to browse around more and go to the bakery.

I felt like you today...I pulled the flowers that looked horrible out of the garden I weeded and planted tomatoes instead. Eventually I'll make some climbers out of bamboo or something...make it all jungley.

I'm marinating some kabobs for dinner and I just made a chocolate cake. I can eat outside, but doing it alone kinda sucks. I guess I have the frogs, tadpoles, fish, birds, mosquitoes, etc., but they're not much for conversation.

Camille:
I hope you and the peepers enjoyed your evening meal. One of the project collaborators was in town from Accra so she, Bob and I walked over to a hotel for dinner and sat by the swimming pool with the two dolphins spouting water from their mouths and watched the moon rise into the sky. Mostly they talked about work, drank beer and I listened, chiming in once in a while with anything I felt I could contribute. After dinner we all walked home. It was a nice evening.

Steph:
I'm already looking for the next assignment...well, I'll get an email when things become available at least. I keep forgetting other parts of the world aren't warm in January though. I think I'd like to try Italy at some point. And god, the men...ugh, I just know I'm gonna fall in love there.

I went to town yesterday with my friend and got this cool Easter egg plant and they feel just like real eggs! I had to have it. Ever seen one before? You can't really eat them but they're super cool to look at. I have it outside and want to put it in a bigger pot. Then I'll plant the seeds and see how they do here. I'm not willing to kill this plant by putting it in the ground.

Then I bought a bike from my neighbor for $80, so I'm happy there. Now...where to ride it and not crash?

Camille:
No, I have never seen an eggplant as perfectly egglike as the one you bought. Well, maybe one time back in Denver. I've heard about those Italian men...

Subject: You're so right
On Aug 20, 2013 Steph wrote:

Just had to sit down now and write this while I was in the moment. I saw one of the big white egrets flying in the distance. I usually only see one, so I stopped to admire it and said, "Wow...cool." Then right after that, about six others flew up after it.

That's when I said to myself, "This place rocks...I can't go backward now." To be able at any given moment to look out the window and see such variety of birds and landscape is just unbeatable, you know? Go back to the States? Uh, not without a fight. I mean, once you've been jaded like this it's just such a disappointment to go back to something that wasn't even a quarter as nice. It was like going to St. Thomas when I was 18. After that, I could never settle for anything but bathtub water. It spoiled me because I knew how good it could be, so why downgrade? I think I'm going to write an essay on this. Thanks for being my springboard.

Camille:
Ha ha! You are spot on! Thanks for the nod. Why settle for bird deprived landscapes and bad water? Totally worth an essay.

After Bob and I moved to Belize we found we were forever unable to enjoy the murky waters of freshwater reservoirs and backyard ponds. During one of our trips from Belize to Colorado we discovered that what we once considered great fun—water skiing at beautiful Horse Tooth Reservoir along the front range of the Rocky Mountains—had lost its allure.

We went out on the boat, dangled our legs over the side and decided to pass on a swim. The water was murky and cold, not at all the bathtub-warm, crystal-clear blue Caribbean waters we had become accustomed to.

16
HAPPINESS COMES IN SMALL DOSES

Subject: Thought of you
On Aug 26, 2013 Steph wrote:

I was at those peoples' farm yesterday and I took a picture of a cute green plant poking out of the dirt floor with no sunshine at all inside their cabin. It reminded me of a blog you wrote a while back about how plants sprout right out of concrete. It looked really out of place.

Camille:
Life will find a way! I do remember that picture I took of a blade of grass coming straight up out of the road in Alaska. Can't believe you've been reading Plastic Farm Animals this many years and then I remember we met before we went to Alaska, in 2005. Wow! Eight years we've been corresponding, pretty much on a daily basis. No wonder we can tell each other anything.

While I should be more jazzed about returning home, the feelings I have are of apprehension. Mostly because I'm worried my 'free time' will evaporate. I'm worried I won't finish the website migration projects I promised myself I'd finish before leaving Africa. But I'll get it done like I always do.

 ***Camille succesfully completed the Family Section of her website, but was unable to finish migrating the Recipes Pages to their new Wordpress platform.***

Steph:
Attaching a photo of the two bouquets I made yesterday. I just saw another flower that I totally want in here but I need to get the boots on before I venture into that grass. It's the coolest thing ever...sort of yellow and feathery/fluffy. Watch, it'll probably wilt once I cut it. I never get to see it outside, so I figure I'll bring it in.

I absolutely LOVE having these great flowers here and they're so abundant that I don't feel bad cutting one or two to enjoy for a week or two, sometimes longer! You know as well as I do that something like this would cost a small fortune in the States so I feel very lucky.

Oh, and one of my new favorite flowers, white ginger, is down the street in abundance, so I want to cut some of those also. The smell is amazing. I want to bathe in them. Too bad there's not a tub here or I would throw some in with me! I really should go take a walk and get the ginger before I get too involved with my work.

Camille:
Morning! What pretty flowers! In Belize, Marta would make beautiful table arrangements every day for the Cantina. Much like the ones you have created, with heliconia and ginger. In NC we planted a lot of flowers and so have continued a tradition of beauty.

So, Europe next! Good choice and I'm jealous. We have had it with Africa and not too keen on what's going on in the States, so Europe is the logical Mecca.

Although I do miss my friends and what we are doing to create resiliency and small scale sustainability. Which, at the end of the day, is the only way to create a sustainable society - one community at a time.

Tribal humans had it right. Small numbers of people within a specific eco-system will endure in a way that empires cannot.

You have done everything right, my friend - setting yourself up with a remote revenue stream and plunging in without any ties to the American Empire. I have no doubt you will find your other half soon enough. At this point in your intellectual and psychological evolution, an American who has never traveled outside his homeland simply will not be enough.

Steph:
I often think of Bourdain's quote, "The more I travel the less I know." I understand it completely. I love learning things from people and being the introvert that I am, I'm trying to semi-crawl out of that shell. Not entirely, but I force myself to be sociable sometimes when I don't feel like it....like other things really can wait. At the end of the day I come home with something new that I didn't know earlier. I like that a lot. Whether it's the language or traditions or finding out something about a bird or a plant. I'm now the happiest person I've ever known! Ha!

ALSO I got my new website up and running today! Wow...what a relief. Now I just have to add more products to it, which is a pain but it's the only way to make money and hopefully I do.

Tomorrow I go to some ruins with a new lady I haven't met yet in person, so we'll see how that goes. I found it strange how meeting her over the phone went down. The homeowner here told me about her, but just said that she would call me after her visitors left within the next week or two. So I get a phone call and I answer but she doesn't bother saying who she is or anything. Just sort of started talking...like I'm a mind reader or something. So I finally had to ask who it was (really?) and she confirmed that she was Astrid, which is what I already thought. Just seemed weird to me. I mean, isn't that typically the first thing you say? Anyway, she's an expat and a lot older than me but has a car and knows the area, so that should be helpful.

Subject: New blue dress
On Aug 31, 2013 Steph wrote:

I love that new blue dress of yours! What a knockout! Jeez, I would love one of those. I can't stop looking at that picture! I literally had to stop writing you and look back at it a few times. Wow, you totally rock that thing. How beautiful! I kind of wish I lived in a place like that where you can have beautiful fabric made to fit. Wow...well, the day that I do, you can bet all of my clothes will be handmade!

Camille in her new Ghana suit

Camille:
Yes, we are quite jazzed to be living in the land of custom-made clothing. I believe this suit cost me about $50 and includes a second, shorter skirt.

I know the woman who batiked the six yards it took to make this outfit, and I saw it drying on the lawn outside her shop at the Cultural Center and had to have it. They were just folding it up as I went back to pay for it.

The fabrics here are incredible. I would love to buy you some fabric if you tell me what colors you like. I can also take a picture of what we've already bought to give you an idea. The variety is endless.

If you tell me what you want made, I can get the measurement requirements from the seamstress, a European trained Ghanaian with a beautiful voice, and send them to you.

How was your day?

Subject: Say cheese
On Sep 2, 2013 Steph wrote:

It was good. I decided to remove the cobwebs from around the outside of the house because of that butterfly that got stuck the other day. I cut a branch of angel trumpets because I needed something to fill the space, and no sooner do I look at it again and the ants are making a bee line for the opened one IN MY HOUSE. So I had to throw those out. I really love the smell of them but it only happens at night and I'm not even sure these smell. Guess I won't know unless I go out to the yard one night.

Then I caught the bus at 1pm to town and it took me an hour to find the second hand store I wanted to shop in. I found ALL THE OTHER American clothing stores, but I really wanted to go to this one. So I was sort of rushed through it and still didn't find anything I liked. Oh, I finally had pizza too. I figured I wouldn't be able to find the one place I wanted to go to, so instead I just ate at the bus terminal. They don't believe in heating it up for you apparently, so it was lukewarm but ok.

Then I ended up spending $12 on two packages of friggin' cheese. What is it with these people and cheese here? One was just a bag of shredded mozzarella and the other a small block of gouda. Then I had to catch the bus again. I was sweating my ass off the whole time in Turrialba, and it really couldn't have been THAT hot, I don't think. But as we climbed the mountain it got cooler as it always does...then the clouds were so thick you could barely see in front of the bus. Right after I got home it started raining and it's cold. I had been on the hunt for some sweat pants but they're all so long. I could find someone to hem them I guess but what a pain. I guess I'll have to go back to the other American shops and see what they have instead. They don't believe in categorizing them in any way so you literally have to sift through all of them, and that takes time.

Gosh, thanks so much for offering me to get me fabric/have something made for me. I would actually love that. And it's funny because when I saw your suit, I thought to myself, "I would have gotten a skirt made to match that." Great minds think alike! But seriously, you look stunning. I also noticed in the picture of the woman with all the fabrics...like she was standing in front of some tunics? I looked at the picture and said to myself, "Which color...green! Wait, orange...no, red..." Of course I won't be greedy, but if you don't mind, tell me what measurements I need and fabric choices. I just LOVE how your dress is pleated at the ends. That always reminds me of two things: octopus and angel trumpets.

Subject: Hummingbird meat
On Sep 7, 2013 Steph wrote:

I was reading part of your blog about the horse and it reminded me of a horrible dream I had this morning where my mom was making something out of hummingbird meat! Jeez, do they even HAVE meat on them? It was terrible! I saw the hollowed out carcass of it and she was describing in detail to me these disgusting things about the dead bird! UGH!

Camille:
Whoa! Where do these dreams come from? Did you talk with your mom

recently? With the dead bird issue and surrounded by hummingbirds it's no surprise have hummingbirds on your mind. Maybe you are the mother who is letting these birds die.

Steph:
Well, now you've made me want to know...so here's what I found:

To dream of dead or dying birds foretells a period of coming disappointments. You will find yourself worrying over problems that are constantly on your mind.

To dream of a cooked bird, suggests that you're feeling guilty about something. You fear that someone will "find you out" or believe they already have.

I'm sure "cooked bird" means turkey or chicken, not hummingbird, but maybe it's all the same. Guilty...hmmmm...I rarely feel guilty about anything. I'll have to chew on that one. No pun intended.

I was thinking about the hummer I buried yesterday though so I'm sure that's where part of it came from. AH! Maybe THAT'S the guilt...knowing I was partially responsible for its death by not putting anything in the windows. Oh, and yesterday I had hung my red shirt over my bed frame and I heard a bird hit the window. It flew away but I'm sure it was a hummer going for the red. Riddle solved.

Camille:
Must chill out. Yesterday woke feeling slightly stoned, very mellow and the feeling persists. What if the rest of my life is like this? It's sobering to realize that there are people who feel like this from birth, people who aren't always on the cusp of irritable and overtaxed like me.

Brain chemistry. Some have theirs set to chill and some don't.

In other news, we're having movie night again, and tonight's movie is "Dr. Strangelove"!

163

Steph:
Aaaah, I love Strangelove! It's one of my favorite movies. "There will be no fighting in the war room!" I should watch that again.

Well, THREE friggin' cows in the yard this morning. Since I closed up the fence I'm not sure how they got over except that the barb wire down the way is low and I think that's where the kid took them through. I went to their house and made him deal with it and told him I didn't like it. The owner of this house said I had permission to make steaks out of them. I guess it's an ongoing issue, although this is the first I've ever seen of them. I bet it'll be every day now. Will have to find a solution.

Subject: Mom
On Sep 10, 2013 Camille wrote:

Okay, so the cattle are ruining your yard. That's a sucky problem to have. They will go through any fence, but sounds like they are being encouraged. How do you fight this kind of battle? Bad position to be in, especially because it isn't your property. Please keep me posted. I'm glad I'm not in your shoes.

Another smooth day for me. Some moments of stress, but not many. Just this; walking the streets to buy bread and chickpeas, ignoring the screaming kids, taxis, etc. as best as I could and then coming home with minutes to spare before my call to my mother.

Then I think: shit, what on earth are you stressing about? So you are hot, late and trying to multi-task? Is this anything close to what you used to deal with? No. So I calmed down, and the cold water took the heat away. Bob came in, picked up my grocery list and went out for the heavy stuff with Eric and my mother told me another incredible story which I typed into her memoir.

Steph:
I'm glad you're writing those stories down...you'll cherish them later. My mom has totally gotten into her father's history and the time he spent

overseas during the war. On their last trip to Wales, they came across a house where they thought my grandfather had stayed right before the invasion of Normandy. Sure enough it was, and on the wall, his two buddies from San Antonio had written their names and hometowns and the date (June 6, 1944, D-Day). The owners had kept it on the wall and were so surprised that she came there and was able to see it. The crazier thing was that my mom was there on June 6th.

She just did a photo book with stories about Grandpa and they're going back to Wales in three weeks again. So yes, it's good to know things while you still have your mom here.

Oh, I finished painting that cheetah eye, too.

Subject: Eyes
On Sep 11, 2013 Camille wrote:

Love that story about June 6. Right between our birthdays, too.

The cheetah eye is your best yet. I can see big progress in your work. I see the beginnings of 3D in that beautiful eyeball. How is it that eyes are ultimately alluring, but eyeballs disgustingly creepy?

The eyes have it—no idea this is what eyeballs really look like, and I do like the idea of your body-of-work focused on eyes. Your command of the medium—you are actually painting HAIRS in water color. Go, Steph, go!

Steph:
Well thanks. I was going to attempt the cuttlefish eye, and I still will, but I think I'll do a half sheet of this cat instead, which could be difficult as well since it's mostly black with subtle hints of shadow. Yeah, not happy with just painting a bird. I want cool stuff. I can fast forward and see a gallery of all my paintings as being eyes of creatures. What fun!

Yeah, that's why I'm thinking watercolor isn't my right medium. I like what it does to the eyes and the base, but I'm using the paint as is to make hairs...and tiny brushes.

I finished the cat...I like the eyes. Knew I was getting into sketchy territory with the shading but whatever. It's not bad for only painting for three days. The nose is too skinny. Everything I sketched on paper disappeared when I painted the black background. Duh!

Camille:
Excellent! Your progress is amazing. Don't know how you did it, but this face pops—you're mastering the art of 3D, something I was never able to achieve. This looks like hours of work. Or at least weeks of technique.

Subject: Serpentarium
On Sep 13, 2013 Steph wrote:

Thanks! Yes, it took about five hours. I should've done better but I was ready to finish it! I like the eyes. But this is really taking from my real work! I worked after the sun went down on my new site though. Going to the serpentarium today! Wheeee!! Maybe I can get some good eye pictures there (no fur!!!).

Camille:
Are you kidding? Your REAL work is being the most creative you imaginable. Heh heh.

I love the dress you wore to the serpentarium, the videos and the picture of you with the tree frog from your blog.

Strange how you are drawn to creatures that writhe and pulse, whereas they give most folks, including me, the heebie jeebies. I really do think you have a career ahead of you as the ambassador of reptiles and sea creatures. There's been a void since the crocodile hunter died.

What are you up to today? I'm going to meet my friends for coffee. I don't drink coffee but that's not the point, of course. Later I'll go back to working on the photo album.

Red eyed tree frog perched on head at local Serpentarium

Steph:

Thanks! Yeah, that was a secondhand dress I got in town for about $4...I love it too! I agree, I'd love to take croc hunter's place! That'd be a blast. I'm just lacking in knowledge unfortunately. Animal Planet doesn't want to train someone I'm sure...you'd just have to know. Sigh...although it'd be easy enough to learn things and I do think they'd dig a female croc/snake wrangler!

Camille:

Oh heck, I don't think you have to know so much to be on TV. They have staff to do research and stuff. They want someone who plays well on camera and you sure have got that. And someone who's willing to mess

167

around with the animals. Surely, they'll help you with a script. Or at least give you a chance to research an episode.

Okay, so I'm making this shit up. I'm just remembering what we learned in Belize about the documentary business. There is a lot going on behind the scenes. The face before the camera is only a small piece of it and I think you would be great.

Steph:
Okay, well you inspired me to write to Animal Planet. I guess it can't hurt right? They won't know who I am unless I tell them! Everyone says I SHOULD be the next croc hunter, so why the hell not!? Now that I'm able to travel and live this freestyle life it seems now is the time to take a chance! Wheeeeeeee!

Camille:
Just remember this. They need you more than you need them. There is a big void waiting for a beautiful, earnest, articulate personality championing the mysteries of the animal world.

17
EXPECTING THE LEAST

Subject: Internet
On Sep 14, 2013 Steph wrote:

So the people with the phone company supposedly came by yesterday to look at my internet problem. TALKED WITH SOMEONE (certainly not me) and said nothing was wrong. Yeah...typical. It's Independence Day so nobody will come out today either...another day down. Guess I will work in the yard.

Camille:
Sucks about your Internet.

Yeah, we're surrounded by slackers too. The power is the issue since last night. Comes in at 50 volts and won't push the refrigerator, etc. I'm afraid to plug in my laptop unless it's through the regulator. Which is better than no electric at all. So I should stop complaining. That's what happens. Things get better and I come to expect better. They get worse and I feel let down.

It's all about expectations at the end of the day. If we lower our expectations we are happier.

I hope I am able to sleep through whatever goes on tonight if anything. Heck, sometimes it's the neighbors, or some rabid Christians with loudspeakers. Chainsaws moan on and on all through the night, cutting up wood at the charcoal plant up the hill behind our house. We live in a loud place. Not like your idyllic hideaway.

But then, we have Internet...

Steph:
Jeez, sorry for the delay. My Internet has been down since Friday, finally got fixed today after having to get snippy with a supervisor...but REALLY? Close my case TWICE and never even came here to talk to me? I can finally catch up on real work and general browsing. I bought a ticket to Panama today for the right price so now to find a place to crash for a couple of days on my border run. Plenty of options but the cheap days of going to Panama are OVER in a big way.

So tomorrow I'm getting torn away from the computer by going to town and the botanical garden...I'm not complaining really, I haven't left since Thursday. Completely losing track of the days.

How has life been over there?

Camille:
All is well here. My friend Elodie from the lake is coming over for dinner and then we are going out to see a French movie at Alliance Française up the street. Kat's going to meet us. I'm already caught up the laundry and made dinner, with 2 1/2 hours before Elodie shows up, so nothing to but work on my projects, do some yoga and wash my hair. A perfect day.

 Kumasi's Alliance Française, located half a mile from Camille's house, is part of a global network of cultural centers which provide exposure to French language and culture.

Subject: Time
On Sep 19, 2013 Steph wrote:

Hey, sounds like you're finally getting some time to yourself! Good for you! I hope you're feeling a little more relaxed and less stressed out.

Went to the botanical gardens (did a blog) with Astrid and it was cool. I would've stayed longer but I felt like she wanted to just walk through and before I knew it, it was over! Very cool stuff there. I got a $10 bag of coffee (gasp!) but it's supposedly best of the best "reserve" so I'm hoping it WILL be. Figure I should support the farmers. Oh, got a bar of chocolate too, even though I rarely eat straight chocolate. It was from Limon, near where I was living down south.

My friends in San Jose offered to pick me up at the airport when I return from Panama, let me stay at their house, and then take me out here the next day. They're really nice. I'm making them lasagna on Monday for lunch. I found out he wants to drop Linda off at my place while he goes to the farm at 9am. I can practice my Spanish with her.

Subject: Fence patching
On Sep 20, 2013 Steph wrote:

During the whole fence patching episode yesterday, something bit me on my middle finger and elbow. I can never see the insect that does it, either, I just get really swollen up for four days. So my finger turned all fat as did my elbow. Finger swelling has gone down a little but not completely. And it doesn't itch until you DO scratch it, then it's crazy intense itchy like my elbow right now. I never should've touched it. Arrrghhh! I need to work on another section of fence eventually. It's weird foggy this morning with no sun, which is unusual so I don't know what the day will be like.

I have to walk to Astrid's to get my pants hemmed and I need to make a coffee cake for Diego (my neighbor) since he put up the one section of fence yesterday, so I wanted to thank him for that. He did a great job and now I know how to do it too! This will look great in the homeowner's eyes, I hope, and strengthen my referral. I applied for a three month sit in Anguilla starting in May of next year. Talk about planning ahead! I'm sure they'll get tons of requests for that place though. Two stories, two cats, pool, car, all bills paid. Weather isn't too bad around that time from what I saw.

Well, I wasn't woken up by the cows this morning at all...no mooing anywhere! Bet they're gonna be mad that their supply got cut off! They may take revenge though!

Camille:
How's your finger and elbow? Nice work shutting out the cows. Maybe they'll stay out. I hope so.

You remind me of myself in the way you get so busy with everyone around you, and yet don't mind spending hours by yourself. I wonder what motivates us to be so outgoing when we are really introverts at heart?

A Caribbean island sounds great. But what will you do until May?

Steph:
Oh, thanks for asking...swelling has gone down but I found myself scratching my elbow today.

Well the sit in Anguilla was filled...I happened to see it. I applied for one in Spain which fit my dates perfectly...in the south, near the beach staying in a guest house next to the villa for a few months...with a border collie which I would love. Won't hold my breath!

Measurements are attached for my new blouse. Thanks again for that! I cleaned this afternoon so I should get back to work. And have a cupcake. ;-)

Subject: Ten weeks!
On Sep 22, 2013 Camille wrote:

Thanks for the measurements. I hope to get over to the seamstress tomorrow. I'm making progress on my Family Photo Album. Got the Camille page done anyhow. How are your projects coming along?

Steph:

Oooo, I loved that photo album! It was so neat to see you from baby 'til '99. Wow...it's so strange, isn't it? Looking back like that in such a short time (how long it took me to look through those photos) and how much time has passed and everything that happened in between. Time is weird. Like what if we lived a Martian year? 686 days instead of 365. I wonder if we'd still feel like time flew by. It boggles my mind.

Well, I can't wait to see some more, but I did enjoy your early life...I'm not sure I remembered or knew about you not living at home. I'm still getting to know you!

Well the church across the road (rather, the hall on the same property) was jumpin' last night. They BLASTED music from about 6pm to 11:30, which sort of pissed me off. I mean it was loud inside my HOUSE why would they play it that loud THERE? Unbelievable. So I stayed up 'til then 'cause there was no way I was getting to sleep.

I failed to take one other pair of pants to the seamstress, so I walked to Astrid's again today to drop them off and give her extra money for taking my measurements the other day. And I'm getting fatter too...I put on a pair of shorts I hadn't worn in a while (ones that were falling off of me in PV) and they were almost tight. Not good. But Camille, those cupcakes are so damn good! And they're light and fluffy and gone within seconds...how could they have so many calories? It's not fair. Okay, so when my site(s) are done I SWEAR I will walk everyday again. I must. 'Cause I love cupcakes.

Linda and Gustavo will come tomorrow for lasagna, so I have to clean up a bit here then prepare for that. I'll just have her help me prep and keep busy 'til he shows up. I'm just becoming alive at 9 though, so that kinda sucks. Today, I work more on my site and hope to have it up this week. Astrid wants to go to SJ (San Jose) on Thursday with me for a fun day so that'll be good.

Camille:
How has your week been?

I had the best day yesterday with my friend Kat. I walked over, which was also cleansing and empowering. It's about 3.5 miles across town. We talked about everything imaginable, and then I caught a ride with Manu and walked the last 25 minutes home. It was a beautiful, bright, blue sky day which is rare in Kumasi between the high humidity and the pollution. Life is good.

Life is good.

Steph:
That's great about yesterday. My week has been crazy. I have a clogged pipe from the kitchen and it's now day four of trying to get it fixed. They're allegedly coming back today (third time) to work on it. I was told 8am, it's 8:04. I won't expect anyone until 9.

Yesterday Astrid and I went to SJ and I finally found some shoes (not the best but better than nothing). Did a little shopping, came back on the bus and there was a wreck that had just happened, blocking the road. But 30 minutes later it was cleared. Then it started raining (cold rain) and we had errands to run in Turri so that was nasty. I built a fire last night but wood burns up fast so it didn't last long and it's still chilly in here.

I launched my second website last night so that's out of the way! Now to start on a third, which will take a long time to input products, and I need to find another theme to use. I leave for Panama in a week so I need to figure out my transportation there soon. Oh, and we're going to see the dancing horses on Saturday I'm pretty sure. So watch for a new video! They're so darn cute!

Camille:
Wow, your site is beautiful. Great picture of a life-crushing wave. I can see all the work you put into this.

I wish I was going to see the dancing horses with you. Would you say it's harder to get things done in Costa Rica than in Texas? God knows it's nearly impossible to get anything done in Ghana here. They will tell you anything and lie, lie, lie.

Subject: Service
On Sep 30, 2013 Steph wrote:

Thanks for taking a look at the site...and the compliment! Yes, it did take a while.

And yes, it's impossible to get the same level of service here. They figuratively repainted the car instead of washing it. The drain was clogged. Easy enough, right? No. They claimed it couldn't be cleared out so they drilled two huge holes in the wall (outside) to install two new pipes from the Tico sink in the wash room and the kitchen sink instead of just trying to physically clean out the existing pipe. Then the hot water pipe (plastic) either broke or just came out and they said it'd be two days until I had hot water in the whole house. I almost screamed at that point. Luckily my nice neighbor who speaks English came to the rescue and drove to the hardware store to get the effin' $6 part and it was fixed in 10 minutes. Unbelievable. So I was finally able to take a shower and do the dishes and clean the kitchen and floors for the fourth time this week.

So now we'll see what the owner has to say. I've been keeping him up to date on the situation, but I don't think he was prepared for what happened today and neither was I! Crazy. At least the labor shouldn't be that expensive. Parts were $50.

So here I am, basically, at the end of another day. God only knows what tomorrow brings. Hope you sleep soundly tonight (and I mean WITHOUT sound).

Steph:
We went to watch the horses yesterday and considering there were well over 150, they were quite peaceful. But you could tell that one in particular was having a bad day or just wasn't liking the crowds. Astrid, Jane and I were sitting on a concrete bench on the sidelines of it all. That horse in particular was giving me the heebie jeebies because I could tell it was stressed. Every time it got too close to me, I'd get up and out of the way.

At one point, another horse that was tied to the not-so-great fence bucked up and broke the fence, which in turn freaked out this other horse we were next to...I jumped up out of the way and the horse kicked and bucked and ended up kicking Jane's foot (her bad one, at that). Had I not gotten out of the way, I would've gotten the brunt of it and I'm sure a broken bone. I felt bad for her but at this point it was so crowded we couldn't leave if we wanted to since the horses were now parading up the street we came in on. Her foot swelled up and bruised but she was a trooper.

It was surely an experience I won't forget. Once all of the horses had left the field people started trying to leave, including us. Horses and riders passed by us doing their cute side kick trots, beers in the riders' hands (sometimes multiple). People in their stopped cars went into the trunks to pull out beers while waiting. When the street became a parking lot though, it was either "if you can't beat 'em, join 'em" or wait it out. So wait we did! The cops finally made an appearance directing traffic. Had they not, we might still be there. Then it rained like crazy all night...I can't imagine how many drunk people driving with horses in a trailer were out last night.

I have to go into town today to buy my bus ticket to San Jose for Friday.

I think I'll chance it and just go direct the same morning I fly out. Jeez, I need to get my shit together for that trip too, like find hiding places for things in case the house gets robbed (which it probably won't), but you never know.

18
DISCONNECTING

Subject: Panama City
On Oct 5, 2013 Steph wrote:

Wow...It's neat here! Did a bunch of shopping yesterday when I arrived, great prices, great grocery store, too! All around U.S. prices and products. Never see this stuff in CR. Going to the canal for a couple hours today, then a mall (not that I need to shop at this point but what the heck). Figure I'd kick myself if I didn't see the canal while here. Not sure what else I should do after all of that though.

Anyway, good times!

Subject: Hired help
On Oct 9, 2013 Camille wrote:

Our housemates upstairs have hired a woman to cook and clean for them, and Bob and I are not so comfortable with the arrangement. Although they've done their best to reduce her impact on us, the fact remains there is another person in the house to deal with. I now think twice before going upstairs to use the washing machine or borrow the blender. To us, it looks like an elitist entitlement born of privilege, and we are hoping this new development doesn't compromise security.

Steph:
I agree with you on your stance of hiring people...I can't do it either. When I was in Arenal, they had a woman come to clean the house once and she spent SEVEN HOURS there...for about a two hour job. Of course that included catching up with the neighbors, talking to me, and eating lunch, with only about three hours of actual work being done at a very slow pace. So the only worker here is the gardener who only trims the grass...that's not something I would really want to do and the owners pay for it. It's only once a month so I'm okay with it...I do the rest.

It looks like a nice day...yesterday I don't think it even rained at all which is strange! But the electricity went out at some point last night...odd. I really need to ride my bike (or attempt to) to Astrid's to fix her keyboard this week. Will also talk to the guy about doing a small blog page for his cabins, which will earn me $100. Not sure I'm up for it today though. Astrid has started getting on my nerves a bit and although she's nice, she tends to dig at me. Plus her driving makes me nuts.

Camille:
Life's too short to hang around with people who irritate you, who have nothing in common with you and/or a myriad of other Chi-sucking behaviors. Sorry to hear Astrid is not easy to be around.

Because I'm leaving in two months, I'm not as socially gregarious as usual, which is my way of disconnecting. Someone like Astrid would be the first to fall by the wayside.

Last night I was chatting with the French lady who runs Alliance Française and she was saying how she wants to lose some, if not all, of her cynicism. When I thought about her comment later I came to the realization that I LIKE cynical people. I enjoy them more than really positive people. But I definitely do not like mean people.

I don't mind having someone mow either, or the occasional person to clean the house if it goes too far astray as my home in NC did this past year.

Steph:
As for you disconnecting, I can't blame ya there. I think we feel that we should be nice to everyone even if we don't like them that much.

Camille:
Morning! Can't believe it's Sunday already. Bob and I are going to Ingrid's for brunch this morning.

I'm starting to freak! With seven weeks to go (possibly three!) the pressure is upon us to pack up all this shit, get rid of all our furniture and get jobs on the other end. Not to mention my family photo album project. Whatever it is (and god knows, it could simply be hormones, those post-menopausal non-specific angst anxiety attacks) I'm sure I'll be right as rain soon.

Subject: Moving back
On Oct 13, 2013 Steph wrote:

I can understand why you're upset/stressed. With short notice on cutting back your time there, that puts you under a ton of pressure to get things done.

I also think that just the simple fact of moving back "home" and away from a place you've been at so long is also stressful for both of you. Hell, I get a little sad when I think about having to leave THIS place. I just have to think that the next place could be even better and I'll be seeing a different country. In the grand scheme of things, it'll all work out. It's just that fear of the unknown, I guess, and wondering how anything could be better. It's strange that I have this "fear" creeping in when I thought I had gotten over that sort of thing. But I suppose it'll always be with me in one form or another. I've lost my fear of going to a big strange country I've never been to before, which makes me happy.

Either way with you, maybe it is hormonal or just the fact you're quite overwhelmed with emotions right now that are staring you right in your face...It would be hard for anyone to keep an even keel, so don't let it get to you. Just start doing what needs to be done and you'll be ready when it's time to go.

Okay, big hug...you'll be fine. Do a little yoga or something and make the list of things that need to be done. You'll feel better!

Camille:
Thank you for your wonderful advice. I am feeling much better now! We have begun packing, so I feel better about that too. I have a feeling I'll sleep great tonight.

Sorry you had to spend your day at your desk and jealous you are seeing oropendolas. We've only seen them in Guatemala that time we went from Belize to Tikal. I will never forget our convoy of armed boys in open trucks, one of whom had a toothbrush sticking out of his back pocket.

Oropendolas are large basket weaving birds that look prehistoric. Found in Central and South America, they are part of the blackbird family. They have crazy calls they make and as they vocalize them, they look like they're falling forward off the branch. I am only assuming that 'pendulum' is where the 'pendola' part of their name comes from due to the swinging motion. You'll often see the large, long basket nests at peoples' houses hanging up that had fallen out of a tree. They're quite an amazing piece of work.

Bob and I had a good day at Ingrid and Tim's. Kat and Agye picked us up and took us home. No crazy driving except by everyone around us who are seriously bat shit crazy drivers, but hey, it's Africa and we're used to it now. There really are no rules. It's every car for itself most of the time.

Anyhow, we enjoyed great conversations with a small group including Elisabeth and Kirsten. All very smart, intuitive people. Life is too short to

181

hang out with jerks.

Steph:
Another "new" bird hit the window and had some trouble recovering. It's amazing how tame they are when I'm holding them, but they don't have much choice.

I can't imagine how they feel after hitting the window. Ugh....I hate hearing it. This one hit pretty hard too. I've never noticed one like it before, really neat orange colorings.

My Amazon sales have picked up somewhat so that's cool. And I sold a Berkey today, so that paid for my groceries at least. I don't mind keeping even!

Subject: Star fruit drink
On Oct 18, 2013 Steph wrote:

I made this today and it was good. Do you get star fruit there? I used two of them (and they were tart) and a whole lime. Made a simple syrup out of 6 spoons of sugar and it was just right. Goes well with vodka too. ;-)

Star Fruit and Ginger Drink

1 pound star fruit
1 thumb of ginger
1 teaspoon lime juice
4 cups of water
sugar to taste

Blend star fruit and ginger with water and lime juice then strain. Add sugar and serve chilled.

Camille:
We've seen star fruit growing around Lake Bosumtwi, but have not noticed any trees in Kumasi. This drink sounds wonderful. I'm making a

ginger/hibiscus tea we call Zinger and also sometimes a lemon grass tea. Bob stopped drinking juice and Zinger because he is trying to quit drinking and it reminds him of vodka.

Subject: Little birds
On Oct 17, 2013 Camille wrote:

Gina is back in town so I went over for coffee. And then I went shopping and worked in the kitchen all afternoon. Looking forward to watching two more episodes of Modern Family with some spicy Chinese eggplant, rice and sauteed wing beans.

Tell me more about your sweet little bird.

Steph:
Wing beans, wing beans...that's fun to say. Ha ha...Is there anything you'll actually MISS about Africa?

Where the hell did the day go (again)? I worked on a questionnaire for the hotel (cabins) I'm going to do that website for. But I did it hoping I'd be doing more jobs like that, so it turned into a six page doc. I'll have to put my little blurb at the bottom of the site to show my company name. Even got a new Gmail address of warmreptile, which is the name of my new found company...ha ha...Warm Reptile Designs. I just love that name and have always wanted to use it for something. Honestly, I saw it as being Warm Reptile Productions for a movie but no movie is coming out of me. I'm happy to have the email address.

So the birdie.... John said, "It was an orange-billed nightingale-thrush, a species that I didn't see near the house until last year, when it suddenly started appearing." That's really all I have on it...luckily no bird hit the window today.

The tadpoles have sprouted legs and one even ventured out onto a rock the other day. They may have gotten out of the pond, as I'm not seeing the mature ones in there much lately. Cuties. Usually it's a good sign if there are a lot of frogs around because they're very susceptible to toxins and die off fast. There are tons here. I can't walk in the yard at night without kicking one. By accident, of course.

Camille:
That's very cool you have a new Warm Reptile email address. Hmmm. A movie. I'd say you are currently starring in your own movie!

Yes, there are plenty of things I'll miss about Africa; the slow hum of life ongoing, my expat friends, not having to drive, an abundance of fresh, tropical fruit, life without A/C and lots of reasons to complain. Heh heh...

19
THE LAST STRAW

Subject: Weekends
On Oct 19, 2013 Camille wrote:

What are you up to this weekend? Is weekend still a concept for you? We're going to an expat party this afternoon, so that'll be fun!

Steph:
The neighbor's dog barked ALL NIGHT until around 3:30am, when I guess they decided to bring it inside. Then they let it out again around 5:30am, only to have it bark constantly again. Then at 7am, my friggin' neighbors are pumpin' the jams so loud I feel like it's in my room. Of course after it wakes me up playing for 10 minutes, they turn it down. I can still hear the beat, though, which is annoying enough. What is the point of having it so loud so the whole block can hear it?

Weekends mean nothing to me except if I want to venture out, I'll end up seeing more people on the road. I walked yesterday and this guy was digging and another guy standing there watching and the digger literally stopped what he was doing to just look at me. Like I was a green alien who just landed in my spaceship in the middle of the road or something. I said good morning and the other guy smiled and greeted me...the digger said nothing. People just STARE at me...I hate it and I don't understand why. Do I really look that out of place? It's not like I'm wearing Bjork clothes or have a pink mohawk standing four feet high. I guess I'm preaching to the choir here, aren't I? You know all about being stared at don't you? I feel your pain, my friend.

I still didn't ride my bike this week and I sure as hell am not doing it on a weekend either. The guy at the pulperia asked me about it yesterday (I bought it from them) and I wasn't sure exactly what he asked, I just said I was lazy.

Camille:
Amazingly, I slept through the 4:30am call to prayer this morning and got a solid six hours of sleep between my midnight piss and dawn. I felt soooo good, I got up and walked two miles to brunch at the Golden Tulip with BJ. I made a point of letting her talk this time, because she is really bright and interesting and such a good listener that she makes it incredibly easy for me to do all the talking.

I got to hear all about her time in Rwanda and what she learned about the conflict there and how it has affected the people. Honestly, I could listen to her talk all day. Brunch was not as fun as having BJ all to myself. We met with four other 20 somethings, including Jay, who is also awesome, and three young people doing short-term volunteer work at the teaching hospital.

Steph:
Well, it seems that you definitely deal with a lot more annoyances than I do! It stuns me that people don't have common sense when it comes to disturbing others. Do you think it really is a commonsense issue or something that's learned? I mean, when most people sleep, it's at night...most people have day jobs and wake up at a normal hour to conduct business during fairly normal business hours (during the day).

Camille:
So yeah, all of your take on the Muslim mayhem is spot on. And it isn't

just five times a day, it's more like 15 or 30 because the three mosques are within earshot and don't all call at the same moment. So one will call at 3:15, (yup, there they go) and then another and another. They let that sink in for 15 or 20 minutes and then call again, presumably to wind up their special prayer period. So even if it was one mosque, we'd hear it ten times. With three, it's more like 30!

Subject: Getting physical
On Oct 21, 2013 Steph wrote:

Ok, so I DID ride my bike today and almost keeled over dead. My heart actually did start to do funny things...so I came home and now I am positive I want to sell it. Even though I don't like walking on these dirt/rock roads and it hurts my feet, it's about all I've got. I walked to pay my bill and was out of breath at the top of the hill coming back. I went to pot real quick. I've reached out to a couple of English speaking friends to see if they know anyone who wants a bike, so we'll see.

 They ended up paving the road after Steph left the house sit.

I found out where my neighbor's grapefruit tree is. John tells me to just go take them but I won't do that. I'll ask next time I see him...John said he doesn't even eat them. There are a lot too! God, I could have juice! I didn't even think of that! Okay, that's my next mission then.

Well, here's to having a good sleep...

Camille:
That is really scary about your bike ride. Having a heart attack is never a good thing to flirt with! But how can you know? One minute you're doing something you feel isn't too strenuous, the next you're having palpitations.

187

Subject: Kente drama
On Oct 24, 2013 Camille wrote:

I woke up Sunday with the realization that I'd given the seamstress two yards of kente ($70 worth) to make a vest and a jacket and they never gave me one scrap back. So on Monday I went down to ask if they could give me the leftover fabric. I figured I could have some change purses made from it or at least a few bookmarks. By our calculations, we should have had about a yard leftover.

> *Kente cloth is a hand-woven fabric specific to West Africa which originated in the Asante region where Camille is living. Each color and the woven patterns have cultural significance. Camille had traveled to a kente village and purchased two yards from the weavers.*

Bob offered to go with me and I was glad because I might have let them walk all over me and he didn't let that happen. On our way over there he coached me about how to open the conversation. I still messed it up a little, feeling all sheepish and guilty for having to ask, kicking myself for not making this arrangement up front, wishing I didn't need to. They said there wasn't a shred left!

The boss came out and the employees were all like, No, we didn't even have enough to make the waist band as planned. They pulled a wad of kente from a bin under their cutting counter but one of the tailors said that wasn't our wad. Then they scrounged around and found the red material they had used for the rest of the jacket. Presumably, there should have been at least a few threads of kente in the same vicinity.

Bob was pissed. He knew they were lying whether the owner realized it or not. He asked for the two projects I'd left with them Friday and said, we don't need you to make these two dresses and we stalked out.

The boss called us back from her shop balcony after we'd reached the street and we reluctantly returned, climbing back up the stairs, hoping

188

she'd found our $35 wad of kente. She had laid out a yard of kente and starting with "I am very hurt" was going to "show" us why they had to use every scrap for my jacket.

That pissed Bob off even further because now she was going to spank us. He said, we don't have time for this and we turned our backs and left. It was very uncomfortable but I survived, and I'm happy he thought to take the work away, which I thought was over-the-top rash at the time.

I emailed Kat to ask how many yards of kente she gave them to make her dress and she said two and they gave her the leftovers. So there. I hope I can learn to sit down before every interaction and re-school myself in the appropriate self-preservation strategy. Which questions to ask up front, what might go wrong, what to say if they pull a bully on me.

Have I told you the linoleum story? Remind me if I haven't. It's a good analogy for a lot of things.

Steph:
I like what you said Bob's response would have been...that would've been good. I'm glad Bob went with you and you took what was left of the job from them. Were these the people who did your jacket and my top? I hope you don't always think of the missing fabric when you wear the jacket, though. And it IS hard to let things like that go...nobody likes to KNOW they've been taken advantage of.

I hope your day gets a little better, love. ;-) And no, I don't recall the linoleum story...what was it?

Subject: The linoleum story
On Oct 29, 2013 Camille wrote:

Thanks for all your kind words. Yes, this is the shop that made your top and I'm pretty sure I will be able to wear the jacket without pining for the lost kente.

As for the linoleum story—this is about dog training. One of the first things I teach a pet is that the kitchen is off-limits and since the kitchen floor is generally made of linoleum and often leads into a carpeted room (at least in Colorado), the line between the two floors was what I used to mark the territory.

Whenever a dog would slide a toe across the carpet onto the linoleum I would jump up and give it holy hell until it wouldn't even consider going into the kitchen. So "keeping the dog off the linoleum" became a euphemism for pushing pushy people back - lord knows there are plenty of them!

The problem is that pushy people are so used to walking into the kitchen that you have to be very hard on them up front.

So when I'd get a new dog (often got them from the pound and they had a couple of years of bad habits already), I would only let it in the house when I was there to watch it.

To make it understandable, I would line up the kitchen chairs to block it out of the kitchen. Then I would go to work in the kitchen and if it tried to worm its way between or under the chairs, it got reprimanded and pushed back.

From my position in the kitchen I could lunge at it and yell, and every dog understands the concept of territory, so that sunk in within a few hours. Then I'd remove one chair, then two and finally no chair needed. In a week it knew that its world would end if it slid as much as a toe across the linoleum.

20
FLIRTING WITH FAME

Subject: Days zipping by
On Nov 1, 2013 Steph wrote:

So how IS the packing going...are you relaxing some? Feeling like you're gonna make it okay?

Well, have a good weekend...I don't have anything going on that I know of. Oh wait, yes, going to Olivia's on Sunday for lunch.

Camille:
Geez, my days are zipping by! We'll be in winter before we know it. Yes! I finished my project!

Steph:
A birdie hit the window today, a smallish one. And as I was hanging onto it, I noticed it smelled good! Like cologne! It was odd to say the least. Maybe it was something he ate or brushed up against? No idea, but I kept sniffing his little back. Wonder how common that is? Can't say I've smelled a bird before, but from now on I will!

Subject: Eclipse
On Nov 3, 2013 Camille wrote:

Here's a picture of your new tunic. Coming to a mailbox near you soon...

Camille modeling Stephanie's new tunic

That's wild about the birds smelling like cologne!

We're in the middle of a solar eclipse right now. We rigged up two viewing systems, a shadow camera (tin foil with a hole in it and a white pad of paper) and a bucket with water in it.

Steph:
Thanks for the picture...my mom said you looked like a model ;-) and I think so too!

Today was good at Olivia's. There must've been 20+ people there, though, which always weirds me out. Luckily I've already met most of them during the tamale-making thing a while back. It was just enough time...about four hours or so. We went to the trout bar to get something for the party. They can catch, or you can, a trout and have them cook it for you. I'd feel way too guilty doing that, plus I'm not crazy about fish anyway. Might be nice to take Julio up there though. It's a good walk and they have a few pools on the mountainside with trout in them.

Anyway, they also had a birthday cake at Olivia's and I got the happy birthday singing on video so that was fun.

Ok, hope your eclipse day ended well. Oh, I had a dream I was getting married to Julio last night! It was sort of crazy.

Camille:
Please thank your mother for the compliment. Thanks to you, too. I needed to hear that because I have also been eating too much lately. Hard not to when my job is to cook. When we were managing Casa Iguana one of the laundry ladies was asked to move into the kitchen and she said she didn't want to because then she would get fat. Sure enough, she ended up working in the kitchen and she did put on weight.

I dreamed Bob and I had a little baby girl and eventually she was just this creamy liquid in a perfume bottle. This was based on your This was based on your good-smelling bird story, Bob's call to Amy yesterday, and the episode of Modern Family we watched before we went to bed.

What weirded you out about the gathering at Olivia's? Too many people? When will Julio arrive and how long are you staying—until the end of the year?

Steph:
Julio is coming on Nov. 29 - Dec. 8th and I will be here until Jan. 4th or thereabout. I realized that I don't really need to wait until the owners get back just in case another offer comes up a few days before then. The house can be left alone for a few days. Although I would like to meet them...after all this time being alone and it being "my" house, it

would feel weird to hand it back over.

Oh, at Olivia's, it was just awkward being around all of those people and nobody but she spoke English. So I just felt uncomfortable a bit. I don't like being around groups of people at all. Today, went to Gustavo's farm and I had a good time. They even offered to pick up Julio and bring him out here, which was very sweet. It's a long drive, though, and would hate to ask that of them...of course we'd pay them.

There was a really cute guy today on the drive back home...their huge truck was blocking our way. Of course it was marred by him picking his nose...ha ha! Can't have it all I guess. I just wanted a nice long look and then saw that. Gross. Men....

Subject: Fame awaits
On Nov 5, 2013 Camille wrote:

Did you see that Caretaker is looking for a TV journalist?! This may be your stepping stone into Crocodile Huntress fame!

Steph:
Awesome, thanks...email has been sent to them. ;-)

Camille:
You are ON IT! Go, go, go! Someday I'll be able to say I remember you when!

Steph:
Well well...whatta ya know!

> *"Hey Steph,*
>
> *Would love to hear more about your story. Are you available to Skype in the near future?*
>
> *let me know!*
>
> *Jxxxx Txxxxxx"*

194

Subject: Wellll
On Nov 5, 2013 Steph wrote:

I Skyped with the guy...It sounds like they're looking for a nut job though...along the lines of The Shining, so I doubt anything will come about...I'm too serene for them I'm sure. It's a show for Nat Geo though...well, got the foot in the door at least!

Camille:
I'm sure. The Shining, really? I know they mentioned it in the posting, but seriously? Is this what people want to watch on TV these days? The world's going to hell.

Steph:
Yeah, I know...well, drama sells apparently, you know. I'm sure they want some guy out in the cold or wilderness getting hurt, killing stuff, etc. I don't really know. I just got the impression that I wasn't "edgy" enough, but you know, can't win 'em all!

Subject: Bananas, art and worms
On Nov 6, 2013 Steph wrote:

So I went up to the hardware store...yeah, the one that doesn't exist! I don't know why I always think there's one there but there isn't. I don't know where the hell I'm thinking it is. Oh well, I needed the exercise anyway. That hill kicks my ass.

Not too much going on today. The bananas I chopped down turned yellow overnight. I'll give them to my fruit guys when they come by. I hate to see them go to waste. I have plenty on the tree that are literally bursting at the seams they're getting so fat! Something had a go at one last night. Same munch marks on the one bunch out back. I heard something last night on the porch, I didn't bother to look. Wonder if it's a kinkajou?

I'm tired. I finally took that Ivermectin yesterday. I don't think it went

195

well with wine. I should've drunk more of my star fruit juice instead but didn't. I felt weird last night and didn't sleep well. I'm supposed to take the next one in a week. Might as well use them...never know what is in my intestines at this point. I thought I'd have a worse reaction knowing my body, but surprisingly I didn't.

 It is suggested that expats take an anti-parasitic every 6 months while living in the tropics. Ivermectin is sold over the counter quite cheaply.

Camille:
Bananas: In Belize we cut down the bananas when they were still slightly green and hung them from a hook in the ceiling. At night we covered them with a burlap bag to keep the bats from getting them. Everything was open-air there, no screens or window glass. On the nights someone forgot to bag the bananas the bats had their way with the stalk and we arrived in the kitchen to a god-awful mess. Banana pulp and bat shit splattered on everything in the bar, from glasses to crates of soft drinks.

Art: It's all about the practice, not the results. My sketchpad has been sitting on my dresser for a week, prominently opened to a blank page and duly ignored. I even picked out the place where I'll sit to do some sketching—at the top of the steps outside our kitchen on the landing where Nwansane drew her last breath.

Worms: Being tired is to be expected as your body reacts to the Ivermectin. I wonder how many worms are dying right now and how will you know?

Steph:
Ha ha on the worm note...eeewwww I don't really want to know honestly. The one lady said she'd take it when she started feeling run down. I'm interested to see if somehow I perk up. I guess the second round is to kill leftovers of ones that weren't "hatched" yet or whatever.

She said she took them all at once, but that's not what the pharmacist told me to do. Anyway, I'm tired of being reminded of it when I see the pills lying around.

So I went out to get my bananas this morning and saw the birds eating them and then the squirrel came down and sat on the bunch and munched away.

I'm letting the bread dough rise so I can have some nice bread with my lasagna tonight!

BLOG OUT ON a LIMB

Bells and Birds

By Steph

The bell rang and I ran to my math class. Instead of people leaving, they were STAYING after class working out problems on the board, getting ready for the big test. My teacher scoffed at me for coming in right after class had ended. I looked for my 200 pound math book but it wasn't there. I said to him, "I guess you don't care about a missing math book, right?" He replied, with his arms crossed, "NO, I DON'T!" Drag. I thought to myself, "I should just drop this stupid class, I'm going to fail anyway. I hate to buy another boo....." THUD. I slowly come out of my dream and wonder what that noise was. I look at the clock: 6:15. BIRD. God, I hate getting up. I peer out the curtains, eyes blurry...can't see anything. I go to the living room and do the same. Yep! I run outside, look around to make sure nobody can see me, then retrieve the bird.

He smelled good too...REALLY FREEKIN' GOOD. Recovered fine and flew out of my hand after about 10 minutes.

 ***Steph read that birds can smell good because of what their diet consists of.***

Camille:

I loved the way you worked your dream into your latest blog and happy that you were able to take some good photos of the beautiful birds that slam into your windows. As you point out, they often flit about too quickly for a good look.

Bob's trip to Accra was successful. He flew over and back yesterday to repack our crate after they took everything out to fumigate. They threw all our wooden masks together into a plastic bag after unwrapping them. Bob had individually wrapped them in bubble wrap to protect them.

Then he finds out they have two more inspections, requiring two more unpackings. I'm sure there is a good reason why they couldn't go through our stuff all one time. But it is what it is. We'll see what we'll end up with. One small thing was already missing. Ghana, I can't leave you too soon at this point.

I'm making fried rice for dinner, a dish they refer to as oily rice in Kumasi, and I spent four hours in writer's heaven, published this week's blog and wrote next weeks, too!

BJ and Jay rode their bikes to the lake. It took them between four and five hours. We couldn't imagine weaving through Kumasi traffic and riding up the hills that surround the crater lake. Youth is for the young as they say.

Subject: Sweet smelling bird
On Nov 9, 2013 Steph wrote:

It was a pretty good day considering how early I got up. I did a new walk, which is going toward Gustavo's cabin. Ran into a lady and I practiced a little Spanish. Came back and was doing something in the yard when a huge branch fell from the tree. Glad I wasn't near it. Another small tree and some plants took the pounding. So I got out the machete and started hacking it into pieces for firewood. Picked some chayote to give to my neighbors, then walked the grounds a bit. Fed the fish for the third time today. I don't give them much and I like to watch them eat. They act like they're starving.

Then my iPod freaked out AGAIN, but I didn't take an hour to figure out how to get it going like last time. I'm afraid the drive is giving out or something.

Oooo, I was so happy the bird smelled good today! Ha ha...and strange that he smelled just like the other one too. Odd. Oh, and as I was sitting here at the table, he flew into (well, swiped against) the window! I often wonder what they would do if the window wasn't there? Sit on my shoulder? It's the second time that's happened with a bird I rescued.

Well, the sun is out again. I took some pics of more little creatures outside. This mantis has been in that flower for over a week or two that I know of. I had forgotten about it and spotted it today.

Camille:
Thanks for sharing your beautiful pictures. I've always had a soft spot in my head for praying mantises. Is this critter actually eating a bug? My father called the brown mantises walking sticks.

This getting out of stuff I don't want to do just keeps getting easier! I thought it would be a big deal to ditch dinner and turns out Bob didn't care at all.

I walked to the Tulip yesterday both ways, a distance of four miles, walked a mile at dawn to catch some final neighborhood photos and this morning walked another mile and a half. I could feel yesterday's walk in my legs today.

21
BURNING PLASTIC

Subject: Prime minister
On Nov 11, 2013 Steph wrote:

Yeah, he was eating a bug but either he got scared when I got close and dropped it or he was done. I used to call them prime ministers. My British grandmother was shocked when I, at age four, exclaimed that the prime minister was at the door.

I liked your taxi picture. Funny because when you said dawn and pictures, I imagined one while it was still sort of dark, looking down a deserted street. If you ever get up when it is just becoming light (but not too dark to see the street), do a tight shot of it. I'd love to see the taxi with the wheel missing as part of the focal point...like get real close to it then shoot down the street. Maybe hunch down so that the missing wheel takes up most of the bottom portion of the frame. I think that would be cool.

You haven't said much about the Obamacare thing...how do you feel about that? Maybe it is something you will appreciate since it could be cheap for you (I know it will be for me!) and you won't have to worry about health insurance anymore. I can't imagine you guys have spent that much money down there, so Bob should have quite a bit saved up for now, huh? Was your housing paid for? I dropped my insurance in October and haven't renewed it. I figure it was a waste of money and I never really go out anyway so might as well coast along for a while.

Camille:
Well, we paid off our debt and kept paying our mortgage back home, but won't return as rich people if that's what you're asking. Our housing and food was not paid for although it was fairly inexpensive. We rent the whole first floor for $400 and groceries cost us about $350 a month, transportation another $50. Many of our expat friends make a whole more lot money than Columbia is paying for this research project and we decided I wouldn't seek work outside the home.

In Belize, if Bob called Rolando, our assistant manager when he was indisposed (in the outhouse), his wife would tell Bob, "He's in a meeting with the Minister."

Our power was out for 16 hours. Bob started the generator after 12pm to cool down the refrigerators. He noticed right away that the neighbors seemed to have power, so he finally called an electrician, who arrived shortly after the power came back on. It's three-phase power and the house was only receiving one or two phases.

Just found out tonight that Ghanaians always sleep with the lights on. They're scared of the dark! Too many night demons and so on. So when the power goes out (now I understand why they call it "lights out" here) no one can sleep and they all come dragging into work like zombies to fall asleep at their desk or wherever they work.

I guess Ghana is going to keep surprising me right up to the day I leave!

Bob and I are jazzed about Obamacare! For the first time in nine years I'll be insured. We'll sign up for catastrophic insurance so if we get hit by a car we won't lose the house. Bob looked into it (he takes such good care of me) and said, given our income bracket our premium will come out of our taxes at the end of the year. So it won't cost us anything! Everyday stuff we'll still pay for, like dental.

Steph:
That's really funny about sleeping with the lights on. It's really amazing what people will believe isn't it? Or maybe it's we who are crazy. Never know!

I went to find the other access to the stream, but I saw I would have had to walk through someone's property so I didn't. That's when it started raining. Then I heard Joel in the back of my head going, "This isn't rain." I had to laugh. Then it started raining harder and I heard him say, "Now THIS is rain." I didn't get too wet and I'm getting better at walking up that damn hill. Now it's raining again. I guess this is what everyone was saying would happen. Kind of a drag, but at least I have painting to do.

I started sort of working on Plan B if I don't get a house sit. Found a couple spots in Panama that have serpentariums which I would LOVE to work for. Of course I'd have to try to get in touch with the center to see if they'd even accept a volunteer and I still have time to figure it all out. Worst case, I just go there and see what's up.

Took my second Ivermectin yesterday (and didn't drink) but crashed out pretty good.

Then during the small hours I woke up to a heavy smell of oil burning which was odd. Then it went away. I didn't hear any cars or anything.

Then later, I heard what sounded like a big fire...the popping of wood or something which was also odd. Seemed it was quite a while after the oil smell and I have no idea who would be up that early doing that. But then it stopped. It sounded really close too. No idea what it was.

I think you should get together a top 10 list about Africa while things are still fresh in your mind!

Subject: Top ten oily serpentarium lions
On Nov 14, 2013 Camille wrote:

That's a GREAT Plan B!

That oily smell may be the smell of burning plastic. Perhaps your neighbors torched off a pile of garbage and yard waste. Happens here about once a week. Every morning my neighbors light their cook fire with plastic and it smells kind of oily. It stings my nose.

Okay, you're on! Here a list of Top Ten Ghana Moments:

1. What?! All that noise we hear at night actually helps people sleep? Apparently many Ghanaians don't sleep well in the dark and so leave the lights and sometimes a radio on all night.
2. Um? Dog Stew can actually smell good to a vegetarian?!
3. Wow! Even an older obruni like me can look good in a custom made Ghanaian suit.
4. There are can openers for sale! Can openers! I found a whole stack of them for sale on the street after six weeks of opening cans with a knife!
5. Amazing! I just flicked an ant off my neck while deep frying falafel and didn't give it a second thought. Ditto for the ants I shake off our toilet paper.
6. Indescribable! Words and pictures cannot sufficiently convey the sensation of swimming through a river of protoplasm at Kejetia, West Africa's largest market located in central Kumasi.
7. Unbelievable! Never would have thought it possible to ride a bicycle with a pan of oranges on your head until I saw a woman doing this in Tamale.
8. Incredible! You can put a goat in the back seat of a taxi here and no one will blink an eye, but show up at a night club in sandals and they won't let you in.

9. It IS possible to feel completely at home on another continent 5,000 miles away from home. For me that place was astride one of The Green Ranch horses at Lake Bosumtwi.

10. Yikes! The only thing between me and that bull elephant heading our way is our guide's rusty pistol!

Okay, I just had a cry in Bob's arms. I'm leaving all my friends here behind and I'm afraid I won't have any friends left back home because I've been gone so long. Obviously I'm having Transition Anxiety but diagnosis doesn't dry tears.

Steph:
Great top ten! I knew you could pull one off!

Are you having any anxiety dreams about your move by chance? I know you're feeling it in real life...I'm sure something is coming out in your dreams too.

My lion is coming along, I've had to re-do the side of the face though and will finesse it today. I forgot my neighbor paints too, so I may ask to borrow some brushes from him today so I can finish this up. I hope it comes out really neat! I know Julio will love it for his Christmas present!

Subject: Lions in the dark
On Nov 15, 2013 Camille wrote:

I love, love, love your lion! He's just effin' majestic! Can't wait to see him with whiskers.

Thanks for the coaching on the taxi photo. Bob went out at dawn and took a picture I think will work.

A new addition to Dr. J. G. Wood Lane - front wheel rests on a cinder block

I love that we share our art with each other! No bad dreams coming out of my distress yesterday. I think I got it all out of my system.

Steph:
Ahhh, thanks...I've worked on it more today but the under chin is bothering me. I'm not thrilled with the whiskers either, but it is what it is. I didn't get around to putting in the four black ones either. Sheesh, I gotta finish this thing up! But overall I'm pretty happy with it. Nose is too big, but whatever...live and learn.

As for the photo, that's it! He did it. That's what I had in mind!

Oh, it started raining today with the sun out and there was a nice rainbow in the distance. It was over a house, but I liked it against the grass and stuff. It went away quickly when the clouds rolled in. I rarely see a rainbow here.

Well, brownies almost ready. More walking for me tomorrow! My excuse is that I have to use up the cocoa powder.

Subject: Retreat
On Nov 17, 2013 Camille wrote:

What are you planning to do while Julio is there?

Steph:
While Julio is here we plan on going down to where I lived in Puerto Viejo for a few days where I'll be tour guide. Then we'll head over to Arenal, close to where I also lived on the lake. We're staying in a nice hotel and we'll do the hot spring thing. He's never been to either of these areas before, to it should be fun. I did buy my bus ticket to SJ yesterday so I can meet Julio at the airport. Haven't decided how we'll get back here yet.

Camille:
How fun! You two are going to have a blast.

I'm making spaghetti tonight for us and BJ and we're planning to watch a movie. Looking forward to that. I'm pretty tired so maybe today is the day I locate my inner napper.

Steph:
So my morning is your afternoon. This reminds me of the MASH show where Radar would try to explain the time difference to Henry: "Our yesterday is their today..."

OH...I popped into a boutique shop the other day and they had this skirt that looked JUST LIKE these 80's "fashion" pants I used to wear. I couldn't believe it. I really should've taken a picture. I loved those things and actually I still have them...I couldn't get rid of them. Ridiculous looking...big elastic waistband, puffy thighs and super tapered at the ankle. I took them into work for Halloween one year when we had an '80's theme...I did NOT wear them though. I couldn't believe I saw the matching skirt. I should go back and take a picture.

Subject: Getting your fun pants on
On Nov 19, 2013 Camille wrote:

Those pants are hilarious! I can honestly say I've never worn anything quite like that. Went straight from bell bottoms to boot jeans, always been a tee shirt and jeans tomboy who regrettably never learned to navigate the slippery terrain of fashion. You look fabulous, by the way. Such a great smile and so beautiful!

We watched "The Illusionist" with BJ and loved it. BJ is real sick today. So sick she called me on the phone to come upstairs and check on her. I had figured she was catching up on some BJ time up there. No idea her bowel and stomach were turning themselves inside out.

The spaghetti was great. We both ate Italian last night. I don't think dinner is what made BJ sick. She may have malaria. She is now sleeping peacefully, so that's good.

Steph:
Eeeeew, malaria. Not good. I'm glad you never got that while you were there. Is she going to get tested or just let whatever it is run its course? I'm sure over there, like in Guyana, you can find the right tree and make some concoction from the bark to ease the pain. The quinine tree was common there and left no side effects unlike the mass-produced pills can. Drag, well I hope she'll be okay...keep me posted.

I was supposed to write a little about CR each time something good came up, but it fell to the wayside so now I'm four months behind!

Oh gosh, my dream last night. I had (in real life) noticed this HUGE thing hanging from the vines/tree yesterday and I don't know what it is...but fixin' to find out today. It looks like a small watermelon but I also know he was growing a squash vine—but this is like no squash I've seen. So I had a dream that a frog had swallowed this thing WHOLE!

He looked really uncomfortable and I managed to get it out of his mouth after saying, "You'll never digest that!" I cut it up for him and fed him huge chunks of watermelon. In that same dream, I was bitten on the bottom of my foot by a duck and it bled like crazy, like squirting out blood bleeding! I told the girl next to me to help me fast! It was strange.

Subject: Bleeding Jesus malaria
On Nov 21, 2013 Camille wrote:

Turned out BJ did not have malaria, only a stomach bug which she treated with antibiotics, rest and a couple of nights of my cooking. Bob and I have really been enjoying her company as Jay wheels his way north to Mole. She plans on taking a bus up to Tamale to meet him tomorrow.

Yesterday I found myself trapped in a conversation with a young Ghanaian who wanted to know if I had accepted Jesus into my life. Being an atheist who believes strongly in the value of human compassion, this kind of situation always sets off internal conflict between my desire to be nice to others and my impulse to share my thoughts about religion.

Bob and I are going to the lake soon without our computers, so I'm catching up emails before we go. Good god! A day and a half without my laptop! Hee hee. Horses, Elodie, the birds, her delicious cooking and time to relax. Won't be a bad thing.

Thank you for sharing your dreams with me. Bob was bleeding yesterday after grasping a palm frond. I was taken aback to see blood dripping from his hand, not gushing like from your foot in your dream, but I wonder if somehow that and your dream are connected?

22
LEAVING IN 3, 2, 1...

Subject: OMG
On Nov 20, 2013 Steph wrote:

Yeah, about the dream of me bleeding and Bob. You know, lately and maybe it's because we're talking more, but Julio and I dream a lot of the same things too. I told him yesterday I dreamed I had some lady run into the front end of my Prelude. He said he had a dream that we were going to a small town and there was this big dip in the road and I bottomed out and wrecked the front end. But this is like the third dream in the past couple of months that has been similar.

But it could also be that I can clue into things like that, which would be even weirder. I'd like to think it's that! There have been other events in my life where very strange things like this have happened...the whole "getting into your head" stuff. I did used to get heavy ESP, so yeah, maybe I did know he got cut!

Well, I hope you have a good time at the lake...you always do. Oh, and glad she didn't have malaria. I can't believe he is riding that far! Wow. Hope he makes it okay.

Camille:
We're back! We reached home about three hours ago.

I'll bet you do have ESP. Bob and I had the same dream once and it was so uncanny that we decided it meant we needed to leave the country. So we moved to Belize! It was about the beach and the images were incredibly similar, as were our feelings about what was going on. We were each searching for a way out in our dreams and then we saw the ocean and realized, That's it—that's where I need to go!

Only eight more nights in Kumasi for us! We have everything pretty much lined out, but it's easy to start hyperventilating anyway. It was a bit outside our comfort zones to go to the lake for a day, but I think it was a good thing. I went for a nice walk with Elodie down by the shore. We decided not to ride. I think Bob and I are getting sluggish from the hot weather because frankly neither of us had the energy. Elodie was offering but when we said no thanks, she was fine with that. She gets plenty of riding.

Jay made it to Mole on his bike and BJ took the bus up to meet him this morning. Those two! So Bob and I have the whole house to ourselves.

Can't wait to hear your news. Geez, I feel like I've been gone for a week! Guess I'm really hooked on email.

Missed you!

Steph:
I missed you too! I thought you'd be gone longer for some reason. Does she not get Internet out there, or is it just the principle that you "disconnect"? And no riding? Wow, Cookie. Amazing!

HOLY CRAP you're LEAVING SOON! God, I didn't realize it was this soon. Whoa, that must feel crazy, huh? I assume everything is in order? Oh, you're going to Morocco though, right? For five days was it? So when do you actually get HOME? I just got butterflies FOR you! eeeekkkk...weird.

Is there going to be a going away party for y'all? Are BJ and Jay staying there? I think so, but can't remember. And he made it on his bike! Wow! Did he ride at night too? Nothing went wrong?

Anyway, I got the idea to move the mantis (will assume you've seen my cute video already) to the rose bush. Thought she'd like the other bugs on there (plenty) but she didn't eat any. Man, you know you're a hermit when you get excited about interacting with a walking stick.

I'm going shopping tomorrow morning if I can get out of here by 8 to prepare for J's arrival. He'll be here on Friday.

Camille:
Julio arrives the day before we all—BJ, Jay, Bob and I—fly to Accra from Kumasi to catch our flights home. They leave late Saturday morning and we fly to Morocco on the early Sunday morning flight. We'll reach Raleigh late December 7th, exactly two weeks from today. I'm experiencing an odd mix of malaise, relaxation and anxiety.

The reception is so bad at the lake it isn't worth it. I had to climb around on the slope behind the house just to send BJ a text.

Jay called last night and BJ texted to report they were chilling by the Mole Hotel pool with beers after a monkey stole his box of digestives. I called him back to get the monkey story and it was hysterical. He was amazed the monkey didn't snatch his bag with all his money in it. Obviously, he said, the monkey recognized the red biscuit box and went for them, then sat a little ways away and tore open the box, stuffing biscuits into his/her mouth.

I really enjoyed your mantis video. Especially when it turned around and was riding proud on your finger like a captain at the helm of a ship! Nice camera work. You have a gift!

Maybe what I like about mantises is their thoughtful attitude. They seem to be thinking. They really look like aliens. My parents

211

intentionally kept half of our back yard in the Bronx wild so we kids could experience nature, and it was crawling with wild roses and mantises.

Subject: Thieving monkey
On Nov 23, 2013 Steph wrote:

Glad you liked the mantis video! It was so cool! I took her to the rosebush today too but she still didn't catch anything. The roses are crawling with bugs, flies, bees, other insects so you'd think she'd like it there. I guess I could've left her there longer but I was going in and I didn't want to lose her, plus it looks like it's going to rain. I think she's better off in the spot she chose and feels comfortable in, so she went back there. I agree, they do seem really intelligent, the way they cock their heads and waver back and forth. I wonder if it's a male though since it's not that big...I read females are larger. The one time I actually call a creature a SHE and it's probably not.

Mantis perched upside down on a rosebush

212

I slept badly last night. The night before I dreamt I was in an elevator that was falling and falling fast! So fast, that I crawled up to the top without a problem because the gravity was gone. I don't remember what happened though...if we landed okay or crashed.

Went into town today and get this...Some places won't allow you to try on a bra. My god, it's not like it's panties or something. I mean, what could you possibly spread by trying on a bra? THREE places wouldn't let me. In the one place that did, they all fit horribly. Maybe that's why!?

P.S. Hey, lucky for Jay, monkeys don't spend money! What kind was it? They are good thieves. I remember being in a tourist spot here in CR a few years ago and the white faced capuchins sneak up and unzip people's bags or just take anything they leave lying around...but yeah, mostly food.

Camille:
Ha ha! What if a monkey stole Jay's money and then went and ordered a beer and a salad. Would they serve him/her? I think he said it was a patas monkey. When we were there in February we only saw one green vervet monkey.

I am so glad I didn't have to buy a bra down here. I brought three and only wear them with some of my outfits and then only when I go out. Because I have tiny breasts. Lucky me.

You can buy bras on the street here and they probably wouldn't care if you stripped naked and tried them on right there in front of them. A couple of times a week I see a woman with a huge head pan of bras walking down Robteng, the street the next block over. She arranges it with the bras hanging off the side like tassels. They all look huge. Big enough for me to wear as a hat on my tiny head.

I love your praying mantis stories! How would you know if it were a she or a he, anyway?

213

Have a wonderful day. Hope you aren't too itchy or sluggish! Hope you slept well. I slept like a baby, or rather a toddler because babies don't sleep well at all. Just listen to the little one next door!

Subject: Jay
On Nov 27, 2013 Camille wrote:

Just sipping cocoa on a "brisk" not-yet-80-degree white sky morning in Kumasi with only five more nights to go.

BJ and Jay arrived home shortly before we made it back from Kat's. BJ ran down the front steps to meet us in the dark (the power was out, naturally) and to inform us that Jay was lying in bed shivering from malaria.

She had gone out and bought him an over-the-counter malaria test, something like a pregnancy test only using fingertip blood, and it showed positive. Before we left I had set on Jay's desk a package of malaria treatment pills that Bob had bought for him and BJ said he was already taking pills.

Steph:
Hi! how's Jay doing? I'm getting a bad feeling over here for some reason...

Camille:
He's mending slowly but going to make it. As for traveling, it may not be his best trip. Megan the nurse brought him quinine yesterday and he was a sick as a dog. It's really hard on your stomach.

Subject: 3, 2, 1...
On Nov 27, 2013 Camille wrote:

Morning! Well, NOW I'm finally starting to lose it! I think it's a combination of trying to cook a final few meals and the refrigerator leaving. At least three people are also coming over to scavenge through

214

our house. Would be great if I weren't trying to pull off a four pot meal tonight!

Keep breathing, do some yoga, mow the lawn, sweat a bit, admire the order I'll make from chaos and how smooth the grass looks after I'm done, shower and breathe. That's my plan.

Okay, back to you. That is a really lovely cat photo. And oh my god, aren't you going to see Jullo in just a couple of days!

We're staying at the Riad Cherrata in Marrakech's Medina.

Leaving Kumasi in 3, 2, 1... !

Steph:
WOW, that place in Morocco looks awesome! Luxury, huh? Well, you deserve it. Nice end to your looooong trip. You'll have great stories and will look back on it in a different light possibly.

Well, I'm glad Jay is surviving at least.

Okay, I know you're busy so I'll keep it short here...I'm getting excited/nervous/skittish for you if that helps at all!

Camille:
Hi! You are a dear friend. Of course it helps!

I survived my little fit of a day, complete with long, tearful goodbyes and late arrivals, which sent me scurrying to pull together dinner an hour later than usual. But now we're stuffed on Obruni comfort food, BJ went out for dinner and then off to Alliance Française for a movie and all is quiet on the home front.

23
THANKSGIVING

Steph has secured a volunteer job in El Valle, Panama helping an expat couple open a butterfly house. She'll be raising the butterflies and helping with tours and baking in the café.

Subject: Panama tofurky
On Nov 28, 2013 Camille wrote:

Yay, Panama! That is so cool. I do hope it works out. When is Julio arriving? This Saturday or next? I'm thinking it's this Saturday.

I have the day to myself which is good. Seriously yesterday kicked my ass. I'm exhausted and irritable. That cider I drank didn't help. I just want to hide somewhere until this is all over. But today is all mine. I'm going to put my affairs in order, do some writing, cook an easy meal and have movie night with the kids. All is well.

What'd you make for dinner? Any birdies hit your windows lately?

Steph:
Yes, I'm very excited about Panama...I couldn't get to sleep last night with so much running through my head.

Julio comes tomorrow. It's STILL raining! Windy, too. I feel like going out and getting the wet, cold mantis and putting her/him on my flowers here in front of me (and I just might!). That would be fun...hang out together for a while.

It's so strange to have this countdown of sleeping the next to last night in your bed, huh? It's hard to believe how time flies, really. Seemed just like last week Julio and I were saying, three and a half more weeks 'til we see each other! And yeah, I guess people just don't realize all of the last minute stuff you have to do before leaving. I got caught up in that too and could barely make time to see anyone before leaving Texas. They mean well, but the idea of a coming home party is better. ;-)

Love you, friend!

Steph:
No tofurky for you today? Ha ha, I love saying that word. Next to Kentucky Fried Satan, it's my favorite saying I got from you.

I did bring the mantis in from the rain and she seems happy hangin' in the flowers. I cut some of those big red Easter lilies, so she's sitting near those looking out the window.

Camille:
Well, it's the last day of November and today's the day we leave!

The first thing Bob asked me this morning was, what was I looking forward to back home. The only thing that popped into my mind that I'm REALLY looking forward to is Twizzlers. I mean, seriously? That crap candy made from high fructose corn syrup and cattle toes?

 Actually, twizzlers are made with cornstarch rather than gelatin.

I think we overstayed our stay. We are gagging on glee to be leaving. But seriously, I am going to miss a lot of things, most of all my friends and the horses at the lake, our big beautiful house, the national geographic street scenes and the fresh fruit all year round to name a few.

I love that you brought your mantis inside. Geez, you just might be lonely. Perhaps a bit closer to the Jack Nicholson persona than you let on to that TV show. But Julio will fix all that for you.

Steph:
Well, it must feel strange not having all your stuff around you. I'll never forget the last time I looked back into my house the day I left it...all empty. It was odd. All the years I took to collect all my stuff...gone. But hey, I don't regret a single day.

Plastic Farm Animals
blog

Leaving Kumasi – An Exit Interview
By Camille

Q. So, how does it feel to be leaving Kumasi?

A. It feels like the end of a play I've been acting in, like curtains drawing closed across a dirt stage littered in plastic, slowly pinching off the sound of the roosters, taxis, chain saws, crows, bulbuls and Muslims. It feels like a sigh of relief.

Q. Kumasi was that bad, huh?

A. Yes and no. Like any big city, Kumasi was loud, crowded and dirty, although as a friend pointed out the other day, it's really more of a village than a city. A huge sprawling village of two million people all striving to survive. All outside cooking, sleeping, peeing, laughing, yelling, burning trash, and carrying impossible burdens on their heads.

Each time I walked outside our compound gate onto the rutted dirt road

I felt as if I were stepping into the pages of National Geographic. It was fascinating and often an affront to all of my senses. I was intrigued by the childlike innocence I saw in nearly everyone, a strong desire to please, to see the bright side of life, a prayer on their lips for someone bigger and stronger to hold their hand and walk them over to the good life.

Q. Do you think your African experience would have been different if you had lived away from town?

A. Definitely, yes. After living in a small farming community for nearly five years, we found Kumasi a bit outside our comfort zone. It helped that Bob had grown up in Accra when it was roughly the size of Kumasi and that we had lived both abroad and in cities with populations well over two million.

Q. Why did you agree to the move?

A. I have been keen to visit Africa since I was a young girl. When the opportunity presented itself, I encouraged Bob to take the job. I don't think we would have moved to Africa had the job been anywhere other than Ghana. I had long wanted to experience the place of Bob's childhood with him. Also, the pay was sufficient for us to pay off our debt and put a little savings in the bank. We hoped to share the adventure with our daughters and so connect them to their father's African experience. In addition the project—research involving sanitation—fit our values.

Q. Are you glad you went?

A. Yes, and I would do it again in a heartbeat. Bob and I experienced Ghana together, topped up our bank account and shared five months with daughter Amy. Not to mention we saw wild African elephants!

Q. Why are you leaving Ghana?

219

A. The project goals have been accomplished, Bob's contract is finished and our house, property, friends, family and neighbors await our return.

Q. What will you miss about your life in Kumasi?

A. I think I will miss life without A/C, which was reminiscent of my childhood growing up in New Jersey without air conditioning. When the windows are open the sounds of an active neighborhood make me feel connected and alive in a way that sealing myself up in a quiet house does not.

I'm definitely going to miss my friends. Expats bond quickly, forming fast friendships based on need and circumstances. Adrift in a culture that often seems incomprehensible, I reached out to a great variety of personalities and was welcomed into the fold without reservation. We all joke that we probably wouldn't be friends if we met in our native countries. Like war, the act of surviving adversity in a strange world creates strong bonds between a wide range of individuals.

Predictably some of those alliances blossomed into deep friendships with people we may never see again. Which hurts. Fortunately we have the technology to stay in touch.

Q. How will you describe Ghana to your friends back home?

A. Ghana is essentially a nation of five-year-olds, irrepressibly eager, happy, playful, rough around the edges, irresponsible, unruly, naive and often deceitful. The culture is the product of colonialism, Christianity, corruption and tropical malaise. Ghanaians, or at least the majority of people we interacted with in Kumasi, are not problem solvers. The educational system encourages submission and suppresses Independent thought. We see that most Ghanaians are happy to make do, not averse to taking hand outs, have difficulty saying no, and often miss commitments.

Religion is so important that they eagerly attend all-night services at the cost of their daytime performance. Many are convinced that their big financial breakthrough is right around the corner as long as they continue making the church their priority. Many go to church several times a week, to services in which the collection plate is passed multiple times.

Q. What were the highlights of your stay?

A. Our trip to Mole National Park with Amy was highly rewarding. I really enjoyed the walking safaris, seeing elephants and other animals in their natural habitat and learning about the diverse ecosystem. We made enough trips to the beach, Lake Bosumtwi and to parks and botanical gardens with enormous old-growth trees to balance out our time at home in Kumasi.

I also enjoyed tending to our home, compound grounds and gardens, walking to market for food and cooking in our windowed kitchen. I loved looking out at our neighbors and listening to them throughout the day. We lived in a quiet neighborhood a few blocks from a busy road with an eclectic mix of people. I settled into a quiet rhythm of writing, yard work, walking around greeting people in Twi and housework.

Q. Do you have any advice for others headed to Kumasi to live and work?

A. Yes. Don't expect too much! Get out of town on a regular basis. Start a garden and a compost pile, it will keep you grounded. Walk to market at least once a week. Join the Facebook group Kumasi Expats, or find another way to connect with other expatriates. Get used to living with ants. Learn enough Twi to show you care about the people and their culture. Don't touch people with your left hand. Keep antibiotics and a regimen of malaria treatment in the house. They are cheap and easily purchased over the counter from any chemist. Check out Alliance Française near Ahodwo Roundabout. Embrace the adventure.

Subject: Getting gone
On Dec 1, 2013 Steph wrote:

Hi! How does it feel to be "gone?" I LOVED your blog! It made me cry.

Julio and I had a good day yesterday, went to a bar, got drunk, stayed up late...recovering this morning.

Well, have to run but wanted to say hi and hope you're doing okay in Morocco. Let me know how it is when you have a chance.

Camille:
How fun! I can't believe it's Tuesday already. We got up at 2am Monday and traveled most of the day, arriving in Marrakech, schlepping those enormous blue bags from baggage claim, to one train, to a second train (where a porter actually walked across the tracks with each and every one to put us in position for boarding the final train into Marrakech), into a taxi, onto a hand cart, through the streets of the Medina and up the stairs to our room at the Riad Cherrata.

We're here for five days and are being very careful to remember which clothes we take out of what bags so we can put them where they belong and they will weigh the same when we board our flight home.

We ate a beautiful dinner last night—vegan, beautifully presented on rectangular white plates with little sauces. It was so pretty, had I not been hungry I would have just sat and stared at it. Plus we were zooey from lack of sleep.

We are staying in the oldest district of Marrakech, the sprawling walled-in hive of riads (homes) and souk (market.) Last night I slept in the best bed I've slept in since leaving NC. Eight hours, woke up at 5am with Muslims, then went back to sleep for another two hours. We've enjoyed a fantastic breakfast and are heading out to walk around the Medina.

24
REPATRIATION

Subject: Phew
On Dec 8, 2013 Steph wrote:

Just got home. How does it feel for YOU to be home now?

Camille:
It feels great! I just got online for the first time since leaving Morocco nearly two days ago. Our neighbors and other people we know from town that we saw when we went in to buy groceries all welcomed us with happy smiles and snug hugs. I feel like I had never left. Bob said it's like pulling on an old pair of jeans.

So how was your trip? Where did you go and what did you do?

We had a long day of travel Sunday. Got up at 1am EST, out the door at 2am and arrived at our house at 11pm, washed sheets, etc. and got to bed at 1:30am, then up at 7am and over to Jason and Haruka's for brunch. It's real good to be home.

We have a lot of work to do putting the house back together. Everything is a little musty from a summer without A/C. ALL of our clothes, those we left behind and those we brought from Ghana are kind of smelly.

We're washing clothes but the dryer is clogged so not drying very fast. We need to set up the outside line. I spent two hours cleaning the refrigerator and I need to get a driver's license.

Bob got us wifi and phone numbers. We're going to bed early tonight!

Steph:
Weird to be on the same time schedule again! I liked your last photo blog a lot...It made me a little misty in the eyeballs to see you leave. But it sounds like you haven't had reverse culture shock just yet. Nice of your friends to be there waiting for you! I'm happy you're home but sure you have a lot to do.

The trip was really good...poor Julio got stuck waiting around all day yesterday to get home. He had a five hour wait at the airport after he got dropped off here, then a delay in Houston due to the snow in Dallas and some problem with the baggage so he probably got home after midnight.

Well, I won't write too much. We'll catch up when you are ready to write. Woke up to a bird hitting the window, walked right past him looking for one out by the side. Came back and he was there on the ground by the door, dead. I'm taking your old approach and leaving it for the cats...we'll see what happens.

 Camille suggested leaving dead birds for the cats instead of burying them, which is what I had done with this one. I left it under a tree and when I went back later to see if it was still there, it had disappeared.

Camille:
That is so cool the cat got the bird. The circle of life and so on. Did you have a good time with Julio?

Lyle and Tami invited us to meet them for lunch and since we were in town running errands we jumped right on over. They ordered a bottle of champagne and it was so great!

I am seriously feeling like a celebrity. Everywhere we go people gasp, smile, give us big hugs. It's great. I did get a little culture shock in the Piggly Wiggly today trying to remember which brand of toilet paper we used to buy. Sooo many choices. I was just standing there trying to get a grip.

I bought broccoli and made a stir fry with onions and mushrooms and tofu. First time I've eaten broccoli since leaving the States. I had to stop after two bowls so I didn't hurt myself.

We woke at 4am this morning and couldn't get back to sleep. I hope we do better tonight. We woke up with sore throats so are flirting with getting sick. Have not had eight hours of sleep in days.

Steph:
Yeah, it was kind of cool the cat took it. I made sure to smell the poor bird and it also smelled like the other ones. Weird...

I laughed at your toilet paper dilemma, how funny. Wonder what else you'll come across you haven't had in a year!

And you were worried you wouldn't have friends when you got back. Silly woman!

I'm reading up on how to raise butterflies and they had a great idea about pitching the services to wedding planners and funeral homes. A good idea if I take this back to the States and start my own business.

Time is getting away from me and must do dishes and read more...I have so much to do this month!

Plastic Farm Animals
blog

Homecoming

By Camille

Our homecoming was unexpectedly easy. Sure, there was plenty of remediation work to be done with the house, but our neighbors welcomed us with open arms. No need to endear ourselves to them— apparently the social capital we'd put in the bank before we left was still there and had accrued interest.

Jason and Haruka made sure we were fed. They placed a box of freshly-harvested produce in our refrigerator for us to come home to and fixed us breakfast the next morning. Later, Scott and Rachel stopped by to welcome us home with warm hugs. Lyle and Tami took us to lunch the next afternoon and offered to cut down the oak tree that fell on our garage while we were gone. Everywhere we went in town, people stopped what they were doing to rush over and welcome us home, and our neighborhood homies are planning a welcome home potluck at Tami and Lyle's new house.

Amy arrived a few days after we landed to help pull things together, and our friend Sophie flies in today. I think we'll get out the Christmas garlands and dress up the house for the holidays. We are basking in good friends, good food, good cheer and frankly feeling a bit humbled by the unreserved affections of our friends and acquaintances.

We were also surprised at how easy it is to get things done here. The drive to the landfill for a trash sticker so we can self-haul our recycling and refuse was painless. We were met by a smiling clerk who waived the fee and welcomed us home. Ditto for getting our car registered and my driver's license renewed. We keep wondering when we'll stumble upon the potholes, traffic snags, police barricades, burning piles of trash and pestering children. Poised for the lights to go out, the water to stop flowing and the Internet to quit. What's the catch, we wonder?

In only a few short days we were set up with Internet, a fully functioning kitchen, laundry, transportation and have mostly removed all signs left behind by some mice which took up residence earlier this year. Not to mention employment prospects!

All of these things reinforce our decision to invest heavily in our community and have us promising never to leave home again. We are home and home to stay!

Subject: Homecoming
On Dec 14, 2013 Steph wrote:

It does feel oddly strange being back there doesn't it? Even after only being away for three months, then going to VA, it was like I had no clue how I saw things before. I noticed buildings looked really well built, paint on houses wasn't some crazy color, sidewalks with pavers and the general feel of wealth, things were a little too easy. But hey, it's good we know about the "other side" because you'll appreciate things more...at least until you get used to them again, I suppose.

Well, hey, at least you aren't being thrown into the two million people city mix or anything. You're in a pretty chill place so that's good.

Holy god...there was just a huge explosion for the third time today that scared me so bad I actually got goose bumps! I have no idea what that was, electricity didn't go out or anything but I saw a big blast of color out by the street. See, these things don't happen in the U.S. Wow. That scared the hell out of me.

Transformers often blow due to an overload of electrical usage in houses. Not much planning seems to go into supply and demand when it comes to electricity. The solution is to just come out and replace the part instead of upgrading the system.

Steph:
How'd it feel to drive? I haven't driven in nine months...wait I take that back...that millionaire in VA let me drive his Porsche for a little while. That was fun.

Camille:
Driving was a trip. At first, I slid right into it but then there was a moment on a winding road with a pick up truck coming towards me where I panicked and forgot my gear pattern. Thank god for clutch and brake.

I dreamed the giraffe got out and we were about to chase it up the hill when I said, "No, let's put a pan of feed just inside the gate and wait until he comes down, then open the gate and shoo him in." It pays to be smarter than the giraffe.

Steph:
Well, the butterfly guy sent pics of the house and said it'd be 30-35 hours a week...up from the three hours a day he talked about before. That puts a serious damper on my other volunteer activities I had planned as well as my free time. The house is ehhhh...not as nice as this one...very plain, nothing on the walls in any room...very generic and lifeless. Well, whatever...not like I'll be in the house that much.

Looking forward to seeing the pictures you'll work on later. I guess I need to think about a selfie in the sunny yard as my Xmas card to everyone at some point. Should've done that yesterday when I looked half way presentable. Those days are few and far between!

Subject: Wow...Christmas already?
On Dec 22, 2013 Camille wrote:

I spent three hours in the yard in a tank top and got a lot done. I'm very pleased with it. Now it's raining. Still have the front yard and the driveway to do, but I have nine days before our big New Year's Day Party and it's supposed to be warmish and dry again next weekend.

I just realized Wednesday is Christmas. We plan on eating next door with Jason and Haruka. It's tradition. Missed it last year. Family doesn't come to us and we don't go to them. Guess you're in the same boat. Got any plans?

Steph:
Yeah, I could go to Puerto Viejo for Xmas to see my old neighbor and stay with her, but I'm not feelin' it. Three buses, one taxi, seven hours...not an attractive alternative to being alone. And that's just ONE WAY. So two days wasted for travel so I can go there to work on the website with her. Hmmm decisions, decisions.

It doesn't feel like Xmas when the season never really changes, does it? I'm wondering if anyone here will invite me to their house? I won't count on it.

Olivia came by and I gave her a load of my stuff, mostly clothes. Then, while I was bbq'ing, she called saying her brother-in-law was out front and wanted to get my bike for his son. I took a $30 loss on it, but better than not selling it at all I guess. So that was good.

Plastic Farm Animals
blog

Time Warp
By Camille

We've been home for two weeks and I am continually shocked by the sameness of our town. It appears that virtually nothing has changed in a year and a half. With the exception of a rebuilt courthouse and a couple of new businesses, everything looks the same. It's as if I woke from a dream about living in Africa to find myself still here in Pittsboro.

No one has aged a day. I find this a little unsettling. While my hair has turned from grey to white, seemingly overnight, everyone else looks just as they did before we left. Add in the zooey feeling associated with a nasty head cold and I feel like the ghost of Rip Van Winkle each time I leave the house.

I'm astounded when past acquaintances recognize me. My first impulse is to keep moving as if they had called out "Obruni!" And then, before I can decide whether to greet them in Twi or with cheek kisses, I'm enveloped in a warm embrace. When they ask me about my trip to Africa I blink numbly and, thanks to my cold, begin to cough into the crook of my arm, effectively ending the conversation. Part of me wants to say, "Africa?" while another side wants to say, "I could write a book, do you have a couple of weeks?" or "Just read anything John Theroux wrote about Africa."

Truthfully, our time in Africa had a profound impact on us. It would take a book to explain. When I try to describe the nuances of the landscape or the impact it had on my spiritual growth I begin to sound like a bigot. People shrink back at the telling of what I intend as uplifting stories. I have a better picture of Sub-Sarahan Africa now and I'm afraid it isn't pretty. Ditto with what I've learned about myself.

Yes, my return home has been like Rip Van Winkle with a twist. I aged and then traveled back to the past where everyone in my town still looked the same. Even the technology is the same. I slid into the driver's seat of our 1995 Ford Escort, Christine, and knew exactly what to do. Even though I hadn't driven anything more complicated than a wheelbarrow for a long time, within moments Christine and I were flying up the Gum Springs Road. There was one moment where I encountered oncoming traffic, downshifted and forgot my gear pattern, but other than that my car seems to drive itself just like before, pulling effortlessly into my familiar haunts as I make my rounds.

I'm still using the same phone albeit with a new phone number. But all 100 or so phone numbers of people I apparently called in the past are still unchanged in my little cell phone. I flipped it open and called my *mom the other day and was able to stay on the line for two hours without losing service once. Even the ringtone I had assigned to Bob's number remained the same. When I hear the first clarinet and oboe notes of "The Pink Panther" emanating from my pocket, I know it's my one and only. If someone suggests I give so-and-so a call, I don't need to ask for their number. In fact, in many cases I still remember the speed dial number I assigned them.*

It will be interesting to see if the sameness wears off and I begin to notice things that have changed. Or if, after I am able to speak a complete sentence without lung trauma, I feel compelled to share tales from afar. My guess is I'll pick up where I left off, gratefully embrace a community that held open a spot for me and leave my African experience in the dust.

25
CHRISTMAS

Subject: Pond weeding
On Dec 24, 2013 Steph wrote:

So how's your Christmas eve going? I worked on weeding by the pond...and now it looks very bare. It choked out a lot of the impatiens, which I hadn't realized, but I broke off the sections of day lilies and planted those and put the wandering jew there too...maybe in a couple of weeks it won't look as bad.

Camille:
That's so weird! I also weeded around our little goldfish pond and made it look bare today! What the hey. I'm sure your pond plants will fill in. Mine, not until spring.

Even though it is only in the 40's out, the sun was shining, so with gloves, hat, jacket, sweatshirt and leggings underneath my blue jeans, I spent 2 1/2 hours going at it. I also decorated the porches with sparkly Christmas-like garlands. Because, after all, tomorrow is Christmas. However, no gifts will be exchanged and no pets harmed.

Your time is coming soon. Are you nervous?

Steph:

No, not really getting nervous yet. Seems like I just live day to day and don't think too far ahead. It's like a safety mechanism so I don't stress out.

OUT ON a
BLOG   LiMB

Merry Christmas from Costa Rica!
by Steph

It's a beautiful day and figured I'd get a photo with the wild poinsettias that I noticed growing here about a month ago. The butterflies were enjoying them as well. I'd never seen them growing in the wild, only in pots during Christmas, then left to dry out and die by the time New Year's came around. I always tried to save them, but it was a hard fought battle. They simply weren't meant to be in pots in dry hot offices

with no sun. So it's nice to see them flourishing here.

The other day, I got a present from Mother Nature when a yellow-throated euphonia flew into the house and I was able to catch it and spend a little time with it. Sure was a beauty! Small too, only a little larger than a hummingbird. It had beautiful dark blue feathers and the contrasting yellow really made it stand out. Of course, I had to sniff it and sure enough, it smelled good too! I'm beginning to think all birds must smell good. They all seem to have a similar scent. The bird turned out to be okay and flew off fairly quickly, so that was a nice gift!

Merry Christmas from Moncure
On Dec 25, 2013 Camille wrote:

Nice post, my dear friend. I am feeling especially fortunate today for our friendship and all my other good fortune. Your love for the creatures of the world makes me teary-eyed. What a beautiful heart you have!

We're taking the day off from yard work, laundry, etc. doing lots of cooking and eating and hanging around. I hope you also have an excellent day.

A cardinal is perched in the poplar tree and a blue jay has landed in the Bradford pear. Guess they are saying Merry Christmas, too!

Steph:
Aw, thanks. I'm very glad for our friendship too, knowing it'll last a lifetime! The best gift of all. And I'm so glad you're back home too.

My neighbor decided fireworks were in order last night as I was trying to get to sleep...then I think around midnight he popped some off again. I would've gotten up to look at them but it was cold.

Camille:
Here is a picture of the four of us from yesterday.

Haruka, Jason, Camille and Bob

We had a really nice time with our neighbors and stayed from twoish until nearly 9pm. We feel like brothers and sisters. Haruka and I sat on the couch with our feet under a throw after we played cards. Jason played his guitar for us, which we didn't even know he did. Then the guys talked and Haruka and I sang Christmas carols.

Well, fill me in. I'm sure you've been up to something!

Steph:
Glad you had a good time. It's good to be around friends isn't it? You look great, BTW.

Really not much going on here. I cleaned up in the yard a bit today...planted some stuff in the bare spots by the pond and chopped down some limbs off of trees.

I keep finding really big bones in my yard. Jaw bones, leg bones (animal, not people...ha ha). I keep throwing them away in the brush and new ones appear daily now. It's disturbing. I hear the coyotes every night again but wonder who exactly is dragging this stuff over here. No idea

235

what animal it is, but it's big. Would have to assume it's cow, but I really don't know. If I lived here I'd have one of those night cams so I could see what happens in the yard at night.

I had an idea about how to pack my clothes inside those compression bags and gave it a whirl today. It didn't work out exactly as hoped, but pretty good...so I packed some things and went through my other stuff figuring out what I need and don't need. I think it'll be a bit lighter than when I got here.

Subject: Screaming down life's highway on roller blades
On Dec 27, 2013 Camille wrote:

What are compression bags? Why are big bones showing up in your yard? That's pretty weird. It could be the dogs and probably is. They must have found a cow carcass.

It's only 40 degrees out and the sun is filtering through thin clouds, so really too cold for this tropical princess, but that evil boxwood outside our bedroom window continues to taunt me. My car is in the shop, so at some point I'll have to go into town.

Steph:
Sorry, I meant space bags - those plastic bags that you can suck the air out of with a vacuum or pump.

I felt guilty about the lack of flowers by the pond, so I dug up some others and stuck them in there. He's not going to be happy. For rainy season, it's been damn dry. It shows everywhere here, plants thinning out, dirt super dry...so it's not totally my fault. All those weeds made it look full, 'til I picked them out (like you did too). It hasn't rained in a good six days. Odd.

Oh, I had a dream last night that I was roller skating SUPER fast, like 80mph...how I knew that, I don't know, but that's what it was. I worried about hitting a rock or something in the street and killing myself but it didn't happen. So I looked it up this morning:

To dream of roller blading, especially outdoors, signifies that you are moving through life with ease and purpose.

Yeah!

Camille:

Heh heh, moving through life with ease, or screaming down life's highway on roller blades? Sounds like a dream I have versions of. I'm driving down a hill and the brakes don't seem to be working too well. Or the road ahead dips down below the water line but I keep driving.

I had good dreams but don't recall details. Mostly I was in charge and feeling strong and capable. Like I am, heh heh.

Subject: Leezard
On Dec 30, 2013 Steph wrote:

I have dreams about brakes not working too...weird.

I caught myself getting a little tearyeyed on the bus ride to town while overlooking this little village. I don't really know why I'm sad to leave it, but it seems I get that way when I leave any place here. Then I realized I'd be leaving CR altogether! I had to think that Panama will be very similar and it won't be that big of a change really, so that made me feel better. At least I'll be accomplishing something at the end of the day, unlike here.

I saw this little guy in my room trying to get outside. Chase ensued, lost him a couple of times as he ran for his life. Finally got him, then took him outside and he didn't want to get off of me! I thought his back legs were paralyzed! So I tried to get him to move around and finally he did, so I knew nothing was wrong with him. He just liked the warmth or something. I petted him and scratched his chin, then finally had to put him in the bushes. Crazy kid.

Subject: Idea
On Dec 30, 2013 Camille wrote:

I have an idea for a book. It would basically be you and me writing back and forth and telling stories of our day, current events, memories. It was the stories about our music and watching Jason play that triggered this notion. I actually really like books that are set up as a series of letters. Two different voices, two different countries, age groups and climates. What do you think?

Steph:
I DO like your idea for a book. I agree...the letters from you living in Africa and me here might be quite interesting to some people. And it's not like we actually have to WRITE the book, it's already written! Cool idea. People, I think, are inherently curious about other people. It's why people watching is so enjoyable. I think they like to "spy" on others' lives and even live through them. Heck, we could just do an e-book and self-publish it and sell it on Amazon and see what happens!

PART II

PREPARING FOR DEPARTURE

I learned this, at least, by experiment:

that if one advances confidently in the

direction of his dreams, and endeavors to live

the life he has imagined, he will meet with

a success unexpected in common hours.

- David Henry Thoreau

Tourists don't know where they've been,

travelers don't know where they're going.

- Paul Theroux

Here is some practical advice for those considering a leap into a different lifestyle. Stephanie offers the perspective of a woman traveling alone in Central America and Camille the perspective of a married woman traveling to Africa and Central America with her husband, Bob.

BEFORE YOU LEAVE

Have a Backup Plan

Steph says: I used to plan everything far in advance and thought that was the right way of doing things. When I finally started letting that go, I felt freer to let life take me where it may. As John Lennon once said, "Life is what happens when you're busy making other plans." Sometimes you just can't plan for things and often, it's a lot more fun when you don't.

However, in regard to finances, I think you must have something to fall back on and it should be a monetary amount you decide upon. If that means you have to move back to your home country to get a job, a place to live and a car, make sure you have enough money to get by until you can earn more. Then double that amount just in case!

In determining the next place you go, I personally like to have an idea ahead of time. It may not be concrete, but there is some planning involved when you have to buy a plane ticket. There are people who are fine with just showing up in a strange town and finding a hostel or place to crash for the night. Then they start planning where to go after that. In my case, I like to know how much money I will be spending and I don't like surprises. Therefore, I plan. I don't like hostels and sharing bathrooms with strangers.

241

Camille says: We planned and planned and then let go. The image that best illustrates the process is that of a trapeze artist who carefully calculates the distance and then jumps, hands outstretched into thin air. It may look daring and effortless but it takes a lot of forethought, and don't think for one minute that there's no safety net below. Leave money in a bank account back home and do your best not to spend it.

I've seen people travel without much forethought or planning, and while they usually manage to do alright, I would find it quite stressful to wonder where I'm going to sleep and whether or not I can depend on the kindness of strangers. If you know where you are going and what you are doing, you are much less likely to be taken advantage of.

Also, make sure someone at home knows where you are and how to contact you and that you have a plan for checking in with them on a routine basis. If you are traveling alone, find a close friend or relative who will promise to come get you if fall ill or have an accident.

Do Your Homework

Camille says: Do yourself a favor and read up on the culture, history and climate of the place you intend to go or ask the expat community. There are forums and Facebook groups devoted to expats living in the exact location you have targeted for your adventure. Understanding the customs and how the local people think will be immeasurably helpful after you arrive in their homeland. It also helps in terms of packing to know what kind of weather and local customs to expect.

Before I moved to Ghana, I thought to ask a woman who lived there if there was a dress code. Turned out there was a cultural preference for ladies in skirts. So, I packed heavy on the dress and skirt side and never once felt out of place in my host country.

In preparation for our move to Belize, Bob and I immersed ourselves in Mayan history and upon arrival delved into medicinal plant lore. This really helped us in our roles as jungle guides and we earned the respect of our staff and the local vendors.

Beyond making things easier for us and our presence more palatable for our hosts, we found that a little bit of research went a long way towards enhancing our appreciation for our new home. We found our experience much more rewarding when we understood the back story. Many pitfalls were avoided and we were fascinated by nuances we might have missed had we not done our homework.

Steph says: In Central America, it seems most women wear skirts or dresses as well. I didn't follow this protocol, however. I knew I would always look like an outsider no matter how I dressed. However, I made sure not to offend and wore appropriate clothing in restaurants, shops, etc.

Definitely beef up on the local customs. I can recall more often than not that people shake hands differently down there than in the U.S. It's a very limp, weak hand shake, so don't try to overpower your new friend by crushing their hand with your American standard. Follow their lead, and most of the time you should be fine. I'm not just talking about women, it's men as well. Usually they don't do a full on hand clasp either—it's more like taking your fingers instead of your whole hand. It's interesting how hand shaking (or not) differs from country to country.

Some places expect you to pay for your meal at the counter, even though you've been served at your table. You can either politely ask your waiter if you should pay them or at the counter at some point, or find out beforehand what the custom is (or just watch and see what other people do). Find out about tipping also...and run the whole gamut of situations: taxi, restaurant, haircuts, tour guides. Most of the time the rule is that you don't tip but if they give you good service, it's always appreciated.

Locals like it when you ask about their families; be sure to ask if they have pictures. I've found that usually they will have photos of their kids (not so much their spouse, though) and it's a great ice breaker. Ask about their parents or grandchildren (if they're old enough to have them) and you'll usually find you will be asked the same in return. It's a safe subject to start out with and will more than likely lead to more.

Items to Leave at Home

Steph says: In hindsight, I took things I didn't really need and lugged them around for months. Those things included:

- Books
- Snorkel gear
- Dress shoes
- Cooking utensils/spices
- Favorite piece or two of jewelry
- Inflatable pillow
- Multiple bathing suits
- Portable water filter (abandoned this after 3 months due to space limitations)
- Portable coffee filter
- Bedside clock/alarm
- Small laptop keyboard
- Water bottle
- Mouse

Camille says: We ended up using our snorkel gear in Nicaragua and were happy that we brought it. Coffee and alarm clocks were unnecessary because we were there to run a jungle lodge, are morning people and woke with the sun. I'm also real happy that I left my yoga mat at home because I learned that I can do yoga on nearly any surface.

I wished I had not bothered to bring a neck pillow—it took up precious space in my carry-on and didn't help me sleep during the flight. I also wished I had not brought a water bottle in my carry-on. Between airport water fountains and in-flight service I had plenty of water to drink.

244

Items to take

Steph says: I put a lot of consideration into what I would be taking with me when I left the States. It also depended on what would fit in my bags, since I only had a carry on and a medium sized backpacker's bag. I knew beforehand, for the most part, what was available in Central America and how much things cost, so that was considered when packing and purchasing things. Buying travel size items came into play, like a small speaker for my iPod. Here is a list of things I took (besides clothes and basic necessities):

- Portable water filter (I'd suggest this only if your water supply is bad)
- Laptop
- Laptop hard drive with an exact copy of what I had before leaving on it
- Camera
- Flashlight
- Bed pillow (foam and cut in half to save room then packaged in a space bag)
- Pepper spray
- Tools for laptop and iPod (very small screwdrivers and specialized tools for opening iPod)
- Rechargeable batteries with charger
- Sunscreen (it is VERY expensive there)
- Makeup (also very expensive there)
- Natural insect repellent
- Small roll of duct tape
- Anti-bacterial/pain relievers/first aid items
- Portable speaker for iPod
- Two different unlocked cell phones with different bandwidths
- Silica gel packs
- Good knives (one for protection and one for food)

245

- Dental tools
- Suction cup holder for bar soap in the shower (VERY handy to have)
- Space bags with portable pump
- Personal item that reminded me of home that I could always put somewhere in view
- Apple TV
- Spare memory cards
- Copy of operating system install with product ID in case of hard drive crash and other major software
- Watercolors, brushes and paper
- Credit cards (multiple), driver's license with photo copies of them all, with phone numbers to call in case they are stolen
- Ziploc bags (can buy these anywhere though)
- Locks for my suitcase and backpack

In addition to items to take, you should also look into getting shots and vaccinations before going. Check the places you think you'll go to see what they require upon entry. Vaccinations like Hepatitis A, tetanus and others don't last forever. Do you remember the last time you got yours? I barely did, so I got quite a few, including yellow fever since I was going to be in Panama and that is one thing they check if you say you're going to a certain area. Some shots require 6 weeks to complete the session, so plan accordingly. I had to get a TB test before I was allowed to work with monkeys, and some countries may require that you show proof of being tested.

Camille says: Stephanie's list is perfect and yes, it's absolutely mandatory you take what you need to enter your host country. For Ghana it was a visa and a yellow fever card. I get a tetanus shot every ten years so it's easy to know when it's due.

We did not bring a portable water filter, pepper spray, space bags or Apple TV, but it would have been good to bring unlocked cell phones and operating system install disks. I add only the following:

- Can opener
- Ear plugs
- Movies saved to a hard drive
- An extra pair of Tevas (sturdy all terrain sandals)
- A journal, video camera and digital recorder
- Crisp, unmarked currency in various denominations

I think the bottom line is, what you take and don't take totally depends on where you are going. The more remote your destination, the more careful you need to be not to forget anything.

Communications and Electronics

Camille says: Set yourself up with a communication system. In our case we brought laptops and bought a Skype-to-call account so that we could call our friends back home. Unless you have an international cell plan, your phone will become a paperweight as soon as you board your plane. We bought cheap phones in Africa for local calls.

Internet was expensive and a pain in the butt. After unsuccessful attempts to get the house wired for Wi-Fi, we bought pre-pay vouchers, spending $40 at a time which would last about three weeks. Unsurprisingly, topping up was not always as easy as typing in the numbers and sometimes involved the tricky use of cell phones.

Steph says: I made sure to bring two different unlocked cell phones with me. There are different bands for cell phones and data in different countries. If you don't look into this ahead of time, you may be sorry. You'll then end up buying a cheap basic phone there and spending money you didn't think you'd have to.

Some places won't always have Internet/Wi-Fi and you'll have to rely on your phone or a USB Internet stick, which you can put a SIM card into and plug into your laptop. I would suggest buying one from your home country instead of when you get someplace. Mine has come in handy quite a few times. Prices for Internet access can vary, although it was fairly reasonable in Central America. Within the configuration of the USB stick, you can create new profiles depending on your provider. One piece of information you'll need is the APN, so be sure you ask your provider while you're in the store what that is. I've had luck using the wrong APN and still being able to connect, but it's best to find the correct one.

Keeping electronics safe from humidity is another consideration you may want to think about depending on where you go. You can buy large packs of silica gel that you can dry out again in an oven. I know when Camille lived in Nicaragua, they kept their electronics in a Tupperware box with silica packs. However, I've read that for cameras, it's best to not keep them in air tight containers, even with silica, since the camera can't breathe and too much humidity could form inside the box (and the lens).

FINANCIAL CONSIDERATIONS

Surviving Financially

Steph says: Of course the first thing you'll want to know is how you will support your new found travel habit. You may be gone longer than you think so you really should have a long range plan. I would never condone just walking away with no money in the bank or too little—although I've met people who do that and end up finding a way to live. I come from a very financially conservative background so it's always been important for me to have money saved up. Of course, I realized that selling my house and cars would be a fairly large chunk of where my money would be coming from. I had a nice savings account built up, and I also own an online business. I don't make much, but it's enough to help with bills. Something is better than nothing.

Coming from an I.T. background, I knew I could make money anywhere in the world by building websites, consulting, having a little online fix-it business or other computer related services. If you already work remotely, you will have a better and easier time moving abroad. There's no reason for you to have to stay where you are if you don't have to physically report to anyone. This idea of living abroad isn't just for single people. Families do it, some even with small children in tow.

Even though it is not legal to work in other countries without a lot of paperwork or through a company you already work for, people still do it. They even do it for many years, taking that risk of getting caught (and expelled from the country). I've met women who babysit, wait tables, clean houses, do yard work, sew, make crafts or get into the real estate business. Some countries don't even let you volunteer or do a work exchange without a valid permit.

You really won't get a feel for what you can do until you're there for a while. There are a lot of opportunities in third world countries as far as businesses go. However, creating a "legal" business can be an enormous lesson in futility, especially if you don't have time, money, patience and a good understanding of the language. It is possible to invest a certain amount of money into property (land, house, business) and be able to stay in the country that way. The rules for expats and retirees are different everywhere.

I had to decide upon a monetary figure at which point I would have to start making money in order to keep up the lifestyle. After thirteen months of living abroad, I was pretty much where I started financially when I left. The number I set for myself, if I could keep my annual expenses the same, would last seven years. Of course, doing house sitting helped immensely, and I think that's something anyone who wants to travel the world should definitely sign up for. It's like getting free money in a way. You may have to sacrifice some things, but I believe it can really pay off in the long run. It certainly helps when you have to pay hundreds of dollars to fly to your next location, too!

If you want to "retire" abroad, and I put that in quotes even if you're not of retirement age, you must show proof of guaranteed income per month. Usually, it has to go directly into that country's banking system. It could be an annuity, social security, retirement fund, etc. Your business paycheck doesn't count. It also needs to be the minimum amount they set (around $1,500 - 2,500 per month in Central America).

Unless you are really set on legally living somewhere for good, you will have to do visa runs (leave the country for a specified number of days and re-enter) about every three months, depending on where you are. Be prepared to spend money getting from country to country. Finally, figure out what you'll need to show at customs as well (bank and/or credit card statements, possibly a visa and letters for proof of volunteering).

You could also legally work, but that requires a different visa, a letter from your employer and tons of paperwork from what I can gather. You also have to leave the country after your visa is up, but it is a good alternative to living and working in another country if you need the money.

Camille says: Leaving your homeland without a penny in your pocket is a terrible idea. Even though we initially went the route of volunteer employment with room and board, we had a nest egg back home. Bob had left a nice job and so we even had severance pay rolling in for the first six months. While it may have appeared that we dove off a cliff into a new life, we had a safety net of U.S. dollars sitting in a bank back home.

We had a budget, a timeline and contingency plans. We planned to go for one year, spend no more than $1,500 a month and return at once should something catastrophic occur.

As it turned out we remained expats for two years. We stayed in Belize for fourteen months and then Bob accepted a job offer which took us to China for six months after which we decided to live on Guam for a while.

How Much it Costs to Live Abroad

Steph says: When I went back to the States for a visit, a friend told me that her household expenses for the month were $10,000! They live in a large, nice home, have two kids, two big vehicles, are members of the country club and rarely cook for themselves. In contrast, my living expenses in the States by myself were around $4,000 per month. My living expenses for 13 months in Central America were about $7,500. I spent less in one year than they did in one month! Of course, I saved a lot of money by house sitting. Otherwise, I would have spent about $4,000 more during that year on rent and utilities. The $7,500 included travel expenses, food, utilities, rent, cell phone, etc.

Depending on where you want to live will determine how much you spend. I imagine Europe will be more expensive and can only comment on Central America. Costa Rica is more expensive than Guatemala. Places by the beach or in tourist towns and expat communities are higher priced. But you aren't going so you can live among expats, right? You want some cultural exchange and to learn what it's like outside of your own country! I will say it's hard to avoid expats no matter where you live, which isn't necessarily a bad thing. It's nice to be able to connect to someone who speaks your language and to get helpful tips about the place you are living. Sometimes you even make really good, long lasting friendships this way too. Regardless, there will always be an interesting cast of characters.

You will only find real deals once you arrive in the country. Rentals you find on the Internet are geared toward expats, not locals. My suggestion would be to either find a place once you arrive by word of mouth or rent a place through the Internet for a couple of weeks to a month. Don't lock yourself into a three month lease unless it seems really good (but you never really know until you get there if it is). It seems everyone knows somebody who has a house or a room for rent, and you can negotiate a price more easily in person. They will typically start high, so it never hurts to throw around some prices. To them, it's better to get something than nothing. Be sure to check out the place first and then decide whether it's a good fit for you.

Ask locals beforehand how much utilities cost in the area so you can get an idea of how much more you will have to pay, if they are not included in the rent. If you are able to dry your clothes on a line outside instead of using a dryer, take advantage of it! If you have to pay for electricity, it will save you money and you're also being more environmentally friendly. Most of the time, though, you won't have a choice!

Washing clothes in a washing machine uses up a lot of water and most places in Central America have water shortages in the dry season. I get some weird comfort out of doing my clothes by hand, not to mention good upper-body exercise! It takes some time, but I'm saving water that is greatly needed for more important things. Be aware of your water usage and don't waste it. Quite often water will be turned off during peak times of the day, or it may just stop altogether at any moment up to a few days at a time. Ask around, locals will know if it does. Be sure to have a large jug of it for personal use on hand if this tends to happen in your area. Camille's water would go out for days, but they were always sure to have a backup plan.

I'd be remiss if I failed to mention health care costs. Initially I bought an 8 month plan from Ingle Insurance. It will even cover you for a few weeks when you go back to the States for a visit, and you can set up whatever deductible you'd like. Honestly, I stopped buying insurance after it expired. I was living in a place where my risk limit was low and health care was inexpensive enough to just pay out of pocket if need be. Obviously (at the time of this writing) Obamacare isn't going to do a thing for you overseas. That's something you would need to research on your own and is beyond the scope of this book.

Camille says: Living abroad is never as cheap as you hope but definitely less expensive than your lifestyle back home if you do it right. Our budget in the U.S. is between $2,500 and $3,000 a month, and we were able to live on half that in both Central America and West Africa.

These are the things that made living on less than $1,500 a month a pipe dream:

- Travel
- Entertainment
- Internet
- Alcohol
- Western food

Living on the Cheap

Steph says: First, I may suggest using Excel or a similar program to create a monthly spreadsheet of your expenses. Write down everything

253

you spend your money on and do it as you accrue expenses. Create a few columns with headings like Food, Utilities, Entertainment, Clothing, Travel, and then sum them up at the bottom with a final total for each month. You can even figure out what percentage went where and reassess your spending habits if needed. You may be surprised at what you've been spending, plus this exercise helps to keep your budget in check.

The best way to see the world and not pay rent is to become a house sitter. There are quite a few Internet sites out there where you pay a small fee to become a member. It is completely worth it as long as you are a responsible person who can hack living in someone else's home and treating it with the utmost respect and care. Most often, house sits involve taking care of pets. You will have to get references and a few house sits under your belt before people will start trusting you. You will have to be honest, personable, reliable and be good with dogs and cats.

What's great about this type of accommodation is that word can get around quickly once you get to know people and you will find that some house sits don't have to come from a site but from family and friends. It pays to network! Never hesitate to ask an expat who may live in your community if they need a house sitter (or know someone else who might).

There are also help exchange websites which offer opportunities to work for room and possibly food. If it's a farm, they're usually more than willing to share what they grow. The only drawback here is that you will usually be sharing a room and bathroom with other people. Some people are looking for help with their kids or housework...the possibilities are endless.

It pays to trust your gut and to do some research on the person's name/address, etc. before accepting the offer. Google street view is a great way to see the outside of the home and the neighborhood for places that actually have that; third world countries, not so much. Ask for photos of your room, bathroom and the house so you're not surprised when you show up. If it doesn't appear to meet your standard of living, it's better to change your mind before you go than try to get out of it after you get there!

I've also learned to ask things like what time in the morning the pets need to be fed, how long you are able to leave the house during the day or night, if you may have access to their vehicle and how close a grocery store is. If they are not going to give you a car to use, you'll need to know how close public transportation is or ask if they have a bike.

If you like to volunteer, some places will help cover part of your expenses by giving you a place to sleep and maybe eat. Just be aware that the work can be physically demanding or you could be working with younger people or in a large group. Some places even expect you to PAY to volunteer and don't provide anything. There are a lot of sites out there with a collection of free volunteer opportunities. If you have some specific volunteer activity in mind, find the place you want to do it and drop them an email. It never hurts to ask.

I often look for websites dealing with homestays when I can't find a house sit or just want to play tourist for a while without the hassle of staying home all the time. They are usually cheaper than hostels or hotels and you get the added benefit of living with a local. You often have a good choice of locations as well, especially in larger cities. I've found that the host will usually take you out places with them, give you a ride to the grocery store when they go and introduce you to their friends. It's a win-win situation.

As for food expenses, if you don't know how to cook, you'd better start learning! I rarely eat out; it can cost quite a bit, even at the cheapest places once you add it all up. A $7 lunch could buy you enough at the store to last four meals if you cooked it yourself. Buy from the local growers instead of the grocery store. Eat what's in season and plant your own vegetables if you will be in one spot long enough. They don't take long to grow in the tropics. I've seen neighbors growing a lot of veggies...it wouldn't hurt to offer them money directly if they'd be willing to sell some to you.

Be aware that fruits and veggies can and do have worms in them if they have not been sprayed with pesticides. As Camille said once, "Worms or chemicals...which would you rather have?" Never eat fruit that has fallen on the ground. Check that guava carefully after cutting it open (they're notorious for worms). You may even want to look at buying a portable water filter to travel with. Ironically enough, some of the best tasting water I've ever had was in third world countries and I did not get sick from it. Although it seemed the closer to the beach I lived, the worse the water was.

Clothing can be found at second hand stores. Find them, love them and buy them. Most of the thrift stores get their clothes from the U.S. Just make sure you wash them before wearing. You won't feel as bad leaving behind the $2 shirt you got there as opposed to the $25 shirt from your hometown. Giving your unwanted things to the locals means a lot to them, and they are more appreciative than you can ever know.

Convenience items are usually more expensive abroad. Individual tooth flossers cost a lot more than a roll of dental floss. Foaming soap pumps let you take liquid soap four times farther by watering it down. Taking bar soap out of the wrapper to let it harden makes it last longer. Buying paper towels that are perforated into half sheets instead of whole saves money.

Brand name foods from the U.S. cost a lot more when there's usually a local alternative (sometimes just as good). Sodas and bottled drinks are also expensive. Make your own out of fresh fruits or buy powdered and add water. Tea bags are cheap everywhere and you can easily make a pitcher of ice tea which lasts many days. Rice is cheap and you can do a lot with it. Start looking for your favorite recipe website and maybe even get daily emails for recipe ideas so you don't get in a rut. Food will be one of your main expenses, so keeping that low will help your overall budget.

Camille says: Regarding house sits, home exchanges and paid caretaking positions, we subscribe to The Caretaker Gazette (caretaker.org.) The Caretaker is an inexpensive resource listing hundreds of opportunities in a newsletter published every two months. They have an online version, too, and send email updates between publish dates.

Our Ghana budget of roughly $1,500 a month for two of us included travel expenses, food, rent, clothing, transportation and entertainment. Keep in mind that we didn't have A/C, a mortgage or a car. We grew some of our own food, ate tons of cheap, local produce and only ate out once a week. We didn't have a gardener, cook or housekeeper and chose to walk or use taxis for transportation.

As Stephanie stressed, cooking your own meals is an immense saving and also culturally comforting. Bob and I were able to eat very well on less than $175 a month. This figure does not include alcoholic beverages, restaurant meals or propane and kitchen appliances. Depending on how long you intend to stay, it may not be worth your while to set up a kitchen. Street food in Ghana is only a dollar or so per plate and our housemates ate it often with only occasional repercussions.

Laundry can be a thing if your new home is not equipped with a washing machine. In Africa we washed our laundry by hand until we decided to buy a machine for the house. The cost of sending our laundry out was too high and we were averse to having someone come in and do it for us.

Friends of ours in Nicaragua washed their clothes by hand, but had the neighbor's son come in once a week and tackle the bed clothes and towels. Labor is not expensive in the third world if you are comfortable having someone in your home, but this can be risky.

257

Keep in mind that your belongings will seem like unattainable luxuries and therefore are too much of a temptation for the average domestic worker. Even if you are absolutely certain that they would never steal from you, their friends may not be as trustworthy. Your house keeper or night guard may inadvertently inspire one of their acquaintances with some random reference to the wealth of their new employer.

Traveling Expenses

Steph says: it's hard these days to find cheap air fares in foreign countries. I often splurge and fly rather than take buses because I can't stand road traveling. However, I'm hating it a little less every day. It lets you see parts of the country you wouldn't if you flew and if you have the time, it definitely saves money. I find that 6 hours sounds worse than it actually is on a bus. If you do fly, be sure to check local carriers first. Some places near the coast can have boats that will take you where you need to go. If you don't have to go far, offering a local some money to take you there could be another alternative to getting a taxi. Buses can be very crowded but are usually the cheapest alternative (and may be shared with livestock). Some can be very comfortable, others not so much.

Be aware of how long your visa lasts, because typically you will have to leave the country after a few months to renew it. Plan accordingly by living near a border town or find someone else to travel with if they need to do the same thing. Sometimes you can renew your visa at least once by going into a city and paying a fee, which may be cheaper than leaving for a couple of days.

Often, as is the case in Central America, you must show a return ticket to immigration and to the airline (not a one way). People who don't know about this are forced to buy a ticket at the airline counter before entering the country and may get stuck with a cancellation fee if their plans change. Be prepared and do your homework about your specific destination.

Camille says: While it's tempting to save money by taking the cheapest transportation available, it may cost you more in the long run. You might find yourself delayed, robbed or the victim of an accident. We chose to fly whenever possible or took a private taxi.

The ubiquitous" tro tro", a beat up mini van or bus, is the cheapest way to go in Ghana and much of Africa. But we never felt comfortable trusting our luck to the crazy tro drivers, nor did we want to stand and wait for the tro tro to fill, often to suffocating over-capacity. We heard quite a few stories from friends about tro tros rolling off into ditches or ripping each other's bumpers off when passing.

At least one friend reported getting into a shared taxi with his wallet and leaving without it. It's easy for one passenger to jostle you or distract you while the other relieves you of your cash.

The bus is a safer way to travel if you don't mind taking all day to get there while being blasted by preachers and/or cheap Nigerian movies. Make sure you have a robust bladder and ear plugs and don't count on air conditioning.

On one trip, we thought we'd save time by taking the first available bus from Tamale to Kumasi. But it broke down three times and we ultimately found ourselves stranded in a remote village. There we stood face-to-face with a madman chained to a log which he had carried across the street in his arms after seeing us step off the bus. Bob assured me we were safe as we listened to him rail against the white man, proclaiming to have a gun with which he was going to shoot us but I cowered behind a pair of large African women anyway.

It took us 11 hours to travel the return distance of 385 kilometers (240 miles), nearly twice as long to as it took to get there via taxi.

WHAT TO EXPECT

Living Conditions

Steph says: The first thing you need to realize (at least for third world countries) is that your standard of living is probably going to drop. Sometimes it's a far drop. Besides, you didn't move thinking you could have the best of both worlds, did you? As in relationships, there are compromises when you live in a different country. Sometimes it could be above the norm, which is always pleasurable.

In Belize one year when I volunteered to catch crocodiles for tagging, I stayed in a very basic cabin on the beach. It was a small island and I was lucky enough to be one of seven people on it. It had what I needed...a bed, a sink, bathroom and a desk. I thought it was a bonus to have a place to hang my clothes instead of just a wooden plank. No screens on the windows and maybe a fan (I don't recall). Apparently it even had hot water, which I didn't find out until my last night there!

I sat on the beach with the waves lapping at my feet and looked back at my cabin. I asked myself if I could I live in that for a while. It had everything I NEEDED (with the exception of a kitchen). Then I looked out at the vast expanse of the blue ocean, the palm trees gently swaying in the wind and the iguanas sunning themselves. I said, "Yes!" I've never forgotten that defining moment in my life. It helped me give up everything because I knew I would still be ALIVE, even if I only had the most basic accommodations. A place may not be as visually appealing or comfortable, but look at what lies outside!

So keep that in mind as you prepare yourself for living abroad. As long as a place is clean, doesn't leak too much and isn't infested with bugs, you should be fine. Cleaning in one form or another was something I did every day in Costa Rica. The veranda got dusty and dirty easily, so sweeping happened at least twice a day. I needed to do dishes every day and not let them pile up in the sink since there was no dishwasher.

Everyone has a different standard of cleanliness, but I think it is worth mentioning. We're so used to being enclosed in homes with air conditioning, filters and vacuum cleaners. Poor Camille would have Harmattan in Ghana, where dust storms really wreaked havoc on her cleaning schedule. Don't bring it up with her.

Camille says:

If you need and can't imagine a life without strawberries, you may as well stay home. Think instead about a world full of mangoes and avocados. Our travels have mostly taken us to the tropics, where the only place you might find air conditioning is in a bank. But the rewards are enormous as long as you are open to them.

As Stephanie mentions, your standard of living will plummet. At first you will be dismayed when your leather belts and shoes turn green and you will miss your comfy bed and dream of life without bug bites. Soon enough though, you will realize how much simpler your new world is. Time slows down, clocks become a joke, wildlife meanders through your yard and the streets are alive with friendly people who are happy to stop and chat.

Eventually, the critters stop biting (they really do prefer new blood) and you find that your new life offers enough physical challenges to have you sleeping like a baby. You lose weight, your skin tans and you find muscles you may have forgotten about.

Then one day, you will face your departure with trepidation, wondering how on earth you will survive back in the land of A/C and forced-air heat, alarm clocks, commuters and streets empty of life. And yes, strawberries will be "in season" all year round.

Culture Shock

Steph says: The culture in Central America wasn't that shocking to me since I had traveled there so many times before. However, I can see how it might be for someone who hasn't. The language barrier was one of the most difficult things to deal with. Thinking I could get by in Spanish after studying it for about a year was a mistake. Each country has its own slang words, pronunciations and accents. People will tend to speak fast (at least to a foreigner it seems fast), so all I can say is keep practicing.

Playing the dating game is really weird too. Don't expect it to be at all like you're used to. Of course everyone is different, so some may find that it's not a challenge at all to date. I felt that the men were overbearing and pushy and rushed into things way faster than I was used to. It turned me off from even attempting to date. Local women looking for American men may have a different agenda altogether.

Driving can be a bit shocking, whether you're actually doing it yourself or you're just a passenger. I noticed that Central Americans like their half down the middle, which is pretty harrowing when meeting around a bend in the road. Typically, people are really laid back down there and not in a rush to do anything until it comes to driving. It really makes you wonder how anyone in their right mind can do some of the things you see.

Motorcyclists will drive in between cars, people will drive on the shoulder for a really long time, some won't bother stopping for lights or stop signs, and others will drive drunk. Down there, you are guilty until proven innocent and god forbid you're the one driving and you can't speak Spanish.

I've seen manhole covers missing from busy streets, which will completely ruin a car if you happen to drive into that gaping void. I've almost been in wrecks because someone has stopped their car right over a hill on a one lane road while talking to someone on the street. I've heard brakes lock up at night because a sloth was crossing the road. I've seen huge rocks in the road which have fallen off the side of a mountain, and I don't even want to talk about landslides or earthquakes. Basically, just be aware that anything can and will happen when you least expect it.

Being a stranger in a strange land might make you wish for the comforts of home and familiar faces. This is a completely normal and valid reaction. Being on the road for an extended period of time can make one feel vulnerable and lonely.

My advice is to not let it get to you. Venturing out into the world by yourself can be scary, but don't let it keep you from seeing what's out there. Make a phone call or send some emails back home and then keep on trekking. Make friends wherever you are, and you will be able to accept culture shock a little easier each place you go.

Camille says: My first glimpses of Ghana—the sights, sounds, smells and feel of the place—were intoxicatingly foreign and that's the reason I believe we go: to wake up our senses and step out of our shoes long enough to find the commonalities that all humans share. Travel is an adventure in cultural anthropology.

While it certainly helped to study a little beforehand, nothing could have prepared me for the sensation of floating along a sea of human protoplasm in Kejetia market, ducking head pans full of live chickens, winding my way past skyscrapers of giant tubers, past men hacking at slabs of meat inches from my feet. Not to mention the smells! Or our outrage when we realized people were pushing their terrified toddlers towards us to punish them for their little sins.

As Stephanie mentions, transportation is exhilarating and will have you fearing for your life. There are no rules, it's every man, woman and child for themselves, all trying to get from point A to point B without dying.

263

We have never seen so many potholes of such size! If you are driving, do not even think about blinking. If you are a passenger, best to keep your eyes shut.

My advice is drink it all in, mind your feet and use your wonder and horror as catalysts for mind boggling epiphanies.

Creativity

Camille says: Expect a huge burst of creative energy. Stephanie was smart to bring watercolor supplies and I am happy that I brought my journal. We both got a lot of use from our cameras, and our blogs flourished. No matter what your medium, you will see the creative juices flow as soon as you leave the familiar behind.

Steph says: Camille is right, once you can finally relax and step away from the madness you used to call home you may find your creative side will emerge. It could be something you've done in the past and now you have more time to do, or you might pick up a new hobby. I had wanted to paint for well over 15 years but I never had the time; when I did try it long ago, I got frustrated and quit. When I lived in Arenal on the lake overlooking a volcano, I had a favorite tree at the top of the hill. I wanted to paint it and found a set of watercolors in the house. It was a terrible painting, but I wanted it to remind me of that tree and my time there. Somehow, I got better quickly and really started to enjoy the pleasure it brought me.

Time on the beach was spent sculpting sand creatures, and I got pretty good at it. It gave me ideas of things I could sculpt with other media that didn't disappear when the tide came in. When you're not worrying about getting through the week or what time it is, you can give in to the guilty pleasures you always wished you had time for.

YOUR PERSONAL TOOL KIT

Learning to be Happy and Overcoming Fear

Steph says: I read a book before making my jump into a new life called *The Big Leap* by Gay Hendricks. It talked about hitting your upper limit and sabotaging your happiness. I think everyone can find an example in their life of how they do this without realizing they're actually doing it.

In a nutshell, he said that you reach a point where you are having a good time doing something, then all of a sudden something in your head says, "You shouldn't be having this much fun...so RUIN IT!" You never HEAR yourself say this, but you act on it. Typically, you will stop what you're doing for some reason and do something else. This takes you away from the happy feeling you were having and leaves you unsatisfied.

In my case, I can recall sitting outside on my porch listening to the birds sing while admiring my plants and flowers and taking in the feel and sounds around me. Then all of a sudden I would have this urge to go inside and I would. There was no NEED for me to go inside or deprive myself of this lovely relaxing time I was having, but I would do it quite a bit, never allowing myself to just sit there and enjoy it.

I didn't realize I was doing this to myself until I read that book. Once I recognized that this happened, I would take steps to avoid sabotaging my happiness. Since I've started doing that, I've been a happier person and it's made a huge difference in the way I live.

Another example that almost everyone can relate to is not being able to take a compliment. Next time someone throws one your way, be cognizant of how you answer. Is it typically, "Oh no I'm not!" Or do you negate what they say and mention how you hate that particular thing about yourself? I noticed whenever someone would complement a

265

meal I made for them that I would find something wrong with how it was done and respond with that instead of just saying, "Thank you."

I now try to accept the compliment instead of discrediting it. Whenever I meet someone for the first time and something about them stands out, I try to compliment them on it. It could be that they have beautiful eyes or great skin or a lovely dress on. Everyone likes to hear compliments but rarely accept them.

Basically, there's no need to ever be unhappy yet we all feel, for some reason, we don't DESERVE to be happy. It helped me overcome the need to have tangible things, realizing that everything can be replaced (furniture, decorations, cars, etc.). The things that can't be replaced (old photos, writings and sentimental objects) can be packed away and given to someone to hold on to. I sold just about everything I had (gave a lot away, too) and I don't look back with any regret. It only let me be who I am today, and I learned that I can live out of two suitcases quite well.

Addressing your fears and finding ways to overcome them will take you a long way, even if it's not about moving to a different country. Start with something small and you'll be amazed at how much you can continue to conquer fears that hold you back from the life you really want to live. Henry Rollins said, "Kiss your fear on the mouth," which is another piece of advice I took to heart.

Fear in small doses at the right time is fine, but never let it keep you from doing what you want. I truly believe in gut instinct and I have learned to never ignore it. Please don't think I mean that you can travel into the underbelly of a dangerous city at midnight without having fear. Use common sense everywhere you go and listen to your gut. But overcome irrational fears that hold you back from the things you want in life.

I believe that your parents want you to be happy. They want to keep protecting you and give you advice after learning from their own mistakes. It's okay to step out of that zone your parents still expect you to live in. It may not make them happy and they will always worry about you, no matter how old you are. This is now YOUR life and you need to make your own mistakes and learn from them. You need to do things you've always wanted to and without their approval. You may even find that you're too scared to tell your parents what you want to do for fear of criticism. You may be surprised that they will back you and keep their thoughts to themselves. Just keep in mind that you don't need their approval anymore and you are the only one in charge of yourself. Get over the fear of your parents and I promise you will become a happier person.

Camille says: The book that most inspired me and Bob was *Illusions* by Richard Bach. In particular, we got a lot out of the introduction, which basically encouraged anyone who wishes to fully experience life to "just let go" which is exactly what we did.

When we got married in 1994, we wrote the following mission statement for our life together: "Team together to avoid negative influences and create a life of challenge and fulfillment by following our hearts." A few years later we found ourselves living the American Dream and wondering if this was all there was. Something felt slightly off, so we took the time to do some strategic planning and ultimately decided we needed to leave the culture of our births and seek a new perspective.

We met twice a week for months, made lists of what we wanted and what we didn't want in our lives and glued pictures of rain forest, horses and food to poster board. Eventually it became clear we wanted to live in the rain forest of Belize and manage an off-the-grid jungle lodge with twenty horses that we had stayed at a couple of years before.

Like Stephanie, we secured a position, sold our house and seven acre horse farm, finalized our employment, gave away nearly everything and left the country. I strongly encourage going through this process of defining your dreams and getting a handle on what it is you really want out of life.

Playing Nice with Others

Steph says: I think the thing that stands out the most for me when dealing with locals were their customs versus mine. Anything from traffic and how to behave in it, to standing in line waiting for a bus. The personal space between people was a whole lot closer than I was used to, and I found myself getting very annoyed over it. I found most locals to be quite friendly, though, and tried my best to get along and not show my frustration.

It behooves you to remember that you are a guest in their country and must be able to accept their customs. Some of the most memorable times I've had were on their holidays. It's pretty neat to be in a different country for Christmas, New Year's or an Independence Day event.

I was reminded recently by my mother that she used to have to prod me to go outside and meet other kids when I was young. I seem to have this aversion to meeting people and tend to be a loner. I was explaining to her that I have learned (finally) to step out of my comfort zone and meet my neighbors. I find that it can usually do you good.

I always ask people what the crime is like in the area and if there are any shady characters to watch out for. Ask for advice and you shall receive! So if you tend to keep to yourself, get used to being more sociable because you never know who you might meet.

There is a quote that has always stuck in my mind: "Be kind, for we are all fighting some kind of battle." It helps to remember that when someone treats you badly. It especially helps when you're in a store and the clerk couldn't care less about you.

I have only traveled alone on this journey, which makes things a lot easier in terms of getting along with a partner. People ask if I get lonely and the answer is usually, "No." There are times when I wish I had someone to share a moment with or make a nice meal for, but for the most part I am okay with being alone. I feel this has made me a stronger person with regard to having to do everything myself and not rely on anyone else. It keeps me busy and I don't have to worry about someone else's happiness or moodiness.

One thing to realize is that your dream isn't necessarily someone else's dream. I wouldn't have wanted to drag someone along with me who wasn't down with the same goals or even the places I wanted to visit. I think it would be much more difficult to travel with someone than to be alone. That is, of course, unless you are both on the same page, like Camille and Bob (they're an amazing couple).

Camille says: Yes, it is so important to realize that whether or not you can understand and/or respect the ambient culture, you are a guest and a representative of your homeland. There is nothing more embarrassing than seeing someone from your own country acting like a buffoon.

That said, you must have your eyes open and be willing to stand up for yourself. In Ghana, especially, we were seen as cash cows. The people we did business with on a daily basis eventually came to us seeking money. Know up front that this may happen and decide how you will handle it when it does.

Know that it can get worse than just asking for money, as in the case of one of our German friends who was set up by his night watchman and robbed at gun point. So, be polite and generous but stay alert and cautious.

269

MUSINGS

What We Miss about the Third World

Steph says: I miss being outside all of the time. In the third world, it is rare for anyone to stay inside during the day. If they do, their doors and windows are open so they can feel like they're outside. You get to know what's going on in your neighborhood. You recognize the sounds of motorcycles or trucks and who's in them. You smell things, sometimes not so wonderful, but it just adds to the reality. You hear music and sometimes you hear someone burst out into song with no music playing at all. You hear birds and their crazy calls. Trees come alive in the breeze and flowers happily smile up at the sun. There is life EVERYWHERE you look and you become a part of it. You feel connected, grounded and like you belong to something pretty great.

I miss the genuine personalities of the people and their kind nature. I also miss not speaking a different language. I miss the ability to pick fresh fruit, veggies and flowers from my yard and sharing the huge stalk of bananas with the birds. I suppose that ultimately, I miss the challenge and unpredictability that living in a different country provides.

Camille says: I miss life without A/C. I loved the consistency of the tropics in terms of day length and temperature. When the temperature inside and out is pretty much the same all year round, people spend most of their time outside. Laundry gets hung outside, the cooking is done over a fire outside and most of the vendors are outside with an umbrella, perhaps for shelter.

As you might imagine, this affords for a very cheery place to live, with people greeting each other as they go about their business, walking from here to there. I miss the slower pace and the easy-going nature of people who don't take themselves too seriously because they have nothing to lose.

I miss the instant camaraderie of fellow expats. We used to joke that had we not found each other in Ghana, we might not have given each other a second's consideration. There was a kind of war-time foxhole mentality which bonded us together.

Year round fresh fruit was a biggie, too. Sure, you can get mangoes all year at grocery stores in the United States, but they pale in comparison to the freshly picked fruit at the produce stands or right off the tree

As Stephanie pointed out, the wildlife is wonderfully abundant. From the geckos on the wall to the birds singing outside my window, having so many animals around made me feel connected to the natural world in a way I surely don't get during winter in the States.

What We Miss about the United States

Camille says: In the 1990's, I missed the local library when we lived abroad, but fifteen years later with laptop and Kindle, this is not an issue. Fortunately, many of our guests in Nicaragua brought and left behind paperbacks, giving us plenty to read. I thought I would miss the movies, but because my life was so interesting I didn't miss them at all. At least for the first year, when all was new and challenging, I felt like I was starring in my own movie.

During the last five months in Ghana, I found myself pining for (of all things) Twizzlers! Ironically, when I finally pushed through a gaggle of teenaged girls to get my hands on the holy grail of cheap candy at JFK airport, I discovered that my desire was a bit overblown.

I most certainly missed reliable water and power. Power outages were a daily, if not hourly occurrence in Ghana lasting from a few minutes to fifteen hours. Even though we had a water storage tank atop the house and never actually ran out, the dry taps in our bathroom were inconvenient and a source of concern, especially after the third dry day, as we didn't know how long our water storage would hold out.

Something I didn't think I would miss but did was the American accent. While most everyone spoke some version of English, the strain of hearing the words spoken with French, Ghanaian, German and Australian accents took its toll and had me longing to speak to an American.

Steph says: I miss a good bed the most. I think every bed in Central America is made of concrete. I travel with my own pillow, which takes the other possible uncomfortable part of sleeping out of the equation. I would hate to have used any pillow down there as they are all horrible. I just bring my own (and the only way is to use a space bag to compress it).

I also miss a dishwasher. It saves so much time by having one. I really dread doing dishes by hand. It takes a long time and it ends up hurting my neck and shoulders. Unfortunately, it seems nobody ever has a dishwasher down there so it's just one of those things you have to deal with.

I miss certain types of food like ham, a good steak or a turkey dinner. Cold cuts (that are real, not pressed) are almost impossible to come by down there. I miss donuts, Mexican food and BBQ. I also miss the convenience of being able to buy certain things and the availability and pricing of some items. Although, after being in the States for a while, I find that I can't wait to leave again.

In Closing

Steph says: We can give you advice all day long, but ultimately the journey will be different for everyone. When you are in the moment, possibly suffering from heat, illness, bug bites or culture shock, it's easy to have bad thoughts. Then you'll have those moments that make you feel like it was all worth it.

Regardless of the outcome, your travels are sure to provide memories that will last a lifetime. Take advantage of everything you can, even if it means stepping out of your comfort zone. It's the greatest gift you could ever give yourself!

Camille says: Please use our little story as you will, for inspiration, information or entertainment. I hope our propensity for complaining did not obscure the more profound nuances of our experiences.

Each and every time I stepped outside our iron gate onto the baked laterite lane I felt as if I were stepping into the pages of National Geographic. But beyond the sensory immersion I was granted a peek into the human psyche.

It's ironic that you have to walk away from something to really see it. By shedding the mantle of my familiar life I was able to grasp something which had become obscured by routine. In Africa I discovered the core elements of humanity. Love, hope, despair, joy, greed, innocence and guilt flourished at the intersection of our cultural differences.

It's been said that travel is glamorous, but I can assure you this is far from the truth. Glorious, challenging and energizing, but not glamorous. For me, travel is both humbling and empowering. I return mystified and enlightened, with a new appreciation for my place in the world.

Epilogue

Stephanie left Costa Rica and went to El Valle, Panama, for three months to help the owners of a Butterfly House start their business. El Valle was nestled within the only inhabited extinct volcanic crater in the world. They worked on setting up the lab, café and grounds before opening to the public. She helped with decorating the café, creating menu items and baking. She also did some PR work through social media to advertise the attraction and learned how to raise butterflies.

She lived in a mostly expat community of Americans and rarely practiced Spanish there. The wildlife and terrain were not as impressive as Costa Rica. Panama wasn't much of a challenge for her, and although she made good friends there, found it to be too much like the U.S. Unwilling to return there again, she took up a house sitting job for two months in Arizona to regroup. She moved to New Zealand for three months and then on to Australia. Deciding to start checking off her bucket list for the rest of the world, she plans on going to Micronesia, Borneo, Malaysia, Madagascar and Europe.

Camille returned to her little community and resumed life with minimal reverse culture shock. Oh, there were a frightening few seconds when she forgot how to down-shift, and a moment in the Piggly Wiggly when she couldn't make a decision. And then there was the shock of winter accompanied by bloody noses from the dry forced-air heat.

But all in all, the return home was as easy as slipping into an old pair of blue jeans. Her former employers asked her to come back to work, and everyone she met in town gave her a big welcome home squeeze. All that social capital she had earned before leaving was still sitting in the bank, awaiting her return. No one had aged a day and the town looked exactly the same as she remembered it. In fact, it felt to her as if she had dreamed the whole other life she had just lived in Ghana.

Follow Steph's continuing adventures on her blog "Out on a Limb" at: warmreptile.wordpress.com and Camille's at "Plastic Farm Animals": troutsfarm.com/PFA.

39060333R00165

Made in the USA
Charleston, SC
26 February 2015